D0835989

The Crippled Giant

American Foreign Policy
and Its Domestic Consequences

THE CRIPPLED GIANT

*American Foreign Policy and Its
Domestic Consequences*

J. William Fulbright

**CHAIRMAN
SENATE FOREIGN RELATIONS COMMITTEE
THE UNITED STATES SENATE**

Vintage Books
A Division of Random House
New York

Fulbright, James William, 1905–
The crippled giant.
1. United States—Foreign relations—1945–
I. Title.
E744.F888 1972   327.73   72–6303
ISBN 0–394–71846–1 (pbk.)

To those of my countrymen and those from other countries whose participation in educational exchange has helped to change the rules of the game

Contents

The Crippled Giant

*American Foreign Policy
and Its Domestic Consequences*

Introduction—
Concepts of Policy

I do not think the human race is in imminent danger of self-destruction by nuclear holocaust. It is not out of the question, to be sure—an accident is always possible. Nor is our probable survival in the short run a basis for confidence in the long run. Nevertheless, with the abatement of hot and cold war in the early 1970's, a reasonably stable world balance of power seems to have taken hold. Acknowledging the deterrent power of each other's nuclear arsenals, the great powers have stepped back from the nuclear brink, giving the world a prospective breathing spell of a few years, or perhaps a few decades. For such cold comfort as it is worth, it now seems probable that if the human race is destroyed or decimated in this century, it will not be because of nuclear war but because of overpopulation or the poisoning of the environment.

In a book published in 1966 I expressed the opinion that "if the great conservatives of the past, such as

Burke and Metternich and Castlereagh, were alive to-day, they would not be true believers or relentless crusaders against communism. They would wish to come to terms with the world as it is . . ."[1] With significant exceptions and incongruities, that became the general thrust of the foreign policy of the conservative Nixon Administration. It is ironic that the shift from ideological crusade to classical power politics should have taken place—insofar as it has taken place—under the leadership of a President who was recently in the vanguard of that crusade, but Mr. Nixon's impeccable anti-Communist credentials were no doubt an asset facilitating the change. The Nixon Administration remained unreconstructed in certain of its policies—most particularly in the perpetuation of the Indochina war—but on the whole the Nixon-Kissinger policy has represented a significant departure from the ideological anti-communism which so strongly influenced the foreign policy of American Presidents from Truman to Johnson.

American foreign policy since the Second World War has been shaped by three basic concepts: the idea of an international security community, the ideological struggle between "communism" and "freedom," and the traditional conception of international relations as a self-generating struggle for power. For a brief period immediately before and after victory in World War II, there occurred a revival of Wilsonian idealism and belief in the possibility of a world system representing "not a balance of power, but a community of power; not organized rivalries, but an organized common peace."[2] In those hopeful days of 1945 the United Nations Charter was drawn up—"to save succeeding generations from the scourge of war"—and, despite the enormity of the commitment the Charter was then thought to represent, the United States Senate consented to it by a vote of 89 to 2 after only a few days' debate. The onset of the cold war quickly dashed the hopes embodied in the United Nations Charter; advised by such diplomatic traditionalists as Dean Acheson, the Under Secretary and later Secretary of State, the Truman Administration reverted—or attempted to revert—to old-fashioned power politics in the developing postwar struggle with the Soviet Union. The Charter in consequence was put on ice, and so it remains to our own time, neither a failure nor a success but an untested set of new rules for the ancient "game" of international politics.

Confronted with a recently isolationist Congress and country, the Truman Administration judged it necessary—and perhaps congenial as well—to frame its case for resisting Stalin's pressures in Europe not in precise strategic terms but in sweeping ideological terms. At a crucial meeting at the White House on February 27, 1947, the assembled Congressional leadership found Secretary of State George Marshall's matter-of-fact explanation of the proposed Greek-Turkish aid program "rather trivial" and "adverse"; whereupon Under Secretary Acheson asked for the floor and proceeded to describe the threat of communism in the soon-to-be-familiar metaphor of a loathsome and highly contagious disease. "Never have I spoken under such a pressing sense that the issue was up to me alone," Acheson later wrote. Soviet pressures on Greece and Turkey, he declared, "might open three continents to Soviet penetration. Like apples in a barrel infected by the rotten one, the corruption of Greece would infect Iran and all the east. It would also carry the infection to Africa through Asia Minor and Egypt and to Europe through France and Italy." By all accounts the assemblage were deeply impressed. The Chairman of the Senate Foreign Relations Committee, Senator Vandenberg, broke the "profound silence" which followed Acheson's presentation by advising President Truman, "If you will say that to

Congress and the country, I will support you and I believe that most of its members will do the same."[3]

The framing of the Truman Doctrine in broad ideological terms was neither the "cause" nor the definitive substantive event in the launching of America's ideological crusade against communism. The casting of their strategy in quasi-religious terms was probably no more than a domestic political tactic to President Truman and to Acheson. It was, however, a symbolic and seminal occurrence, because from that time forward the American people and their leader responded to the acts, policies and pronouncements of the Communist states not on the basis of their discrete and varying political and strategic merits but in terms, as Senator Vandenberg put it, of "the worldwide ideological clash between Eastern communism and Western democracy . . ."[4]

What statesmen say, they soon enough come to believe, taken in, it would seem, by the force of their own rhetoric. From the time of the Truman Doctrine until, let us say, the Nixon visit to China, American statesmen continued to respond to the actions of Communist states and Communist movements not in terms of specific threats to our interests but in sweeping ideological terms. The brave words of President Kennedy's inaugural still ring in our ears: ours was a generation "granted the role of defending freedom in its hour of maximum danger." In retrospect it is difficult to recall exactly what the "maximum danger" was in that peaceful winter of 1961. More recently, despite the change of emphasis from ideological warfare to classical power politics, President Nixon repeatedly echoed Dean Acheson's metaphor of an infectious disease, warning that American withdrawal from Vietnam—our "defeat and humiliation," as he chose to put it—"would spark violence wherever our commitments help maintain the peace—in the Middle East, in Berlin, eventually even in the western hemisphere."[5]

Advised by a scholar in the field, President Nixon became a practitioner of traditional power politics and his policies came to reflect both the virtues and the defects of that ancient art. With its careful, dispassionate analyses of threat and interest and advantage, the geopolitical approach is an enormous improvement on the ideological crusade which it appears, step by step, to be supplanting. Its virtue is coherence and rationality in terms of its own premises. Its defects are those premises, with their cold, amoral view of the world, with their preference for process over purpose, and for power over people. Under those premises the "game" is nothing but a game, conducted for the sake of the game, not for winning *something* but just for the sake of winning. Under the classic rules of the balance-of-power the "enforcer" of the balance must lend its support to the weaker party to a controversy regardless of the merits of the issue. These rules may put the enforcing power on the side of an authentic victim of aggression, as in the case of South Korea in 1950, or they may put the "enforcer" on the side of a regime engaged in the brutal suppression of its own population, as in the case of American support in 1971 for West Pakistan against the Bengalis of Bangladesh and their ally, India. The criterion is mechanical and political; it does not totally rule out considerations of humanity and justice, but they are secondary. Finally, of all of the defects of balance-of-power politics, the most important is that, however successful it has been in keeping the peace over certain periods of time, it has always broken down in the end, culminating as in 1914 in general war. In addition to being amoral and devoid of substantive pur-

pose, the geopolitical approach is inherently unstable;
managed with agility, it can hold war off for a time, but
war in the end is what it comes to.

In terms of the "laws" of geopolitics there is nothing
optional about the balance of power and the role of the
"enforcer." In a significant interview in early 1971 President Nixon expressed his belief that "for the next
twenty-five years the United States is destined to play
this super-power role as both an economic and nuclear
giant. We just have to do this. We cannot dodge our
responsibilities."[6] This outlook is illustrative of what
Professor Marcuse described as the "totalitarian dictatorship of the established fact." Lost to view is the real
possibility that things may be as they are not because
they *have* to be but because they happen to be.[7] We
"have to" play this super-power role, said the President
—as if the matter were patently beyond the range of
human choice, as if some heavenly force had decreed
it. With minds locked into this kind of certitude, we
cannot even grasp the notion of other possibilities. We
are compelled to do things in the disastrous, self-defeating way we have done them in the past because we
have locked all other possibilities out of our minds.
"Realism" is reduced to the blind repetition of behavior
patterns that have been *proven* to be disastrous. Anything else is "unreal"—not because it has to be but
because our minds are in thrall to a bleak, fragmented
and fearful conception of "reality."

Drawn as it is from long experience, the conception
of international politics as an endless, mindless, purposeless struggle for power is by no means a false or
fanciful one. It is after all a fairly accurate description
of the normal behavior of nations, especially big nations. The very fact that, in international relations, nations refer to themselves as "powers"—not as countries
or communities—is itself indicative of the nature of

international politics. Behind the grandiose euphemisms about somebody's "place in the sun," or the more current "responsibilities of power," is the simple assumption that nations engage in international relations in order to acquire power, and the more you get of it, the more it is your duty or destiny to use it. It can never be permitted to go unused; if you *can* be a bully, then you must be—on pain of being thought a "pitiful, helpless giant."

This conception is false not in the sense of misrepresenting human experience but in the more important sense of its dangerous obsoleteness, and its utter irrelevance to valid human needs. Even the most dazzling success in the game of power politics does nothing to make life more meaningful or gratifying for anybody except the tiny handful of strategists and geopoliticians who have the exhilarating experience of manipulating whole societies like pawns on a chessboard. It is rather less fun for ordinary citizens, whose sons are sent to useless wars, and whose earnings are diverted from their real needs, such as schools and homes and community services. And, if you happen to be an American flyer or prisoner of war, or a Vietnamese peasant, the "responsibilities of power" do very little indeed to make life interesting or gratifying—even if you succeed in staying alive.

In his book *Six Crises* President Nixon referred to his hesitation as a young man to enter the "warfare of politics."[8] The conception of politics as warfare seems to have shaped the outlook not only of Mr. Nixon's Administration but, as far as international relations is concerned, of every Administration since World War II. It is assumed, a priori, that the natural and inevitable condition of the world is one of basic antagonism. Generalizing from the monstrously atypical experience of Hitler and Nazi Germany, we assumed—until geopolitical considerations dictated a change of assumptions—that China was determined to conquer and communize Asia, that the Russians were motivated by an unshakable ambition to overrun Western Europe and destroy the United States, and that the only thing that stopped the Communist countries from executing their evil designs was the intimidating effect of American military power. I do not contend that this assessment of Russian and Chinese ambitions was untrue, but only that it was not *necessarily* true, that, as Mark Twain would have said, we may have derived from the experience of World War II more wisdom than was in it. My own belief is that Russian and Chinese behavior has been as much influenced by suspicion of our intentions as ours has been by suspicion of theirs. This would mean that we have had great influence on their behavior; that by treating them as hostile, we have assured their hostility. If indeed politics is warfare, it is not because the Lord decreed it but because nations, including our own, have made it so.

In the interview cited earlier President Nixon expressed dismay at what he perceived as the conversion of "former internationalists" into "neo-isolationists." This raises the question of what an authentic internationalist is. It is true that many of us who supported the United Nations Charter, the Marshall Plan and the NATO treaty have become critical of our world-wide military involvements and of bilateral foreign aid. Nonetheless, I still consider myself as an internationalist. I believe that we should honor all of our duly contracted treaties, both in their requirements of military support as in the case of NATO, and in their requirements of nonintervention as in the case of the Charter of the Organization of American States. I further and especially believe that, even at this late date, we should be doing everything in our power—and that there is a great deal we can do—toward building the United Nations into a genuine world security organization.

There has been in this century one great new idea in the field of international relations, one great break in the "totalitarian dictatorship of the established fact": the idea of an international organization with permanent processes for the peaceful settlement of international disputes, the idea of an international legal instrument through which someday we might hope to replace the "warfare of politics" with something more civilized and humane.

That is the conception of internationalism which was held by Presidents Wilson and Franklin Roosevelt and the entire generation who led the United States out of its nineteenth-century isolation. It arose not only out of the obsoleteness of isolationism but, far more importantly, out of deliberate repudiation of the power politics which had culminated in two world wars. Both might go under the name of "internationalism," but they are radically different conceptions: the one represents the outlook of Wilson and Roosevelt; the other reverts to Bismarck and Metternich. Having participated in the hopeful initiation of the United Nations Charter and then in the bitter disillusion of hot and cold wars, the people who are now being called "neo-isolationists" are by and large those who make a distinction between the new internationalism and the old, who welcome the reversion to the old power politics as an improvement on the ideological crusade but regret it in all other respects, and who retain some faith in the validity and viability of the United Nations idea.

That faith, it must be admitted, hangs on a slender thread. That thread is the belief that there has been some evolutionary advance in generally accepted standards of international behavior. In this respect it is noteworthy that although German aggression in the twentieth century was not fundamentally different in motive or method from the earlier aggressions of the English, the French, the Spanish or the ancient Romans, it evoked moral indignation of an intensity and universality unknown in previous eras. The technology of killing was of course much improved by the twentieth century, resulting in far more of it, but that fact alone does not account for the world-wide condemnation of German aggression in the two world wars. In earlier times most people expected wars to take place and, unless they themselves were the victims, accepted it with equanimity when the losers were killed or enslaved. The new factor in the twentieth century is not the killing but the condemnation of the killing, the infiltration into political life of the idea that human life is valuable and that it is a *crime*—for nations as well as for individuals—to destroy it.

If indeed there has been some advance in moral standards, then the concept of an international security community may be more than a utopian dream. It may be an idea whose time, if it has not already come, at least is at hand. It may be that, through limited, practical measures, we can begin to change the rules of the ancient game, that we can begin to move beyond the conception of politics as warfare.

In the past, epochal innovations—such as the Covenant of the League of Nations and the United Nations Charter—have been undertaken in the wake of disaster. Perhaps that is one reason they have not worked: tragedy fosters the will to innovation but it also fosters the excesses of both hope and despair which reduce the likelihood of success. Quiet times, on the other hand, may facilitate sober judgment but they also drain us of interest in innovation because it does not seem necessary. It is exceedingly difficult to believe that a system that seems to be functioning tolerably well at the moment is likely to break down eventually—even though that is the conclusion to which all previous experience forces us with respect to the present international system.

The war in Indochina now seems perpetual, but some day it will end, and when it does, we may hope for a period of relative stability. The great powers seem relatively "balanced" against each other and, owing to certain innovations of the Nixon Administration, some of the crusading fervor has been drained from our conflict with communism. It is an open question whether the American people and their leaders would have the will and the wisdom to use a period of relative stability to try to bring about fundamental changes in the international system. It seems less than likely, but what a worthy project that would be—to try to establish peace on the durable basis of international institutions at a time when we could pursue the project with deliberation rather than desperation.

If we could do that, we might also begin to free ourselves from the costs, both material and spiritual, which three decades of war and cold war have extracted from us. We have gone astray by trying to do things for which we are ill-suited. Our national experience and the values in which our Republic is rooted did not prepare us for the role of power broker of the world. It was we Americans who provided the principal leadership for both the League of Nations and the United Nations, and in those endeavors, disappointing though they have been, we were as true to ourselves as ever we have been in our foreign relations. For reasons partly of necessity, partly of misjudgment, we have strayed from the course for which our experience and values prepared us into the uncongenial practices of power politics and war. The diversion has depleted our resources and our spirits; it has crippled the giant.

PART I

American Foreign Policy

Let every nation know, whether it wishes us well or ill, that we shall pay any price, bear any burden, meet any hardship, support any friend, oppose any foe to assure the survival and the success of liberty.

John F. Kennedy, Inaugural Address
January 1961

Wherever the standard of freedom and independence has been or shall be unfurled, there will be America's heart, her benedictions, and her prayers. But she goes not abroad in search of monsters to destroy. She is the well wisher to the freedom and independence of all. She is the champion and vindicator only of her own.

John Quincy Adams, Washington Address
July 4, 1821

1

The Truman Doctrine in Europe and the World

For reasons still not wholly known and understood, the grand alliance of World War II broke up almost as soon as victory was won, and the powers which had called themselves the "United Nations" fell into the pattern of hostility, periodic crisis and "limited" war that has characterized world politics for the last twenty-five years. At Yalta in February 1945 the United States, Great Britian and the Soviet Union pledged to maintain and strengthen in peace the "unity of purpose and of action" that was bringing victory in war. Just over two years later, on March 12, 1947, President Truman proclaimed the Doctrine that came to be recognized as the basic rationale, from the American standpoint, for the cold war. President Truman based the appeal he made to Congress for support of Greece and Turkey not primarily on the specific circumstances of those two countries at that time but on a general formulation of the American national interest which held that "totalitarian regimes imposed on free peoples, by direct or indirect aggression, undermine the foundations of international peace and hence the security of the United States." President Truman went on to say that at that moment in world history "nearly every nation must choose between alternative ways of life," the one based on democratic institutions like our own, the other based on "terror and opression," for which the model, of course, was the Soviet Union.

Most of us thought we knew how and why this great transition—from "unity of purpose and action" to Truman's declaration of ideological warfare—had come about in so short a time. The cause was Soviet Communist aggression, limited at the outset to Stalin's subjugation of Eastern Europe but shown by Marxist-Leninist doctrine to be universal in design, aimed at nothing less than the communization of the world. American policy and opinion were profoundly influenced in the early postwar period by the thesis of George Kennan's famous "X" article, in which Soviet policy was depicted as relentlessly expansionist, committed by a fanatical ideology to filling "every nook and cranny available . . . in the basin of world power," and "stopping only when it meets with some unanswerable force." Warning against bluster and excessive reliance on military force, Kennan called nonetheless for an American policy of "unalterable counter-force," of "firm and vigilant containment," which, he anticipated, would "increase enormously the strains under which Soviet policy must operate," and encourage changes within Russia leading to "either the breakup or the gradual mellowing of Soviet power."[1]

From Korea to Berlin to Cuba to Vietnam the Truman Doctrine governed America's response to the Communist world. Tactics changed—from "massive retaliation" to "limited war" and "counterinsurgency"

—but these were variations on a classic formulation, based on assumptions which few really questioned. Sustained by an inert Congress, the policy makers of the forties, fifties and early sixties were never compelled to reexamine the premises of the Truman Doctrine, or even to defend them in constructive adversary proceedings.

Change has come not from wisdom but from disaster. The calamitous failure of American policy in Vietnam has induced on the part of scholars, journalists and politicians a belated willingness to reexamine the basic assumptions of American postwar policy. Induced by the agitations of the present moment, this new look at old events may well result in an excess of revision, or of emotion, but the corrective is much needed if we are to profit from experience and recast our policies. It cannot be said that the assumptions underlying the Truman Doctrine were wholly false, especially for their time and place, but there is a powerful, presumptive case against their subsequent universal application: the case deriving from the disaster of our policy in Asia. And it seems appropriate to look back and try to discover how and why the promise of the United Nations Charter gave way so quickly to ideological warfare between East and West.

I. Anti-Communism as a National Ideology

Until fairly recently I accepted the conventional view that the United States had acted in good faith to make the United Nations work but that the Charter was undermined by the Soviet veto. In retrospect, this seems less certain, and one suspects now that, like the League of Nations before it, the United Nations was orphaned at birth. Whereas Woodrow Wilson's great creation was abandoned to skeptical Europeans, Franklin Roosevelt's project was consigned to the care of unsympathetic men of his own country. President Roosevelt died only two weeks before the opening of the meeting in San Francisco at which the United Nations was organized. The new and inexperienced President Truman was naturally more dependent on his advisers than President Roosevelt had been; among these, so far as I know, none was a strong supporter of the plan for a world organization, as Cordell Hull had been. The Under Secretary of State, Dean Acheson, was assigned to lobby for Senate approval of the United Nations Charter and he recalled later, "I did my duty faithfully and successfully, but always believed that the Charter was impractical." And with even greater asperity and candor, he told an interviewer in 1970: "I never thought the United Nations was worth a damn. To a lot of people it was a Holy Grail, and those who set store by it had the misfortune to believe their own bunk."[2]

Disdaining the United Nations, the framers of the Truman Doctrine also nurtured an intense hostility toward communism and the Soviet Union. Stalin of course did much to earn this hostility, with his paranoiac suspiciousness, the imposition of Soviet domination in Eastern Europe and the use of Western Communist parties as instruments of Soviet policy. All this is well-known. Less well-known, far more puzzling and also more pertinent to our position in the world today is the eagerness with which we seized upon postwar Soviet provocations and plunged into the cold war. Even if it be granted that Stalin started the cold war, it must also be recognized that the Truman Administration seemed to welcome it.

By early 1947—a year and a half after the founding of the United Nations—the assumptions of the cold war were all but unchallenged within the United States government and anti-communism had become a national ideology. It was *assumed* that the object of Soviet policy was the communization of the world; if Soviet behavior in Europe and northern China were not proof enough, the design was spelled out in the writings of Lenin and Marx, which our policy makers chose to read not as a body of political philosophy but as the field manual of Soviet strategy. It is true of course that by 1947, with the United States virtually disarmed and Western Europe in a condition of economic paralysis, the Soviet Union might plausibly have tried to take over Western Europe through the manipulation of Communist parties, military intimidation, economic strangulation, and possibly even direct military action. The fact that Stalin could have done this, and might well have tried but for timely American counteraction through the Marshall Plan and the formation of NATO, was quickly and uncritically taken as proof of a design for unlimited conquest comparable to that of Nazi Germany. Neither in the executive branch of our government nor in Congress were more than a few isolated voices raised to suggest the possibility that Soviet policy in Europe might be motivated by morbid fears for the security of the Soviet Union, and by opportunism, rather than by a design for world conquest. Virtually no one in a position of power was receptive to the hypothesis that Soviet truculence reflected weakness rather than strength, intensified by memories of 1919 when the Western powers had intervened in an effort—however half-hearted—to strangle the Bolshevik "monster" in its cradle. Our own policy was formed without the benefit of constructive adversary proceedings. A few brave individuals like former Vice President Henry Wallace offered dissenting counsel—and paid dear for it.

When Great Britain informed the United States in February 1947 that it was no longer able to provide military support for Greece, the American government was ready with a policy and a world view. The latter was an early version of the domino theory. *Knowing* as we thought we did that Russian support for the Communist insurgents in Greece was part of a grand design for the takeover first of Greece, then of Turkey, the Middle East and so forth, we were not content simply to assume the British role of providing arms to a beleaguered government; instead we chose to issue a declaration of ideological warfare in the form of the Truman Doctrine. It is true, as noted earlier, that the grand phrases were motivated in large part by a desire to arouse this nation's combative spirit, and so to build Congressional support for the funds involved, but it is also true—at least according to Joseph Jones, the State Department official who drafted President Truman's appeal to Congress, under Acheson's direction (and with Clark Clifford's editing, Clifford then being a close adviser to President Truman)—that the new policy was conceived not just as a practical measure to bolster the Greeks and Turks but as a historic summons of the United States to world leadership. "All barriers to bold action were indeed down," as Jones has written. Among the State Department policy makers it was felt that "a new chapter in world history had opened, and they were the most privileged of men, participants in a drama such as rarely occurs even in the long life of a great nation."[3]

The Truman Doctrine, which may have made sense for its time and place, was followed by the Marshall Plan and NATO, which surely did make sense for their time and place. But as the charter for twenty-five years of global ideological warfare and unilateral military intervention against Communist insurgencies, the Truman Doctrine has a different set of implications altogether. It represents a view of communism and of our

role in the world which has had much to do with the
disaster of our policy in Indochina. Even in the country
to which it was first applied, President Truman's basic
formulation—that "We shall not realize our objectives
. . . unless we are willing to help free people to maintain
their free institutions"—has been reduced to a mock-
ery. But who remembers now that the Truman Doctrine was initially designed to preserve democracy in
Greece?

Acheson, who prided himself on being a realist, may
not have taken all that ideological claptrap seriously,
but his successors Dulles and Rusk certainly did, and
they framed their policies accordingly. Whatever merit
the Truman Doctrine may have had in the circumstances of early postwar Europe, the bond with reality
became more and more strained as the Doctrine came
to be applied at times and in places increasingly remote
from the Greek civil war. Operating on a set of assumptions that defined reality for them—that as a social system communism was deeply immoral, that as a political
movement it was a conspiracy for world conquest—our
leaders became liberated from the normal rules of evidence and inference when it came to dealing with communism. After all, who ever heard of giving the Devil
a fair shake? Since we know what he has in mind, it is
pedantry to split hairs over what he is actually doing.

Political pressures at home intensified the virulence
of the anti-Communist ideology. In retrospect the surprise Democratic victory in the election of 1948 was
probably a misfortune for the country. Frustrated and
enraged by their fifth successive defeat, the Republi-
cans became desperate in their search for a winning
issue. They found their issue in the threat of communism, at home and abroad, and they seized upon it with
uncommon ferocity. They blamed the Truman Administration for Chiang Kai-shek's defeat in the Chi-

nese civil war; they attacked President Truman for the bloody stalemate in Korea, although they had strongly supported his initial commitment; and they tolerated and in many cases encouraged Senator Joseph R. McCarthy's attacks on reputable and even eminent Americans. Every American President since that time has been under intense pressure to demonstrate his anti-Communist orthodoxy.

More by far than any other factor the anti-communism of the Truman Doctrine has been the guiding spirit of American foreign policy since World War II. Stalin and Mao Tse-tung and even Ho Chi Minh replaced Hitler in our minds as the sources of all evil in the world. We came to see the hand of "Moscow communism" in every disruption that occurred anywhere. First, there was the conception of communism as an international conspiracy, as an octopus with its body in Moscow and its tentacles reaching out to the farthest corners of the world. Later, after the Sino-Soviet break, sophisticated foreign policy analysts disavowed the conspiracy thesis, but, at the same time they disavowed it, they said things which showed that the faith lingered on. Secretary Rusk and his associates professed to be scornful of the conspiracy thesis, but they still defended the Vietnam war with references to a world "cut in two by Asian communism," the only difference between the earlier view and the later one being that where once there had been one octopus, they now saw two.

If you accepted the premise, the rest followed. If Moscow and Peking represented centers of great power implacably hostile to the United States, and if every local crisis from Cuba to the Congo to Vietnam had the Communist mark upon it, then it followed logically that every crisis posed a threat to the security of the United States.

The effect of the anti-Communist ideology was to

spare us the task of taking cognizance of the specific facts of specific situations. Our "faith" liberated us, like the believers of old, from the requirements of empirical thinking, from the necessity of observing and evaluating the actual behavior of the nations and leaders with whom we were dealing. Like medieval theologians, we had a philosophy which explained everything to us in advance, and everything that did not fit could be readily identified as a fraud or a lie or an illusion. The fact that in some respects the behavior of the Soviet Union and of China and North Vietnam has lived up to our ideological expectations has made it all the easier to ignore the instances in which it did not. What we are now, belatedly, discovering is not that the Communist states have never really been hostile but that they have been neither consistent nor united in hostility to us; that their hostility has by no means been wholly unprovoked; and that they have been willing, from time to time, to do business or come to terms with us. Our ideological blinders concealed these instances from us, robbing us of useful information and promising opportunities. The perniciousness of the anti-Communist ideology of the Truman Doctrine arises not from patent falsehood but from its distortion and simplification of reality, from its universalization and its elevation to the status of a revealed truth.

II. The Khrushchev Interlude

Psychologists tell us that there is often a great difference between what one person says and what another hears, or, in variation of the old adage, that the evil may be in the ear of the hearer. When Khrushchev said, "We will bury you," Americans heard the statement as a threat of nuclear war and were outraged accordingly.

The matter was raised when Chairman Khrushchev visited the United States in 1959, and he replied with some anger that he had been talking about economic competition. "I am deeply concerned over these conscious distortions of my thoughts," he said. "I've never mentioned any rockets."[4]

We will never know, of course, but it is possible that an opportunity for a stable peace was lost during the years of Khrushchev's power. As we look back now on the many things he said regarding peaceful coexistence, the words have a different ring. At the time we did not believe them; at best they were Communist propaganda, at worst outright lies. On the occasion of his visit to the Foreign Relations Committee on September 16, 1959, for example, Chairman Khrushchev suggested that we lay aside the polemics of the past. Mr. Khrushchev said:

> We must face the future more and have wisdom enough to secure peace for our countries and for the whole world. We have always had great respect for the American people. We have also been somewhat envious of your achievements in the economic field, and for that reason, we are doing our best to try to catch up with you in that field, to compete with you, and when we do catch up, to move further ahead. I should say that future generations would be grateful to us if we managed to switch our efforts from stockpiling and perfecting weapons and concentrated those efforts fully on competition in the economic field.[5]

Now, in retrospect, one wonders: why were we so sure that Khrushchev did not mean what he said about peace? The answer lies in part, I believe, in our anti-Communist obsession, in the distortions it created in our perception of Soviet behavior, and in the extraordinary sense of threat we experienced when the Russians proclaimed their desire to catch up and overtake us economically. In our own national value system competition has always been prized; why then should we have been so alarmed by a challenge to compete? Perhaps our national tendency to extol competition rather than cooperation as a social virtue and our preoccupation with our own primacy—with being the "biggest," the "greatest" nation—suggests an underlying lack of confidence in ourselves, a supposition that unless we are "Number 1," we will be nothing, worthless and despised, and deservedly so. I am convinced that the real reason we squandered $20 billion or more getting men to the moon in the decade of the sixties was our fear of something like horrible humiliation if the Russians got men there first. All this suggests that slogans about competition and our own primacy in that competition are largely hot air, sincerely believed no doubt, but nonetheless masking an exaggerated fear of failure, which in turn lends a quality of desperation to our competitive endeavors. One detects this cast of mind in President Johnson's determination that he would not be the "first American President to lose a war," and also in President Nixon's specter of America as a "pitiful, helpless giant."

This kind of thinking robs a nation's policy makers of objectivity and drives them to irresponsible behavior. The distortion of priorities in going to the moon is a relatively benign example. The perpetuation of the Vietnam war is the most terrible and fateful manifestation of the determination to prove that we are "Number 1." Assistant Secretary of Defense for International Security Affairs John T. McNaughton, as quoted in the Pentagon Papers, measured the American interest in Vietnam and found that "to permit the people of South

Vietnam to enjoy a better, freer way of life," accounted for a mere 10 percent and "to avoid a humiliating United States defeat" for up to 70 percent.[6] McNaughton's statistical metaphor suggests a nation in thrall to fear; it suggests a policy-making elite unable to distinguish between the national interest and their own personal pride.

Perhaps if we had been less proud and less fearful, we would have responded in a more positive way to the earthy, unorthodox Khrushchev. Whatever his faults and excesses, Khrushchev is recognized in retrospect as the Communist leader who repudiated the Marxist dogma of the "inevitability" of war between Communist and capitalist states. Recognizing the insanity of war with nuclear weapons, Khrushchev became the advocate of "goulash" communism, of peaceful economic competition with the West. During his period in office some amenities were restored in East-West relations; the Berlin issue was stirred up but finally defused; and, most important, the limited nuclear test-ban treaty was concluded. These were solid achievements, though meager in proportion to mankind's need for peace, and meager too, it now appears, in proportion to the opportunity that may then have existed. One wonders how much more might have been accomplished—particularly in the field of disarmament—if Americans had not still been caught up in the prideful, fearful spirit of the Truman Doctrine.

Even the crises look different in retrospect, especially when one takes into account the internal workings of the Communist world. A British writer on Soviet affairs, Victor Zorza, has traced the beginning of the Vietnam war to a "fatal misreading" by President Kennedy of Khrushchev's endorsement of "wars of national liberation."[7] The Kennedy Administration interpreted Khrushchev's statement as a declaration that the Soviet Union intended to sponsor subversion, guerrilla warfare, and rebellion all over the world. Accordingly, the Administration attached enormous significance to Soviet material support for the Laotian Communists, as if the issue in that remote and backward land were directly pertinent to the world balance of power. It was judged that Khrushchev must be shown that he could not get away with it. We had taught Stalin that "direct" aggression did not pay; now we must teach Khrushchev—and the Chinese—that "indirect" aggression did not pay. In Zorza's view, Khrushchev's talk of "wars of national liberation" was not a serious plan for world-wide subversion but a response to Communist China, whose leaders were then accusing Khrushchev of selling out the cause of revolution and making a deal with the United States.

In the spirit of the Truman Doctrine, the Kennedy Administration read the Soviet endorsement of "wars of national liberation" as a direct challenge to the United States. Speaking of Russia and China, President Kennedy said in his first State of the Union message: "We must never be lulled into believing that either power has yielded its ambitions for world domination —ambitions which they forcefully restated only a short time ago." I do not recall these words for purposes of reproach; they represented an assessment of Communist intentions which most of us shared at that time, an assessment which had been held by every Administration and most members of Congress since World War II, an assessment which had scarcely if at all been brought up for critical examination in the executive branch, in Congressional committees, in the then proliferating "think tanks," or in the universities. Perhaps no better assessment could have been made on the basis of the information available at that time, but I doubt it. I think it more likely that we simply chose to ignore evidence that did not fit our preconceptions, or—as is more often the case—when the facts lent themselves to several possible interpretations, we chose to seize upon the one with which we were most familiar—the Communist drive for world domination.

In the amplified form it acquired during the Johnson years, the conception of "wars of national liberation" as part of the Communist design for world domination became the basic rationale for the Vietnam war. All the other excuses—defending freedom, honoring our "commitments," demonstrating America's resolution —are secondary in importance and are easily shown to be fallacious and contradictory. But no one can *prove* that Mao Tse-tung and Brezhnev and Kosygin, or Khrushchev for that matter, have not harbored secret ambitions to conquer the world. Who can prove that the desire or the intention was never in their minds?

The truly remarkable thing about this cold-war psychology is the totally illogical transfer of the burden of proof from those who make charges to those who question them. In this frame of reference Communists are guilty until proved innocent—or simply by definition. The cold warriors, instead of having to say how they knew that Vietnam was part of a plan for the communization of the world, so manipulated the terms of public discussion as to be able to demand that the skeptics prove that it was not. If the skeptics could not, then the war must go on—to end it would be recklessly risking the national security. We come to the ultimate illogic: war is the course of prudence and sobriety, until the case for peace is proved under impossible rules of evidence—or until the enemy surrenders.

Rational men cannot deal with one another on this basis. Recognizing their inability to know with anything like certainty what is going on in other men's minds, they do not try to deal with others on the basis of their presumed intentions. Instead rational men respond to others on the basis of their actual, observable behavior, and they place the burden of proof where it belongs—on those who assert and accuse rather than those who question or doubt. The departure from these elementary rules for the ascertainment of truth is the essence of the cold-war way of thinking; its weakened but still formidable hold on our minds is indicative of the surviving tyranny of the Truman Doctrine.

With a decade's perspective—and without the blinders of the Truman Doctrine—it even seems possible that the Cuban missile crisis of 1962 was not so enormous a crisis as it then seemed. Khrushchev in the early sixties was engaged in an internal struggle with the Soviet military, who, not unlike our own generals, were constantly lobbying for more funds for ever more colossal weapons systems. Khrushchev had been cutting back on conventional forces and, largely for purposes of appeasing his unhappy generals, was talking a great deal about the power of Soviet missiles. President Kennedy, however, was applying pressure from another direction; unnerved by Khrushchev's endorsement of "wars of national liberation," he was undertaking to build up American conventional forces at the same time that he was greatly expanding the American nuclear-missile force, even though by this time the United States had an enormous strategic superiority. Khrushchev's effort to resist the pressures from his generals was of course undermined by the American buildup. It exposed him to pressures within the Kremlin from a hostile coalition of thwarted generals and politicians who opposed his de-Stalinization policies. In the view of a number of specialists in the Soviet field, the placement of missiles in Cuba was motivated largely if not primarily by Khrushchev's need to deal with these domestic pressures; it was meant to close or narrow the

Soviet "missile gap" in relation to the United States, without forcing Khrushchev to concentrate all available resources on a ruinous arms race.

Lacking an expert knowledge of my own on these matters, I commend this interpretation of Khrushchev's purpose not as necessarily true but as highly plausible. So far as I know, however, none of the American officials who participated in the decisions relating to the Cuban missile crisis seriously considered the possibility that Khrushchev might be acting defensively or in response to domestic pressures. It was universally assumed that the installation of Soviet missiles in Cuba was an aggressive strategic move against the United States—that and nothing more. Assuming Khrushchev's aggressive intent, we imposed on the Soviet Union a resounding defeat, for which Khrushchev was naturally held responsible. In this way we helped to strengthen the military and political conservatives within the Soviet Union who were to overthrow Khrushchev two years later. If we had been willing to consider the possibility that Khrushchev was acting on internal considerations, we would still have wished to secure the removal of the missiles from Cuba but it might have been accomplished by means less embarrassing to Khrushchev, such as a quid pro quo under which we would have removed our Jupiter missiles from Turkey.

Khrushchev had paid dearly for his "softness on capitalism" in an earlier encounter with President Eisenhower. After his visit to the United States in 1959 Khrushchev apparently tried to persuade his skeptical, hard-line colleagues that Americans were not such monsters as they supposed and that President Eisenhower was a reasonable man. This heretical theory— heretical from the Soviet point of view—was shot out of the sky along with the American U-2 spy plane in May

1960. When President Eisenhower subsequently de-
clined the opportunity Khrushchev offered him to dis-
claim personal responsibility, Khrushchev felt compelled to break up the Paris summit meeting. The U-2
incident was later cited by Khrushchev himself as a
critical moment in his loss of power at home. It shat-
tered his plans for a visit to the Soviet Union by President Eisenhower—for which, it is said, he had already
had a golf course secretly constructed in the Crimea.[8]

There were of course other factors in Khrushchev's
fall, and perhaps more important ones; nor is it suggested that his intentions toward the West were necessarily benevolent. The point that must emerge, however—more for the future than for history's sake—is
that if *we* had not been wearing ideological blinders, if
our judgment had not been clouded by fear and hostility, we might have perceived in Khrushchev a world
statesman with whom constructive business could be
done. When he fell, his successors put an end to de-
Stalinization, began the military build-up which has
brought the Soviet Union to a rough strategic parity
with the United States, and greatly stepped up their aid
to Communist forces in Vietnam.

III. Relics of the Cold War in Europe

Cold-war tensions have abated in Europe—partly as
the result of deliberate acts of policy on the part of the
Soviet Union, the Western European countries and the
United States; partly, too, because of the "benign neglect" necessitated by American involvement in Vietnam; finally—and most important—because of general
acceptance of the results of the Second World War,
tacit until 1972, made all but explicit in the Moscow
summit and the German-Soviet and German-Polish

treaties of 1972. The durability of the results of World
War II is the governing reality of contemporary European politics; however little they may like it, Europeans by and large have come to terms with the status
quo of their continent—not because it is just, as indeed
it is not, but because it is effectively unchallengeable.
Insofar as the nations accommodate to this fact and
direct their energies to the abatement of lingering tensions, there is hope for a stable peace and also, with
lessening tensions, for improvement in the lives of the
Czechs and the Poles and all the other nations which
are dominated by the Soviet Union. Insofar, on the
other hand, as we raise false hopes with provocative
propaganda, maintain high troop levels, and continue
the arms race, we retard the natural progress of European reunification, lingering morbidly and uselessly in
the graveyard of cold-war relics.

In Europe if not elsewhere, the power balance which
emerged from World War II has become stabilized.
Unlike the formal, contractual settlement of 1919,
which collapsed, the de facto settlement of 1945, determined essentially by the lines of military demarcation
at the end of the Second World War, has shown itself
to be durable. All of the significant territorial gains
made by the Soviet Union after World War II, including
the establishment of a sphere of domination in Eastern
Europe, were made in the few months immediately
before and after the surrender of Germany in May
1945. Direct Soviet military action since then—as in
Hungary in 1956 and Czechoslovakia in 1968—has been
employed not to expand the empire but to put down
rebellion within it. In classic, Metternichian terms—the
terms which the Nixon Administration understands
well—the great powers are in deadlock, deterred by
each other's nuclear power from expansion or major
adventure.

The Soviet-American agreements reached at the Moscow summit in May 1972 signify the final, belated acceptance by the United States of the postwar balance of power in Europe and in Soviet-American relations. Over and above the specific agreements reached—the treaty limiting the United States and the Soviet Union each to two antiballistic missile sites, the agreement curtailing the deployment of offensive missiles, the agreements for cooperation in space, science and health—the great importance of the Moscow summit was the acknowledgment by the two "super powers" of mutual vulnerability to each other's devastating nuclear power; the acceptance by the United States of the Soviet Union as an equal, "legitimate" great power; the acceptance by the Soviet Union of a stabilized, non-revolutionary status quo; and reciprocal acknowledgment of each other's "spheres of influence"—that term being a euphemism for zones of domination.

For many years the new balance of power was either ignored or denied by American leaders even though its existence was readily discernible. One reason it was not discerned was the absence of a formal peace treaty sanctifying the results of the Second World War—although the reason for the failure to conclude a peace treaty was unwillingness to accept the de facto power balance which had come out of the war. Another reason perhaps was the unfamiliarity of the state of equilibrium: Europe had been in profound disruption since 1914, and statesmen have not easily gotten used to the idea that a leader such as Stalin might be ambitious or opportunist and still not be "another Hitler," if only because the circumstances which allowed Germany to bid for the mastery of Europe ceased to exist after 1945. The redoubtable cold warriors still do not acknowledge the new balance of power simply because they dislike it: it has put a crimp in their crusade. Others of us—in the Wilson-Roosevelt tradition—welcome the new equilibrium but would like to use the breathing spell to try to establish peace on a more stable and durable basis. Nonetheless, the facts are that Soviet preeminence in Eastern Europe is established; that Western Europe is evolving into a formidable economic confederation with increasing bonds to the East; and that the Soviet Union and the United States are in nuclear deadlock. The acceptance of these realities must be rated a solid achievement in statesmanship on the part of the Nixon Administration.

These facts were long obscured by the ideological outlook of the Truman Doctrine, under the influence of which we perceived the Soviet Union as relentlessly expansionist, committed by Marxist-Leninist doctrine to the communization of the world. As recently as 1969 President Nixon warned ominously against "those great powers who have not yet abandoned their goals of world conquest. . . ."[9] The outlook expressed in those words was exactly that contained in the portentous language of President Truman's proclamation in 1950— which is still in force—of a state of national emergency: "Whereas world conquest by Communist imperialism is the goal of the forces of aggression that have been loosed upon the world. . . ." Through such doctrines we inflicted upon ourselves a disabling myopia. Failing to distinguish between practice and precept, we tended to perceive Soviet and Chinese policies not in terms of what these countries have actually done—and not done —but in terms of our own suspicions of what they might wish to do. Obscured to our view, as a result, were such pertinent facts as that the Russians—whatever they might dream in their secret hearts—have not since the end of the Second World War conquered anybody outside of their sphere of regional domination in Eastern Europe.

Relics of this myopia survive in our policy. One of the more striking—though ineffectual—survivals of cold-war mentality in our European policy is represented by our so-called "information" programs directed to Eastern Europe and the Soviet Union. For many years "Radio Free Europe" and "Radio Liberty" defrauded the American people by pretending to be private organizations relying on private contributions and committed to broadcasting the "truth" to the peoples of Eastern Europe. In fact, the two broadcasters received hundreds of millions of dollars from the Central Intelligence Agency from 1950 until the identity of their secret benefactor became known in 1971. Since then, the two nominally independent propaganda organs have been financed by public appropriated funds. The amount proposed for them by the Nixon Administration—but not appropriated by Congress—for fiscal year 1972 was $36.2 million, an amount not far below the total budget of $44 million for the Voice of America, which is the official overseas radio of the United States Information Agency, and hardly less than the $40 million requested for 1972 by the Nixon Administration for our entire world-wide Educational and Cultural Exchange Program.

Purporting to keep the "truth" alive behind the "Iron Curtain," Radio Free Europe and Radio Liberty are in fact hardy survivors of the old cold-war mentality. If our foreign propaganda activities had anything at all to do with an authentic interest in freedom and truth rather than anti-communism, we would presumably be providing funds for a "Radio Free Greece" or a "Radio Free Brazil," both countries whose governments impose a degree of censorship. The rationale for Radio Free Europe and Radio Liberty, and for much of the official propaganda put forth by the United States Information Agency, derives from the old crusading anti-

Communist ideology; it is wholly inconsistent with—
and detrimental to—our emerging policy of accommodation with the Soviet Union. The cold-war outlook has
been clearly enunciated by the Director of the United
States Information Agency under the Nixon Administration, Frank Shakespeare, who has instructed Agency
personnel not to refer to the people of Russia as "Soviets" nor to the "Soviet nation" because, "to call it so,
apart from being grammatically incorrect, is to foster
the illusion of one happy family rather than an imperi-
alistic state increasingly beset with nationality problems, which is what it is."[10]

In this quarrelsome, troublemaking spirit we not only
antagonize the government of the Soviet Union, with
whom we are supposed to be trying to improve relations; we also perpetrate a cruel deception upon the
people of Eastern Europe. Purporting to show them
that there is a better "way of life" outside of the "Iron
Curtain," we foster futile discontent, not for any discernible purpose of policy but for purposes of ideological mischief. In this way we detract from the broader
purposes of our own policy and of world peace, which
require us to live in the greatest attainable harmony
with the Communist governments of the world, however litte we—or their own people—may like those
governments.

The maintenance of over 300,000 American troops
on the European continent is another, more significant
anachronism in our policy. These forces are said to be
essential to permit of a "flexible response" on the part
of the NATO alliance in the event of a Soviet ground
attack on Western Europe—despite the fact that the
nuclear stalemate has made such an attack all but inconceivable. When American troops were first assigned
to NATO in 1951, Western Europe was still enfeebled by

the ravages of World War II; Stalin was alive and the Soviet threat, though probably exaggerated, was plausible. In the early 1970's Western Europe is, for the most part, politically stable and economically powerful, with national economies by and large healthier than that of the United States and collective resources at least as great as those of the Soviet Union. At the same time the Soviet Union, under cautious leadership, has shown itself to be far more interested in formalizing the European status quo than in trying to alter it and shows no inclination to try to occupy Western Europe with ground forces. Under these markedly altered conditions it would seem both safe and sensible gradually but steadily to reduce the American ground force in Europe to half of its present number, as proposed by Senator Mansfield, or even fewer. Under the changed circumstances of Europe, a symbolic ground force is desirable as a demonstration of American loyalty to the North Atlantic Alliance, more specifically as token of the availability of American nuclear power for the defense of Europe, but there is no need of an American army of 300,000 men to protect Europeans who are perfectly capable, if they care to make the effort, of mobilizing and maintaining the necessary ground forces to protect themselves against an all but inconceivable Soviet ground attack.

Some Europeans profess distress over the danger of American "neo-isolationism," but a more accurate measure of their anxiety over the danger of Soviet attack is provided by a comparison of European and American defense expenditures. In 1970, for example, the European NATO countries spent approximately $24 billion on defense, representing 3.7 percent of their collective gross national products; in the same year the United States spent $76.5 billion on defense, representing 7.8 percent of its gross national product. Since 1970 the gap between European and American defense expenditures has narrowed, but it remains considerable, and the fact remains incontestable that if American forces in Europe were reduced, the European countries have the capability of replacing them with their own troops should that seem essential for their security. Under pressure from the Nixon Administration, the European NATO allies agreed in 1971 to increase their overall financial contributions to NATO, and West Germany agreed to contribute a larger share of the cost of maintaining American forces in Germany. Nonetheless, at the end of 1971 the United States was maintaining an establishment in Europe consisting not only of 307,000 military personnel but also 230,000 dependents, with the overall cost of the total American commitment to NATO running at approximately $14 billion a year.[11]

Even if an invasion of Western Europe by the Soviet Army were a real possibility, the overall balance of forces makes the maintenance in Europe of over three hundred thousand American military personnel something less than a matter of life and death for our European allies. The Soviet Union has over three million men under arms, but a large number of these are stationed on the borders of China, while the Soviet Union's allies in the Warsaw Pact have only a little over a million men under arms—many of doubtful political reliability. By contrast, the United States has about 2.5 million men in its armed forces and the European NATO allies have another three million, of whom almost half make up the armed forces of Britain, France and West Germany.[12] On the basis of these figures it is clear that, even with only a "hostage" American force in Europe, our NATO allies would retain a favorable balance of manpower in relation to the Warsaw Pact. In any case, as already noted, our European allies have sufficient population and resources to increase their conventional forces to a higher level if they should judge that necessary for their security. For all these reasons, it seems evident that the maintenance of a large American army in Europe is not a military necessity but a political instrumentality whose importance diminishes greatly as East-West détente is developed.

In the spring of 1971 Senator Mansfield introduced an amendment to the then-pending Draft Extension Bill calling for a reduction by half of the number of American troops in Europe, to a level, that is, of 150,000 men. In the course of Senate debate on this proposal, proponents were assailed by an avalanche of criticism, consisting in the main of clamorous protests over the danger of "neo-isolationism" and an alleged "flight from responsibility." In the wake of an intensive lobbying campaign organized by the White House, the Mansfield proposal was defeated on May 19, 1971, by a vote of 61 to 36. A more modest version of the amendment, calling for a troop reduction of only 50,000 men, was defeated in the Senate in November 1971. The principal argument made by the Nixon Administration, with the strong support of the Chairman of the Senate Armed Services Committee, was that troop levels in Europe could be safely reduced only on the basis of an agreement with the Soviet Union for "mutual and balanced force reduction." Having persuaded a majority of Senators of the need of reciprocity, the Nixon Administration did virtually nothing to try to attain it until the Moscow summit of May 1972, when general agreement was reached for future talks on mutual force reduction. A false start had been made in late 1971, prior to the annual meeting of the NATO Foreign Ministers in Brussels, when it was announced that the former Secretary General of NATO, Manlio Brosio, was about to be received in Moscow for purposes of discussing "mutual and balanced force reduction." The announcement apparently was news to the Russians, because they did not in fact receive Mr. Brosio, whom they regarded as a NATO "hawk." The effect of the Brosio episode and of the intense opposition of the Nixon Administration to the Mansfield amendments was to cast doubt on the interest of the Administration in reducing American force levels in Europe, with or without an agreement with the Soviet Union. The agreement of May 1972 to proceed with mutual troop-reduction talks indicated a change, or at least an evolution, of American policy. Here as elsewhere one detects a certain ambivalence as between the new détente and the old habits of the cold war.

In this as in other areas of our foreign policy, foreign and domestic problems overlap and interact. In our armed forces as in American society as a whole, problems of crime, racial hostility and drug addiction are taking a heavy toll, undermining the morale and combat readiness of our soldiers stationed abroad. In Europe and elsewhere—according to an extended study of the condition of the United States Army by two journalists—many of our soldiers are deeply disaffected from the Army and its mission. Some of them defy discipline and some have been heard to refer to their own military leaders as war criminals. In Europe, where our soldiers have little to do, problems of morale are aggravated by boredom. "Tell Mansfield to come over here if he wants to get some headlines," one soldier told the two journalists. "The most I ever work is two days a week." One officer, an anthropologist working with the Army's drug education program at Fort Bragg, North Carolina, commented as to the young people entering the military service: "They hate the Army. They just hate it. It blows their minds. And some of them use drugs to rebel."[13]

As we evolve haltingly from the ideological animosity of the cold war toward a more conventional kind of balance-of-power politics, we are compelled to reconsider the kind of relationship we wish to have with the European countries, both Eastern and Western, and we are also compelled to take respectful account of the kind of Europe desired by the Europeans themselves.

In the nineteen-fifties and sixties, and to a great degree even now, American policy makers have been preoccupied with the idea of an "Atlantic Community," conceived by Dean Acheson as a community united not only by common economic and strategic interests but also by "common institutions and moral and ethical beliefs" and "the effect of living on the sea."[14] Precisely what "living on the sea" is supposed to do to bring people together is not clear, but one detects in such formulations a kind of romanticized view of Europeans and Americans as superior people. Whatever it connotes, the abatement of the cold war and the desire of a resurgent Europe for independence have reduced the idea of an "Atlantic Community" to little more than a lingering sentimentality. To General de Gaulle the moral and ethical trappings of the Atlantic Community were nothing more than a façade or rationalization for the "messianic impulse" which drove the United States toward "vast undertakings" in the wake of victory in World War II. "The United States," the General wrote in his memoirs, "delighting in her resources, feeling that she no longer had within herself sufficient scope for her energies, wishing to help those who were in misery or bondage the world over, yielded in her turn to that taste for intervention in which the instinct for domination cloaked itself."[15]

From its inception in the late nineteen-forties the notion of an Atlantic Community has been closely associated with the ideology of the Truman Doctrine.

Whatever the effect of "common institutions and moral and ethical beliefs," the driving force behind the Atlantic idea has always been the same as that behind NATO, the presumed need of a Western coalition *against* communism. To the extent, therefore, that the cold war and the Truman Doctrine are obsolete, so too, it would appear, is the aspiration to an Atlantic Community organized and led by the United States.

An alternative and more realistic and promising concept of the new Europe underlies West Germany Chancellor Willy Brandt's *Ostpolitik*. The essence and core of Chancellor Brandt's policy is the acceptance by West Germany of the outcome and consequences of the Second World War, including the division of Germany and the permanent loss to Germany of the territory east of the Oder-Neisse line. The *Ostpolitik* is realistic in that it purports to accommodate to an unalterable status quo; it is promising as a means of alleviating, and ultimately perhaps eliminating, the tensions of the cold war in Europe. The heart and core of the new German policy are Chancellor Brandt's treaties of nonaggression with the Soviet Union and Poland under which the German Federal Republic accepted the postwar frontiers of Europe including, in effect, those of East Germany. Concluding these treaties, the Federal Republic went far to alleviate the profound, surviving fear of Germany harbored by the Soviet Union and the countries of Eastern Europe. A closely related event, also contributing to the alleviation of cold-war tensions, was the conclusion of an agreement made final in June 1972, after the Moscow summit, on the status of Berlin and the access routes to it across the territory of East Germany. Taken together, these agreements represent a turning away from the ideological concept of Atlantic Community and a general movement in the direction of General de Gaulle's "European Europe," reconciling East and West, from the Atlantic to the Urals.

Despite doubts and hesitation, rooted, it would seem, in a lingering attachment to the spirit of the Truman Doctrine, the United States has given its benign approval to Chancellor Brandt's *Ostpolitik* and more grudging approval to a project long desired by the Russians, the convening of an all-European security conference, in which the United States and Canada as well as the European NATO countries and the Warsaw Pact countries would participate. In a speech on December 1, 1971, Secretary of State Rogers said that in the wake of a Berlin accord the United States would be prepared to proceed with "concrete preparations" for a European security conference. The Secretary added that the United States would oppose any effort to use such a conference as a means of legitimizing the status quo of a divided Europe. Here one perceives the lingering spirit of the Truman Doctrine, since a general European security agreement could hardly do anything except to confirm the status quo; which is to say, it would in effect ratify the outcome of the Second World War. In the more current outlook represented by Chancellor Brandt's *Ostpolitik*, confirming the status quo is tacitly recognized not as the means of perpetuating the division of Europe but as the necessary precondition for progress toward ending that division. Agreement "in principle" for the convening of an all-European security conference was reached at the Moscow summit in May 1972.

At the same time that the European states were moving gradually in the direction of a "European Europe," the Soviet Union and the United States engaged in the long, tortuous Strategic Arms Limitation Talks (SALT), without substantive agreement prior to President Nixon's visit to Moscow in May 1972. During the years of

SALT talks the arms race continued apace: the Russians sought "parity" with the United States by deploying their giant SS-9 intercontinental ballistic missiles (ICBM's) and also by accelerating their construction of missile-firing submarines; the United States, for its part, deployed both defensive antiballistic missiles (ABM's) and offensive "multiple independently-targeted reentry vehicles" (MIRV's). Both sides regarded this rapid and enormously costly expansion of their overkill capacity as providing "bargaining chips" for the SALT talks.

The agreement reached at Moscow in May 1972 limiting ABM sites and the deployment of offensive weapons was more important as an act of mutual commitment to coexistence than for the actual arms limitations it imposed. Indeed, giving up the ABM—except for each side retaining the option to two sites—is probably the single most significant commitment the two super powers have made to the principle of coexistence. Insofar as each side abandons the effort to make itself invulnerable to attack or retaliation by the other, it also commits itself to peace and to the survival of the other's power and ideology. The Russians in effect abandon the Marxian dream of a world communized by war; we in turn lay to rest the last vestiges of the old idea of a global crusade for freedom.

These are the symbolic implications if not the immediate fact of the Moscow agreements. The immediate situation is still conditioned by vestiges of the cold-war spirit. Both sides remain capable of destroying each other many times over and, in the wake of the Moscow agreements, the Nixon Administration hastened to call for an increase of over $1 billion for offensive strategic weapons, citing the need for "bargaining chips" in the next round of SALT talks. The Secretary of Defense indeed hastened to make known his doubts as to the wisdom of the Moscow agreements unless we accompanied their ratification with an accelerated program for the development of a missile-launching submarine called Trident, the new B-1 supersonic bomber to replace the giant B-52, and other offensive weapons not covered by the Moscow agreements. The possibility, therefore, arises that, in our ambivalence as between the new coexistence and the lingering spirit of the Truman Doctrine, we may engage the Russians in an accelerated arms race at the same time that we have mutually conceded the survival of each other's power and political system.

With or without an intensified arms race, the balance of nuclear power now, however, seems likely to remain about as stable as so tenuous an equilibrium can be. Despite the continuing enormously costly arms race, the proxy conflict in Southeast Asia, and recurrent tensions in the Middle East, the Soviet Union and the United States have achieved something of the kind of peaceful coexistence advocated by Nikita Khrushchev a decade ago. The basis of that coexistence is fear, the continuing receptiveness of both sides to the warning of Albert Einstein, the man whose formula first made the nuclear bomb possible, that "at the end, looming ever clearer, lies general annihilation."[16]

2

The Truman Doctrine
in Asia

While our response to Soviet communism has been marked by hostility, tensions and fear, our response to communism in Asia has been marked by all of these and, in addition, a profound sense of injury and betrayal. Russia never was a country for which we had much affection anyway: it was the bleak and terrible land of the czars, which, when it went to the Communist devils, was merely trading one tyranny for another. But China had a special place in our hearts. We had favored her with our merchants and missionaries and our "open door" policy; we had even given back much of the Boxer indemnity so that Chinese students could study in America. In the Second World War we fought shoulder-to-shoulder with "free" China; we were filled with admiration for its fighting Generalissimo Chiang Kai-shek and utterly charmed by his Wellesley-educated wife.

I. China in Perdition

When the Chinese darlings of our patronizing hearts went to Communist perdition, we could only assume that they had been sold or betrayed into bondage. It was inconceivable that our star pupils in the East could actually have willed this calamity; it had to be the work of Chinese traitors abetted by disloyal Americans, joined in unholy alliance to sell out China to those quintessential bad people, the Russians. A white paper on China was issued in 1949, and Secretary of State Dean Acheson's letter of transmittal recounted accurately the intense but futile American effort to salvage a Kuomintang regime whose officials and soldiers had "sunk into corruption, into a scramble for place and power, and into reliance on the United States to win the war for them and to preserve their own domestic supremacy." Then, having exonerated the United States from responsibility for the loss of China, Secretary Acheson wrote:

> .... The heart of China is in Communist hands. The Communist leaders have forsworn their Chinese heritage and have publicly announced their subservience to a foreign power, Russia, which during the last 50 years, under czars and Communists alike, has been most assiduous in its efforts to extend its control in the Far East. . . . the foreign domination has been masked behind the facade of a vast crusading movement which apparently has seemed to many Chinese to be wholly indigenous and national. . . .

> . . . however tragic may be the immediate future of China and however ruthlessly a major portion of this great people may be exploited by a party in the

interest of a foreign imperialism, ultimately the profound civilization and the democratic individualism of China will reassert themselves and she will throw off the foreign yoke. I consider that we should encourage all developments in China which now and in the future work toward this end.[1]

In these words the United States government enunciated what became its Truman Doctrine for Asia. By the end of 1950 we were at war with China in Korea, but even then our belief in Moscow's control of the "Communist conspiracy," or our sentimental unwillingness to believe that China of its own free will would make war on the United States, or some combination of the two, made it difficult for us to believe that the Chinese Communists had intervened in Korea for reasons directly related to their own national interest. The fact that General MacArthur's sweep to the Yalu was bringing American ground forces within striking distance of China's industrial heartland in Manchuria was not at that time widely thought to be a factor in China's intervention in the war. The view of Dean Rusk, then the Assistant Secretary of State for Far Eastern Affairs, was that "The peace and security of China are being sacrificed to the ambitions of the Communist conspiracy," and that "China has been driven by foreign masters into an adventure of foreign aggression which cuts across the most fundamental national interests of the Chinese people." Mr. Rusk went on to say, "We do not recognize the authorities in Peiping [sic] for what they pretend to be. The Peiping regime may be a colonial Russian government—a Slavic Manchukuo on a larger scale. It is not the government of China."[2]

Nonetheless, for the first time in our history we were coming to regard China as our enemy, departing from a half-century's policy of supporting a strong, independent China. One China scholar has provided this summary:

> The great aberration in American policy began in 1950, as the people and their leaders were blinded by fear of communism and forgot the sound geopolitical, economic and ethical basis of their historic desire for China's well-being. Having always assumed that China would be friendly, Americans were further bewildered by the hostility of Mao's China, leading them to forsake their traditional support of Asian nationalism, not only in China, but wherever Marxist leadership threatened to enlarge the apparent Communist monolith. With the full support of the American people, Truman and his advisors committed the United States to a policy of containing communism in Asia as well as in Europe—and in practice this policy became increasingly anti-Chinese, an unprecedented campaign of opposition to the development of a strong, modern China. There was no longer any question of whether the United States would interpose itself between China and her enemies, for the United States had become China's principal enemy.[3]

Over the years the notion of a "Slavic Manchukuo" gave way to a recognition of the Chinese Communists as the authors of their own deviltry. This was not a fundamental change of outlook toward "international communism" but an accommodation to a fact which had become obvious to all save the most fanatical and self-deluded cold warriors: that, far from being an instrument in Moscow's hands, the Chinese Communist leaders had become defiant and hostile toward Soviet leadership of the Communist world. Now, from the

American viewpoint, there were two "Communist conspiracies," and of the two great Communist states, China was judged to be the more virulent and aggressive. The Chinese had withdrawn their troops from Korea in 1958, limited themselves to a border adjustment with India in 1962 (when they could have detached a large area after defeating the Indian Army), and assumed no direct combat role in the developing conflict in Vietnam. But these facts were judged to be less important than the fact that they were Communists, who openly advocated subversion and "wars of national liberation." Communist China was not judged to be aggressive on the basis of its actions; it was presumed to be aggressive because it was Communist.

In much the same way that Khrushchev terrified us with his talk of "burying" us, the Chinese sent us into a panic with their doctrine of "wars of national liberation." While the Russians had become relatively benign, contained by America's nuclear deterrent, China claimed to be impervious to the horrors of nuclear war and was still intensely revolutionary itself, committed to the promotion and support of "wars of national liberation" throughout the world. The Kennedy and Johnson administrations concluded that still another gauntlet had been flung down before the United States. Russia had been shown that direct aggression would not pay; now both Communist powers, but especially China, had to be shown that "indirect" aggression would not pay. To meet that presumed threat our military planners invented the strategy of "counterinsurgency," which they undertook to put into effect in Vietnam.

None of this is meant to suggest that China would have been friendly to us if we ourselves had not been hostile. I do not know whether the Chinese Communists would have been friendly or not: nor, I think, does anyone else know, since we never tried to find out. Most probably, in the turmoil of revolutionary change, the Chinese Communists would have been deeply suspicious and verbally abusive of the citadel of capitalism and the leader of the Western "imperialist camp" even if the United States had been willing to come to terms with them. Be that as it may, an objective observer must admit that, on the basis of their actual behavior, the Chinese Communists have never proved the Hitlerian menace we have taken them to be. They have not tried to conquer and subjugate their neighbors. Nor, upon examination, does the doctrine of "wars of national liberation," as set forth by Lin Piao, constitute a charter of Chinese aggression. It stresses self-reliance and the limitations of external support. Lin Piao wrote:

> In order to make a revolution and to fight a people's war and be victorious . . . it is imperative to adhere to the policy of self-reliance, rely on the strength of the masses in one's own country and prepare to carry on the fight independently even when all material aid from outside is cut off. If one does not operate by one's own efforts, does not independently ponder and solve the problems of the revolution in one's own country and does not rely on the strength of the masses, but leans wholly on foreign aid—even though this be aid from socialist countries which persist in revolution—no victory can be won, or be consolidated even if it is won.[4]

The sudden reversal of American policy toward China in 1971 necessarily invites our attention back to the basic causes of these two decades of conflict between the United States and the Communist countries of Asia. In the course of these years we have engaged

in armed conflict with all three of these countries—
with Communist China, North Korea and North Vietnam—but we have never fought a war with the Soviet
Union, which is the only Communist power capable of
posing a direct strategic threat to the United States.
Although it was assumed from the outset of the cold
war that our real strategic interests lay in Europe rather
than in Asia, it has been in Asia that we have thought
it necessary to fight two wars to enforce the Truman
Doctrine. Looking back, one is bound to ask whether
these conflicts were inescapable. Having avoided war
in the region we judged more important and with the
power we judged the greater threat, why have we
found it necessary to fight in Asia at such enormous cost
in lives and money and in the internal cohesion of our
own society? Apart from the North Korean invasion of
South Korea, which was a direct violation of the United
Nations Charter, the Communist countries of Asia have
done nothing that has threatened the security of the
United States, and little if anything that has impaired
our legitimate interests. We intervened in the Chinese
and Vietnamese civil wars only because the stronger
side in each case was the Communist side and we assumed that, as Communists, they were parties to a conspiracy for world domination.

II. China in Wartime

There were Americans in official positions who provided a more objective, less ideologically colored view
of the Chinese Communists back in the days before
they won their civil war. These wartime observers in
China, who included John S. Service, John Paton Davies
and Colonel David D. Barrett, were themselves sympa-
thetic to the Nationalist government of Chiang Kai-

shek, at least to the extent of urging it to make the reforms that might have allowed it to survive. Nonetheless, they reported objectively on the weakness and corruption of the Kuomintang and on the organization and discipline of the Communists in their headquarters in Yenan. They also provided information suggesting that at that time Mao Tse-tung and his associates had no intention whatever of becoming subservient to the Soviet Union and hoped to cooperate with the United States. Not only did the observations of these men go unheeded; they themselves were subsequently denounced and persecuted. Colonel Barrett did not attain the promotion to brigadier general that his career in the Army merited, and Service and Davies were hounded out of the Foreign Service, charged with advocacy of, and even responsibility for, the Chinese Communist victory which they had foreseen. The nation was deprived thereafter of their accurate observations and valuable insights and, what is more, their surviving colleagues in the bureaucracy got the unmistakable message that it was unhealthy to deviate from the anti-Communist line. To survive and get ahead, it was necessary to "see" the world as defined by the Truman Doctrine.

Having been thoroughly educated in the catechism of the cold war, we look back now with astonishment on the reports of Service, Barrett and others from China in 1944. Barrett and Service, who have both published books on their experiences in wartime China,[5] came to know the Chinese Communist leaders well through the "Dixie Mission," which was the name given to the mission of the United States Army Observer Group, headed by Colonel Barrett, at Chinese Communist headquarters in Yenan in late 1944 and early 1945. Their assignment was to assess the potential contribution of the Chinese Communists to a final assault against Japanese forces in China. They came to respect the Communists, not for their ideology but for their discipline, organization, fighting skills and morale.

In his book, published in 1970, Colonel Barrett commented: "The Chinese Communists are our bitter enemies now, but they were certainly 'good guys' then, particularly to the airmen who received their help."[6] Colonel Barrett found that, as sources of information about the Japanese, the Communists were "all we had hoped they would be and even more,"[7] among other reasons because they "could almost always count on the cooperation and support of a local population. . . ."[8] American observers sent out into the countryside from Yenan "all expressed the belief that the Communists were being supported by the entire civil population."[9] In retrospect, Colonel Barrett felt that he had been "oversold" on the Communists in Yenan, but nonetheless, he comments, "the overall look of things there was one which most Americans were inclined to regard with favor." American observers were impressed by the absence of sentries around the leaders, in contrast with the Nationalist capital in Chungking where there were "police and sentries everywhere"; by the tough, well-nourished and well-dressed troops, in contrast with the poorly nourished, shabbily uniformed Kuomintang soldiers; and by the general atmosphere of rough-hewn equality and shared sacrifice. "As a whole," Colonel Barrett commented, "the Communist outlook on life was old-fashioned and conservative."[10]

Even the flamboyant and volatile General Patrick Hurley, Roosevelt's special emissary and later Ambassador to Chungking, was at first favorably impressed with the Chinese Communist terms for a settlement with Chiang Kai-shek. Hurley flew to Yenan in November 1944, where he signed an agreement with Mao Tsetung calling for a coalition government; Hurley pro-

nounced the agreement eminently fair and even told
Mao—in Barrett's hearing—that the terms did not go
far enough in the Communists' favor.[11] Chiang Kai-
shek rejected Hurley's plan out of hand; nonetheless,
Hurley thereafter supported Chiang as the sole leader
of China and publicly blamed the failure of his mediation on his Embassy staff, whom he accused in effect of
being pro-Communist. Although he contended in
November 1944 that "if there is a breakdown in the
parleys it will be the fault of the Government and not
the Communists,"[12] and although he told President
Truman in May 1945 that the Communists were holding back "in my opinion with some degree of reason-
ableness,"[13] Hurley still backed the Nationalist regime
to the hilt and, in the spring of 1945, even reimposed
the ban on nonmilitary travel by Americans to the
Communist headquarters in Yenan. Thus began the
process, culminating in the failure of the mission undertaken in 1946 by General George C. Marshall, through
which, without having ascertained their attitudes and
intentions toward us, the United States came to identify
the Chinese Communists as enemies.

This was not at the outset the result of decisions made
at the highest level. President Roosevelt wrote to a
friend on November 15, 1944: "I am hoping and praying
for a real working out of the situation with the so-called
Communists."[14] And in March 1945, in reply to a question by Edgar Snow about whether we could work with
two governments in China for purposes of prosecuting
the war with Japan, Roosevelt said, "Well, I've been
working with two governments there. I intend to go on
doing so until we can get them together."[15] Within a
few weeks after that interview Roosevelt was dead, and
the conduct of American foreign policy had passed into
the hands of the inexperienced President Truman. Neither Roosevelt nor Truman, however, seems in the last

days of World War II to have given serious and sustained thought to the internal problems of China. Both Presidents were preoccupied with the defeat of Japan, and it had been clear for some time that China was unlikely to play a decisive role in bringing that about.

There was no lack of information available to the United States government in 1944 and 1945 about either the weakness and corruption of the Kuomintang or the strength and aspirations of the Chinese Communists. The views of the professional diplomats were rejected, however, and their reports ignored—that is, until the witch-hunters in the State Department and Congress got hold of them. In June 1944, for example, a warning was conveyed to Washington in a memorandum written principally by John Service:

> The situation in China is rapidly becoming critical. . . . There is a progressive internal breakdown. . . . The fundamental cause of this suicidal trend is that the Kuomintang, steadily losing popular support . . . is concentrating more and more on putting the preservation of its shrinking powers above all other considerations.
>
> These policies, unless checked by the internal opposition they evoke and by friendly foreign influence, seem certain to bring about a collapse which will be harmful to the war and our long-term interests in the Far East.[16]

At the same time that they were reporting the enfeeblement of the Kuomintang, American observers in China provided detailed accounts of the growing military and political strength of the Communists. Service summed up the importance of these circumstances for the United States:

From the basic fact that the Communists have built up popular support of a magnitude and depth which makes their elimination impossible, we must draw the conclusion that the Communists will have a certain and important share in China's future.[17]

His colleague John Paton Davies put it even more succinctly: "The Communists are in China to stay. And China's destiny is not Chiang's but theirs."[18]

The Communists were not only strong but—at least so they said—willing and eager to cooperate with the United States. Service reported on a long conversation he had with Mao Tse-tung in Yenan on August 23, 1944, in which Mao emphasized that the Chinese Communists were "first of all Chinese," and appealed for American help for China after the war. "The Russians," Mao said, "have suffered greatly in the war and will have their hands full with their own job of rebuilding. We do not expect Russian help."[19] America, he thought, could help China, and he told Service:

China must industrialize. This can be done—in China—only by free enterprise and with the aid of foreign capital. Chinese and American interests are correlated and similar. They fit together, economically and politically. We can and must work together.

The United States would find us more cooperative than the Kuomintang. We will not be afraid of democratic American influence—we will welcome it. We have no silly ideas of taking only Western mechanical techniques. . . . America does not need to fear that we will not be cooperative. We must cooperate and we must have American help. This is why it is so important to us Communists to know what you Americans are thinking and planning.

We cannot risk crossing you—cannot risk any conflict with you.[20]

We do not know of course whether Mao was sincere
in his repeated appeals for American friendship. The
reason we do not know is that we never tried to find
out. In our postwar anti-Communist hysteria we assumed that the Chinese Communists were hostile simply because they were Communists and we also
assumed, despite impressive evidence to the contrary,
that they were subservient to the Soviet Union. We
thereupon made our fateful commitment to the losing
side in the Chinese civil war—the side of whose weakness and probable defeat full warning had been provided by our own highly competent observers.

This is not to say that Mao might have been expected
to put Sino-American relations back on their prewar
basis. He most assuredly would not have done that.
Certainly our pretensions to a benevolent paternalism
toward China would have been given short shrift; the
age of missionaries and the "open door" was at an end.
But whatever our relations might have been if we had
not intervened in the civil war, they would at least have
been initiated on a more realistic and promising basis.
We might long ago have established a tolerable working relationship: the sort of relationship toward which
—belatedly but most commendably—the Nixon Administration began to work in 1972.

III. Ho's Vietnam

The anti-Communist spirit that governed our relations
with China after World War II also shaped—and distorted—our involvement in Vietnam. Our interest in
China's civil war, though tragic in consequence, was

attenuated and limited in time. Vietnam was less fortunate. In a test application of the new science of "counterinsurgency," it has been subjected to prolonged, though inconclusive, devastation. But for the American intervention, the Vietnamese civil war would have ended long ago—at infinitely less cost in lives, money and property—in a nationalist Communist victory under the leadership of Ho Chi Minh. In retrospect it seems difficult to understand how we could have accepted the "loss" of China and not the "loss" of the small undeveloped countries on China's southern border.

In the months following the defeat of Japan in World War II, Ho Chi Minh, then leader of the Vietnamese provisional government seeking independence from France, was doubtful that the United States would take an interest in so small and remote a country as Vietnam, although he hoped it would. Major Frank White, a major in the Office of Strategic Services (predecessor to the CIA), then acting as observer for the United States government in Hanoi, recalled a conversation with Ho in 1946:

> The United States, Ho said, was probably in the best position to aid Vietnam in the post-war years. . . . He dwelled at some length on the disposition of Americans as a people to be sympathetic to the self-determination of nations and generous in making contributions to less fortunate states. But here again he doubted that the United States Government could be counted on to come to the aid of Vietnam. He said he felt that the U.S. Government would find more urgent things to do. He said something to the effect that, after all, Vietnam is a small country and far away. Vietnam could not be expected to loom large in the preoccupations of the

United States. In short, he was saying that he hoped America would interest itself in Vietnam but he didn't believe, in the final analysis, we would.[21]

Ho was in due course to be astonished at how greatly the United States interested itself in Vietnam. Ho, it appears, was more realistic about America's self-interest than our own Presidents from Truman to Nixon. Only in the context of the assumptions of the Truman Doctrine could the Vietnamese civil war ever have been rationalized as having something to do with American security or American interests. Looking through our anti-Communist prism, we saw Ho Chi Minh not as a Vietnamese nationalist who was also a Communist but as a spear carrier for the international Communist conspiracy, the driving force for a "world cut in two by Asian communism." The Johnson Administration, as Mr. Johnson's memoirs showed clearly, believed itself to be acting on President Truman's doctrine "that totalitarian regimes imposed on free peoples, by direct or indirect aggression, undermine the foundations of international peace and hence the security of the United States." President Johnson and his advisers believed this despite a set of facts which did not fit the formula: the fact that the issue was not between a "free people" and a "totalitarian regime" but between rival totalitarian regimes; the fact that the war was not one of international aggression, "direct" or otherwise, but an anticolonial war and then a civil war; and the fact that, in any case, the country was too small and the issue too indigenous to Vietnam to pose anything resembling a threat to the "foundations of international peace," much less to the "security of the United States." In practice the issue had resolved itself down to a corruption of the Truman Doctrine, into fear of a "humiliating" defeat at the hands of Communists. It was not so much that we needed to win, or that there was anything for us to win, as that our leaders felt—for reasons of their prestige abroad and their political standing at home—that they could not afford to "lose." As President Johnson said soon after he took office: "I am not going to be the President who saw southeast Asia go the way China went."[22]

The notion that a country is "lost" or "gone" when it becomes Communist is a peculiarly revealing one. How can we have "lost" a country unless it was ours to begin with—unless it was some part of an unacknowledged American imperium? To my eye, China under Mao is in the same place on the map as it was in the days of Chiang. Where then has it "gone"? To the moon? Or to the devil? The "lost" and "gone" concept is indicative of a virulent sanctimoniousness which is only now beginning to abate. In October 1971, members of the Senate gave President Tito of Yugoslavia a cordial reception at an afternoon tea. In September 1959, a similar reception was held for Chairman Khrushchev, but one Senator refused to sit in the room with him, for fear, apparently, of ideological contamination. As we move toward lifting of the "quarantine" of China, as we recognize at long last that there really still is a China, Communist though it may be, the tragic irrationality of the Vietnam war is thrown once again into high relief. All that bloodletting—not just for ourselves but for the Vietnamese—could have been avoided by an awareness that communism is not a contagious disease but a political movement and a way of organizing a society.

In the case of Ho Chi Minh, as in the case of Mao Tse-tung, we might have come to this awareness twenty-five years—and two wars—ago. Ho in fact was a lifelong admirer of the American Revolution, of Lincoln, and of Wilson and his Fourteen Points. As a young man, in 1919, he went to the Paris Peace Conference to appeal for self-determination for his country in accordance with President Wilson's principles, but no attention was paid him, and Vietnam remained within the French Empire. In 1945 Ho Chi Minh started his declaration of independence for Vietnam with words taken from our own, "All men are created equal." In 1945 and 1946 Ho addressed a series of letters to the United States government asking for its mediation toward a compromise with France, but none of these letters was ever answered, because Ho was, in Dean Acheson's words, "an outright Commie."[23]

President Roosevelt, during the Second World War, had favored independence for Indochina, or a trusteeship, but in any event he was opposed to letting the French recover Indochina for their colonial empire. Roosevelt's attitude was spelled out in a memorandum to Secretary of State Hull, dated January 24, 1944, which appears in the Pentagon Papers:

> I saw Halifax last week and told him quite frankly that it was perfectly true that I had, for over a year, expressed the opinion that Indochina should not go back to France but that it should be administered by an international trusteeship. France has had the country—thirty million inhabitants—for nearly one hundred years, and the people are worse off than they were at the beginning.
>
> As a matter of interest, I am wholeheartedly supported in this view by Generalissimo Chiang Kai-shek and by Marshal Stalin. I see no reason to play in with the British Foreign Office in this matter. The only reason they seem to oppose it is that they fear the effect it would have on their own possessions and those of the Dutch. They have never liked the idea of trusteeship because it is, in some

instances, aimed at future independence. This is true in the case of Indochina.

Each case must, of course, stand on its own feet, but the case of Indochina is perfectly clear. France has milked it for one hundred years. The people of Indochina are entitled to something better than that.[24]

British intransigence and the requirements of military strategy prevented Roosevelt from acting on his anticolonialist preference. When the Truman Administration took office, American policy was changed and the French were officially assured that the United States had never questioned, "even by implication, French sovereignty over Indochina." The United States would advocate reforms but would leave it to the French to decide when, or even whether, the peoples of Indochina were to be given independence: "Such decisions would preclude the establishment of a trusteeship in Indochina except with the consent of the French Government."[25]

Whether this initial commitment to France—and therefore against Ho—was the result of growing anti-Communist sentiment within the Truman Administration, or of friendly feelings toward the colonial powers on the part of President Truman's old-line advisers, or both, American policy was constant and firm from that time on. Later, when Acheson and his colleagues were attempting to build up France as the centerpiece of the anti-Communist coalition in Europe, the commitment to France's position in Indochina became stronger than ever. By 1951 the United States was paying 40 percent of the cost of France's war against the Vietminh, and by 1954, 80 percent. After the Geneva settlement, American military aid to South Vietnam averaged about $200 million a year between 1955 and 1961. By 1963 South Vietnam ranked first among the recipients of our military assistance, and only India and Pakistan received more in economic assistance. In this way foreign aid served as a vehicle of commitment, from our initial support of French colonial rule in Indochina to sending an American force of over half a million men to fight in a war which is still going on.

As with China it might have been different. The Pentagon Papers show that between October 1945 and February 1946 Ho Chi Minh addressed at least eight communications to the President of the United States or to the Secretary of State asking America to intervene for Vietnamese independence. Earlier, in the summer of 1945, Ho had asked that Vietnam be accorded "the same status as the Philippines," a period of tutelage to be followed by independence. Following the outbreak of hostilities in Vietnam in the early fall of 1945, Ho made his appeals to President Truman on the basis of the Atlantic Charter, the United Nations Charter and Mr. Truman's Navy Day speech of October 27, 1945, in which the President expressed the American belief that "all peoples who are prepared for self-government should be permitted to choose their own form of government by their own freely expressed choice, without interference from any foreign source." In November 1945 Ho wrote to the Secretary of State requesting the initiation of cultural relations through the sending of fifty Vietnamese students to the United States. On February 16, 1946, in a letter to President Truman, Ho referred to American "complicity" with the French, but he still appealed to the Americans "as guardians and champions of world justice" to "take a decisive step" in support of Vietnamese independence, and pointed out that he was asking only what had been "graciously granted to the Philippines." On September

11, 1946, Ho communicated directly with the United States government for the last time, expressing to an American Embassy official in Paris his own admiration for the United States and the respect and affection of the Vietnamese people for President Roosevelt; again he referred to America's granting of independence to the Philippines.[26]

As far as the record shows, neither President Truman nor any of his subordinates ever replied to any of Ho Chi Minh's appeals. He got his answer, nonetheless, clearly and unmistakably. By late 1946, with the first Vietnam war underway, American military equipment was being used by the French against the Vietnamese. As far as the United States government was concerned, Vietnam was a side show to the real struggle against communism in Europe. If the price of French support in that struggle was American support of French colonialism in southeast Asia—and we seem never to have questioned that it was—the Truman Administration was ready and willing to pay that price.

Ho after all was just another "Commie." In a cable to the United States representative in Hanoi in May 1949 Acheson said:

> Question whether Ho as much nationalist as Commie is irrelevant. All Stalinists in colonial areas are nationalists. With achievement national aims (i.e., independence) their objective necessarily becomes subordination state to Commie purposes. . . .[27]

In February 1950 the recognition of Ho Chi Minh's government by the Communist powers moved Secretary Acheson to declare that this recognition "should remove any illusion as to the nationalist character of Ho Chi Minh's aims and reveals Ho in his true colors as the mortal enemy of native independence in Indochina."[28]

As with Mao Tse-tung in China, we might have gotten along tolerably well—maybe even quite well—with a unified, independent Vietnam under Ho Chi Minh, if our leaders' minds had not been hopelessly locked in by the imprisoning theory of the international Communist conspiracy. Ho was an authentic Vietnamese patriot revered by his countrymen. He had led the resistance to the Japanese within Vietnam and had welcomed the allies as liberators. His unwillingness to submit to foreign domination was clear—or should have been clear —from the outset. When he was criticized by pro-Chinese elements for agreeing in 1946 to a French military presence in Vietnam for the next five years, Ho declared:

> You fools! Don't you realize what it means if the Chinese stay? Don't you remember your history? The last time the Chinese came, they stayed one thousand years . . .!
>
> As for me, I prefer to smell French shit for five years, rather than Chinese shit for the rest of my life.[29]

Nonetheless, without evidence or exploration, we applied to Ho Chi Minh the same set of assumptions which were soon thereafter to be applied to China.

If the evidence of Ho Chi Minh's Vietnamese nationalism ever reached the American policy makers, it certainly did not persuade them. Acting Secretary of State Acheson instructed an American diplomat in Hanoi in December 1946: "Keep in mind Ho's clear record as agent international communism . . ."[30] In February 1947, by which time the war between France and the Vietminh was well under way, Secretary of State Marshall conceded that colonial empires were rapidly becoming a thing of the past but, as to Vietnam,

> . . . . we do not lose sight fact that Ho Chi Minh has direct Communist connections and it should be obvious that we are not interested in seeing colonial empire administrations supplanted by philosophy and political organizations emanating from and controlled by Kremlin.[31]

General Marshall's words were prophetic of what was to become a guiding principle—or, more accurately, a guiding aberration—of American foreign policy for at least two decades to follow: where Communists were involved, the United States would depart from its traditional anticolonialism and support the imperial power. Assuming as we did that Communists by definition were agents of an international conspiracy, we further assumed that a Communist leader could not be an authentic patriot, no matter what he said or did. If the choice was to be—as we then rationalized it—between the old imperialism of the West and the new imperialism of the Kremlin, we would side with the former. Where possible, we told ourselves, we would support or nurture "third forces," genuine independence movements which were neither colonialist nor Communist; and where such movements existed, as in India, we did support and welcome independence. Where they did not exist, as in Vietnam and Cuba and the Dominican Republic, we intervened, making these countries the great crisis areas of postwar American foreign policy and, in the process, earning for the United States the reputation of foremost imperialist power.

Until a generation ago America was regarded throughout the world—and deservedly so—as the one great nation which was authentically anti-imperialist. It was Woodrow Wilson who introduced into international relations the revolutionary principle of "justice to all peoples and nationalities, and their right to live on equal terms of liberty and safety with one another, whether they be strong or weak."[32] Perhaps it was a utopian dream, but Americans meant it at the time, and the world believed we meant it, and we had a plan for realizing it: first the Covenant of the League of Nations and then the United Nations Charter, both purporting to introduce the rule of law into international relations, both purporting to supplant the old imperialist anarchy with a principle of "trusteeship" for the weak and the poor, both purporting to supplant the old balance of power with a new community of power.

The dismay and disillusion which have overtaken so many of us in America are the result, I believe, of our departure from these traditional American values. The corrosive, consuming fear of communism has driven us into a role in the world to which we are unsuited by temperament and tradition. I think that the American people have sensed this all along and are moving to an active, conscious awareness of their own real preferences. It is no easy matter to knock over the household gods we have been taught for a generation to worship, but I think the American people have all along had an uneasy awareness that the dictators and war lords with whom we have been in league for so long are not really our kind of people. I suspect too that if Khrushchev and Mao and Ho had not had the name of "Communist," we might have recognized them as men we could respect: tough and sometimes ruthless, but patriots nonetheless; committed to an ideology we would not want for ourselves, but also committed to the well-being of their own people.

With China's entry into the United Nations, the

President's trip to China and the prospect of increasing, continuing contacts, we may find that we can do business with the Chinese just as we have done with the Russians. We may even find it possible to be cordial, as President Nixon was during his visit, and as we have been for many years with the Yugoslavs. Eventually (who knows?) we may even kick over the household gods once and for all and become friends—like Huck Finn when he helped Jim escape: he knew it was a sin, and he knew he was going to go to hell for it, but he liked Jim, so he did it anyway.

3

Vietnam—
The Futile Crusade

Whatever else may have been proved or disproved by the great North Vietnamese spring offensive of 1972, several things were shown beyond dispute: that "Vietnamization" had failed and the war was still on; that despite great losses, the enemy was still formidable; that despite their own considerable air force provided by the United States, the South Vietnamese were still desperately dependent upon American air power; and that despite troop withdrawals, the United States was still heavily involved in the war, with no hope of either victory or peace as long as it continued to adhere to the war aims of Presidents Johnson and Nixon.

In his campaign for the Presidency in 1968, Richard Nixon said that he had a "plan" to end the war, although he did not reveal the contents of his plan at that time. On November 3, 1969, President Nixon outlined his program of "Vietnamization," which he said would "end the war" and "win the peace." At that time he also said, quite correctly, that if his "plan" did not succeed, his Administration would and should be held accountable. As Mr. Nixon campaigned for reelection in 1972, it was clear that, by the President's own definition of its aims, "Vietnamization" was a failure; the policy followed by the Nixon Administration between 1969 and 1972 had served not to end the war but to perpetuate it. By the spring of 1972 the Nixon policy in some respects had come full circle back to that of President Johnson four years before. In April 1968 President Johnson had partially suspended the bombing of North Vietnam and initiated the Paris peace talks; in April 1972 President Nixon suspended the peace talks and, when the Communist offensive began, resumed massive bombing of both North and South Vietnam, using giant B-52's—as President Johnson had not—to devastate Hanoi and the North Vietnamese port of Haiphong. To round out the ironic circle, Secretary of State William Rogers and Secretary of Defense Melvin Laird appeared before the Senate Foreign Relations Committee (on April 17 and 18, 1972), just as Secretary of State Rusk had four years before, to assure the Committee, and the American people, that the enemy was being defeated and the achievement of our objectives was in sight. Then, a few weeks later, when it appeared that the South Vietnamese Army might crumble and Mr. Thieu's regime fall, President Nixon escalated the air war to unprecedented heights of devastation and initiated the blockade of the North Vietnamese ports; in so doing, President Nixon raised the level of violence beyond any of President Johnson's successive acts of escalation.

In March 1968 Richard Nixon, then a candidate for the Republican Presidential nomination, said: ". . . if in November this war is not over after all of this power has been at their disposal, then I say that the American people will be justified to elect new leadership and I pledge to you that the new leadership will end the war and win the peace in the Pacific and that is what America wants."[1] In January 1969, having repeated that pledge many times in his campaign, Mr. Nixon was inaugurated President. By early 1972, three years later, even prior to the great North Vietnamese spring offensive and the massive retaliation it provoked, President Nixon had dropped a greater tonnage of bombs on Indochina (some three million tons) than had his predecessor, President Johnson, in the preceding five years. Between January 1969, when Mr. Nixon took office, and April 1972, during all of which time the war was said to be "winding down," 3.2 million tons of bombs were dropped on Indochina; 20,000 Americans died and another 110,000 were wounded; 340,000 Asians died; some 600,000 civilians became casualties; and four million people became refugees.[2]

Having dropped more than one ton of bombs for every minute of his Administration, President Nixon had by early 1972 established himself, in the words of the Washington *Post*, as "the greatest bomber of all time. . . ."[3] Nonetheless, employing the insane antilogic which has characterized this war from its beginning, the Nixon Administration pointed with pride to its troop withdrawals, as if the substitution of a devastating, permanent air war for large-scale American participation in the continuing ground war represented the course of prudence and moderation as between the radical "extremes" of expanding the war and ending it.

A stalemated war can be ended only one way, by a negotiated settlement such as the French made with the Vietnamese at Geneva in 1954. Failing that, the war can only continue, although it may be escalated or "wound down," "Americanized" or "Vietnamized." We may offer six-point plans or sixty-point plans and then use the "other side's" rejection of these as an excuse for fighting on; we may wait for the enemy to expire of his grievous wounds, celebrating his failures and dismissing his successes as death throes, as "one last throw of the dice." Still, he fights on, because the North Vietnamese are not interested in a "reasonable settlement," or in who violated this agreement or that "understanding," or in whether indeed there were such. Nor are they interested in "free elections" or "self-determination" in a land where no one, least of all our ally in Saigon, is interested in these things. The Vietnamese Communists are interested only in expelling the foreigners from their country and in its ultimate reunification. For these purposes they fight on, fanatically and at enormous cost; and so, perforce, must we, as long as we insist upon the survival of a client regime in Saigon.

How and why our adversaries have persisted is difficult to understand. They might have accepted President Johnson's "San Antonio formula" or any of President Nixon's various proposals and left it to a more favorable day to work their will, which, as the strongest indigenous nationalist force in Indochina, they would quite probably have been able to do, and someday, in all probability, still will be able to do. Why we have persisted is far more puzzling: living in a world with a number of Communist states, including two great powers with whom we are doing our best to live in peace, we have somehow gotten it in our heads that the establishment of one more Communist government in one small half of an underdeveloped Asian country, or in all three countries of Indochina, would represent a fearsome threat to our security or to our "vital interests," or to our pride or reputation, or to some other nameless abstraction.

I. The Phantom of Victory

The war in Vietnam cannot adequately be characterized as another instance of reversion on the part of
President Nixon and Mr. Kissinger to the old power
politics. Metternich and Bismarck were rational in their
amorality; it is hard to conceive of them persisting in
anything so stupid and self-defeating. I do not really
feel adequate to the task of gauging the meaning for
America of this war which, like a virulent organism in
an otherwise healthy body, has drained our society of
confidence and hope. If I had to try to sum it up, I would
judge that it represents a grotesquely miscarried effort
to apply traditional American values of self-determination and collective security. Americans will be debating
for many years how and why the involvement in Southeast Asia became so great a disaster. The obvious factors
include the simple fact of our inexperience in world
affairs; our obsessive fear of communism and the ob-
scure causes of that fear; the bitterness of our disillusion
with the United Nations and the supposition that we
could substitute ourselves for it; the infatuation with
science which caused us to suppose that we could make
foreign policy—and wars—with computers; and, perhaps most important, that self-righteous certitude of a
nation at the peak of its power which I have called the
arrogance of power.

It seems fair and reasonable to suppose that President Nixon, convert that he is to Dr. Kissinger's brand
of nonideological realpolitik, would not, since his conversion from ideological crusader, have deliberately
undertaken so useless and perilous an adventure. Mr.
Nixon, as he so often has reminded us, inherited the
war; he did not initiate it, although, as a private citizen,
he endorsed President Johnson's repeated escalations
and sometimes criticized the Johnson Administration

for failing to use even greater force. Be that as it may, President Nixon profited from President Johnson's misfortunes and came to recognize the political unfeasibility of further escalation. Nixon, the convert to realpolitik, thereupon scaled the war down to the extent of gradually eliminating American participation in ground combat; but enough of the "old Nixon" seems to have survived—Nixon the redbaiter, Nixon the battle-scarred veteran of the "warfare of politics"—to have made the President unwilling actually to end the war. Something of his state of mind may have been shown in his reported comment to a member of Congress after the bombing of Haiphong and Hanoi in April 1972— "You have to let them have it when they jump on you."[4] The crusade, therefore, continues, alternately escalating and "wound down," but it continues, a stalled crusade against communism in one small corner of the world.

Although different tactics have been employed, the objective of the Nixon Administration in Indochina by all available evidence has been the same as that of the Johnson Administration: to win the war in the sense of establishing anti-Communist client regimes in South Vietnam, Cambodia and Laos. A compromise political settlement, which could only mean a sharing of power between Communists and non-Communists, or an arrangement leaving all the indigenous forces some opportunity to seek power, peacefully or otherwise, but without further interference by foreigners, has been effectively ruled out. That is why the Paris negotiations have failed—because there has been nothing to negotiate from the standpoint of the North Vietnamese and the Vietcong, except the terms of their surrender.

Clearly a political settlement, which would involve some sharing of power with the Communists, has not been the Nixon Administration's aim in Vietnam. Nor,

as we have often been encouraged to believe, has the
Administration's aim been simply to get the American
forces out in good order—to "back out of the saloon"
with both guns blazing. It insults the intelligence of the
American people to tell them that we had to resume
the heavy bombing of North Vietnam in the spring of
1972 in order to protect the lives of our remaining
forces, just as it insulted the intelligence of the American people to tell them that we had to invade Cambodia in 1970 and Laos in 1971 simply in order to cover
our withdrawal. I do not think the North Vietnamese
and the Vietcong would be so stupid as to try to interfere with an authentic, total American withdrawal. Indeed, it is only in a political atmosphere dense with
obfuscation and mendacity that it becomes necessary to
deal with these arguments at all. The real meaning of
"Vietnamization," and of the expansion of the war
across all of Indochina, is that, for President Nixon as for
President Johnson, the objective has been military victory.

Again and again the mirage of victory has receded
from our grasp. When the "incursion" into Laos began
in early 1971, President Nixon suggested that decisive
battles might be at hand, and he predicted that the
North Vietnamese would "have to fight here or give up
the struggle to conquer South Vietnam. . . ."[5] When the
North Vietnamese launched their spring offensive in
1972, we were told that this was "one last throw of the
dice," following which the "other side" could be expected to negotiate on our terms. The Laotian incursion of 1971 ended in a "mobile maneuver"—which is
Pentagonese for "headlong retreat"—and the North
Vietnamese offensive of 1972 (as of this writing in the
summer of 1972) seemed likely to end inconclusively. It
appears that the North Vietnamese will *not* have to
give up the struggle, that indeed, even though they fail

of victory in any one instance, they may launch new offensives every year or two or three, and the war, therefore, will go on for as long as the South Vietnamese Army can continue—in Mr. Nixon's felicitous term—to "hack it," for as long, perhaps, as the tortured peoples of Indochina have blood to shed. At best—assuming the greatest possible success of the policy of Presidents Nixon and Thieu—the prospect is for a war of indefinite duration, with Asians doing the fighting on the ground while Americans provide air power, sea power, supplies and money. At worst, if the South Vietnamese Army falters, they and any American force remaining in South Vietnam will be confronted at last with military disaster—with the very specter of "humiliation and defeat" that has so preoccupied President Nixon over the years.

What would we then do? Hastily pull out our remaining forces or raise the stakes by launching an all-out attack on North Vietnam? President Nixon has repudiated any intention of using nuclear weapons—and for that we must be grateful—but it must also be remembered that people are least likely to behave rationally when their backs are to the wall, and President Nixon himself has not always responded prudently in conditions of adversity.

The Vietnamese Communists have been fighting for twenty-five years, and they have given us every reason to believe that they will continue to fight until they gain power in South Vietnam or until a new government emerges in Saigon with which they can come to terms. They have withstood many reverses in their long years of fighting but they have not been subdued. As Mr. Kissinger noted before he became one of the managers of the war, if a guerrilla army is not defeated, then it has won. "And how long do you Americans wish to fight?" North Vietnamese Premier Pham Van Dong asked in

Hanoi in 1967. "One year? Two years? Twenty years? We will be glad to accommodate you."[6]

Never to be forgotten either—for people who wish to preserve the United States as a humane democratic society—is that the morals of this war are as twisted as its strategy. Our leaders point with pride, when they can, to reduced American casualties, but they have little to say about the million or more South Vietnamese civilian casualties since the war began; these, in the military phrase, are the "wasted" people—some killed by Vietcong terror, many times more by American fragmentation bombs, gunships and napalm. Indochinese peasants never actually see a B-52 because it flies so high, but they know well what it can do. "We hear nothing, nothing at all," a South Vietnamese farmer told an American reporter. "Then a thunder louder than the loudest rainstorm strikes, the earth shakes . . . and we wait to see who dies."[7]

Implicit in this strategy of indiscriminate killing is the cruel and ignorant old supposition that Asians are indifferent to human life. In truth, as anyone who knows Asia at all can testify, the Chinese and Vietnamese and Cambodians and Laotians value their lives and the lives of their children as much as do Americans and Englishmen. They have simply been less successful at surviving, and their cries have been beyond our hearing. As much for the sake of our survival as a civilized society as for their physical survival, we cannot allow ourselves to forget that the victims of our bombs and bullets are people like ourselves, and although they die unheard and in great numbers, they do not die with indifference. The meaning of the war for the Indochina people was summed up by a South Vietnamese soldier fighting on the northern front in the 1972 offensive. He told an American reporter that he thought the war would never end, because "the Americans will never go away and the Communists will never stop trying. . . . My father was a soldier," he said, "I am a soldier, and very soon my sons will be soldiers, too. I have no hope for the future."[8]

Perhaps, as the Nixon Administration has seemed to suppose, the American people will tolerate an endless war as long as it is Asians rather than Americans who are being "wasted" on so prodigal a scale. But I do not think so; I think that the American people are offended and outraged by the prolongation of this useless killing even though most of those now being killed are foreigners, even though President Nixon and Dr. Kissinger have largely succeeded in "changing the color of the corpses."

I think too that the American people are disgusted by the obsession with victory, even in its various, euphemistic disguises. I think they know that the continuation of a devastating air war and the recurrent acts of escalation have been designed not to protect our remaining troops or to cover their withdrawal but to protect Mr. Thieu and his regime and to preserve our own President's personal prestige and political career. I think the American people know that the policy of Vietnamization is a program not of ending the war but of perpetuating it, not of extricating the United States from Indochina but of maintaining a dominant American influence through client regimes. What the American people do not seem to understand—and what I surely do not understand—is why our leaders have clung so tenaciously to the phantom of victory on behalf of a client regime whose survival confers no benefits on either the American people or the Vietnamese people.

I have always been puzzled by our gratuitous tender-

heartedness toward right-wing dictators. It is one thing
to tolerate such regimes, because it is not our business
to be overthrowing foreign governments anyway. But
in the case of such unsavory military dictatorships as
those in South Vietnam—or Greece or a number of
other countries—we have been much more than toler-
ant; we have aided and supported these regimes
against their own internal enemies. I do not think this
is done out of genuine soft-heartedness—although our
Embassy in Saigon has seemed extravagantly solicitous
of Mr. Thieu. Nor is it the result of anything resembling
the hard-headed "realism" in which the Nixon Administration has taken great pride. It takes more than
realpolitik to explain such gratuitous friendliness toward right-wing dictators. Here again the explanation
can only lie in that surviving attitude of crusading anti-
communism which has colored so much of American
foreign policy over the years. The charm of the right-
wing dictators has been their staunch anti-communism,
and that appears to have been enough to compensate
for such trivial defects as their despotism and corruption. I recall a member of the Senate, not so long ago,
going so far as to defend the Greek colonels as "democratic" because they were resisting communism.

This is not the hard-headed "de facto-ism" favored by
the old-school diplomats. It is ideological obsession on
the part of old-school cold warriors. The inspiration for
such an outlook comes not from the practical Metternich but from John Calvin. Fortified by pride—the
pride of a nation which has "never lost a war," the pride
of a President who subscribes to the code that "You
have to let them have it when they jump on you"—the
surviving crusading spirit of the Truman Doctrine provides the only plausible motive for our continuing bid
for a military victory in Indochina.

II. Vietnam on Its Merits

From the start this war has been rationalized in terms of abstractions, analogies and conjecture, to the neglect of tangible, ascertainable facts. As the Pentagon Papers showed so strikingly, our policy makers have been preoccupied with ideology and with geopolitical abstractions having to do with our prestige and our power interests, with the possible effects of the war on countries not involved, and hypothetical future conflicts that our inaction now might cause or our action prevent. At the same time, our policy makers have given short shrift to what is happening here and now, to the effects of the war on those directly involved, not ten or twenty years in the future but right now.

Most of all—and in this respect the Pentagon Papers have been most revealing—our policy makers have given short shrift to the human costs and consequences of the war, both for the American people and the peoples of Indochina. From the outset of this war—in the view of two former National Security Council staff members—our leaders fell into a "dehumanized pattern of decision making," treating the life and death and suffering of human beings not as significant in themselves but as "factors" in strategic and political calculations.[9] Why and how this came to be so is puzzling indeed; the men who led us and have kept us in Vietnam are not monsters but decent, honorable and intelligent public officials. Nonetheless, something about this war, or perhaps something about foreign policy in general, or about our own recently acquired status of super power, has caused us to abandon considerations of humanity at the water's edge and to deal with the war in Vietnam in terms of bloodless, computerized abstractions. Our policy has been made in a world apart from the bombed villages, the piles of decomposing bodies, the mutilated children, and even the cemeteries and veterans' hospitals here at home, which are the tangible human results of the war.

The virtue of tangible facts is not that they represent the whole truth but that they represent the whole of the ascertainable truth, which must be the principal basis on which rational men make decisions and formulate courses of action. We would think it monstrous if a jury were to condemn a man on the strength of analogy, conjecture or intuition. Inevitably, these play a greater role in public policy, but ought they to be considered great virtues, as marks of wisdom and statesmanship, when the matter is not simply one of condemning one man to prison but of subjecting whole societies to the horrors of war?

It is not enough to contend, as President Nixon has never ceased to contend, that if we did not fight here we would have to fight elsewhere, and that it would almost certainly then be a bigger war if not indeed a world war. With all respect to Mr. Nixon's sincerity and knowledge of foreign affairs, he simply does not know that—he has no way of knowing. He is a politician not a prophet, and politicians cannot predict the future, they can only guess at it on the basis of fragmentary information about other people's intentions. Sometimes too, a political leader may draw upon history, but if he knows anything about history at all, he knows that, as analogy, the past is more likely to deceive than to instruct, that the real use of history is in the broad, general insights it may foster, in the kind of informed intuition it may facilitate, allowing us to make tentative judgments about the sort of political action that is likely to prove rewarding and the sort that is not. Of and by itself history provides us with no definitive guidance as to whether we ought to commit our soldiers and resources to any particular war at any particular time and place. That can only be determined by the facts of the here and now, set if possible in historical context, but never to the exclusion of an active awareness that, whatever our fears of repeating past mistakes, and whatever we think we owe to generations yet unborn, we have a prior obligation to those already born and now alive.

Among the abstractions which influenced our policy makers with respect to Vietnam, consider the concept of an "exemplary war," often invoked by both President Johnson and President Nixon. This thesis holds that the major purpose of the war in Vietnam is external to Vietnam: to retain the trust and confidence of our friends and allies all over the world by demonstrating America's fealty to her "commitments." Aside from the fact that the demonstration has been an exceedingly costly one, by no stretch of the imagination proportionate to its objective, there is the equally distressing fact that it has not worked: most of our friends and allies have deplored our involvement in Indochina, regarding it as an indication of something erratic, unsound and unstable about America. One of our closest associates, Israel, has made it clear that, Vietnam notwithstanding, she has no confidence whatever in our readiness to honor a commitment and that is why she insists upon retaining Arab territory. In a major speech on April 26, 1972—as on many previous occasions—President Nixon predicted that "If the Communists win militarily in Vietnam, the risk of war in other parts of the world would be enormously increased. If Communist aggression fails, it will discourage others to do the same thing." The President's own chief foreign policy adviser, Mr. Kissinger, effectively contested the notion of an "exemplary war" in an article written shortly before he went to work in the White House. "Whatever the outcome of the war in Vietnam," he wrote, "it is clear that it has greatly diminished American willingness to become involved in this form of warfare elsewhere. Its utility as a precedent has therefore been importantly undermined."[10]

Closely related to the "exemplary war" thesis is the highly conjectural Munich analogy, with which we are all familiar. Equating conciliation with appeasement and appeasement with the prospect of world war, this thesis takes no notice of the enormous differences in the two sets of circumstances, including the fact that Nazi Germany was the most powerful military and industrial state in Europe, while North Vietnam is a small, undeveloped country, capable of challenging the United States only in the kind of jungle warfare in which we have so obligingly engaged the tenacious North Vietnamese soldiers. The men who led us into Vietnam were, by their own admission, much influenced by the experience of Nazi aggression and Western appeasement in the thirties; they derived from the experience, as Mark Twain once put it, "more wisdom than was in it."

For obvious reasons our leaders have given somewhat less emphasis over the years to their once-favored contention that our mission in Vietnam was an idealistic or humanitarian one, designed to give to the South Vietnamese people the right of "self-determination" or to save them from a "blood bath" at the hands of a conquering Communist regime. The case for self-determination has always been robbed of credibility by the dictatorial character of the succession of Saigon regimes. The staging in October 1971 of a rigged, one-man "election" to ratify the rule of the incumbent military dictator was not exactly the fault of the Nixon Administration, which made desperate efforts to create the *appearance* of a genuine contest. Nonetheless, it should have laid to rest the ludicrous fiction that the war had anything to do with giving the South Vietnamese people the right—or even the chance—to determine their own future. If Mr. Thieu was unwilling to risk the loss of power to an ideological blood brother like Mr. Ky, it is inconceivable that he would ever permit a free election including Communists or even neutralists. As to saving the South Vietnamese from a Communist "blood bath," Secretary of State Rogers invoked that prospect once again, rather feebly, in testimony before the Senate Foreign Relations Committee in April 1972, and so did President Nixon in his address of April 26, 1972, but, for the most part, the Nixon Administration has shown little inclination to try to explain why it is better for South Vietnamese civilians to be blown to bits by American fragmentation bombs or burned alive by American napalm than to face the hypothetical possibility of a future Communist "blood bath."

Then there is the thesis, also highly favored by President Nixon, that we must, in his words, "play out the game" in order to retain our unblemished record of never having been defeated in war and in order to redeem the sacrifices already made by our soldiers. In this context the war becomes its own justification: like a baseball game, it is played to be won because winning is what the "game" is all about. Robbed of all human and even valid political significance, the war is trivialized into a mindless contest to prove that we are "Number One." And as far as "redeeming" the sacrifices of our GI's is concerned, the assumption here seems to be that a victorious war is a justified war, that you can wipe out a mistake by succeeding at it. Of all the rationalizations used to justify our continuing involvement in Indochina, none is more extraneous to the *merits* of the war than this one. Rooted in an assumption that victory redeems error, it is practically indistinguishable from the primitive notion that "might makes right."

Hardly worthy of serious comment—except for the fact that great stress has been laid upon it by the Nixon Administration—is the spurious and circular contention that the United States must engage in air and naval warfare against North Vietnam in order to protect the lives of our remaining servicemen on the ground in South Vietnam and prevent the enemy from interfering with their withdrawal. The argument is disingenuous, since it is quite obvious that the most effective way of protecting the lives of our men is by bringing them home and not by expending more lives and losing more prisoners to the North Vietnamese in a continuing air war. Again and again, during the years of Vietnamization, observers and commentators, including former Pentagon officials, pointed to the likelihood that, at exactly the time when the American force level was minimal, probably in the election year 1972, the North Vietnamese would launch a massive assault confronting the United States with the awful choice between "defeat and humiliation" and radical re-escalation. Our own staff investigators reported as follows to the Senate Foreign Relations Committee after a trip to Vietnam in December 1969:

> Were the North Vietnamese to launch a massive attack at any point in the course of this withdrawal, the United States would be faced with the agonizing prospect of either halting—or even reversing—the process of withdrawal, on the one hand, or being forced, on the other hand, to effect an accelerated, complete withdrawal which would be interpreted at home, and probably abroad, as a military and political defeat.[11]

President Nixon and Mr. Kissinger may have anticipated these contingencies—it seems inconceivable that they did not—but they persisted, nonetheless, confident that by inventiveness and agility they could hold off the day of reckoning at least until after the election of 1972. They have indeed shown themselves to be well endowed with these qualities, but rather less so with the more mundane virtues of level-headedness and common sense. For all the fancy sophistries concocted to explain it, "Vietnamization" was never a promising means of strengthening the American hand; reducing our military strength on the ground while retaining the same political objectives that President Johnson tried in vain to achieve with over half a million men, Vietnamization served only to widen the gap between the objective sought and the means available for achieving it. This policy led inevitably to the denouement of 1972—at which juncture the Nixon Administration re-escalated the war by launching one of the most devastating bombing campaigns in the history of warfare and then appealed most piously to the Congress and the country to ratify its desperation measures with a vote of confidence.

There is one final argument for our continued presence in Vietnam which is said to have carried great weight with the Nixon Administration although it is highly speculative, rooted in far-fetched analogy, and as extraneous to the merits of the war as all the other rationalizations cited. This thesis, said to have been derived from the experience of Germany under the Weimar Republic and also said to have been favored by Mr. Kissinger, holds that an overhasty withdrawal from Indochina will bring on a violent outcry from the radical right in the United States, plunging us, as Mr. Nixon put it in his speech of April 7, 1971, "from the anguish of war into a nightmare of recrimination." For all I know there will be an outcry from the radical right if the war is ended short of total victory—they usually do make an uproar when the government does something sensible—but is that any reason to continue the killing of Americans and Vietnamese? Are our fliers and support troops and the people of Indochina to be sacrificed for the appeasement of the lunatic fringe at home? If there is to be recrimination, I say let's get on with it; it will be better than useless killing.

III. The Geopolitics of the War

For a long time our policy makers conceived of the war in Indochina as a testing of the Chinese liberation-war doctrine and therefore as a proxy war in a grand Chinese strategy for the conquest of Asia. Secretary of State Rusk used to warn of a "world cut in two by Asian Communism"; Vice President Humphrey warned of the threat of "Asian Communism with its headquarters in Peking"; even President Nixon, early in his Administration, warned that "Our defeat and humiliation in South Vietnam would without question promote recklessness in the councils of those great powers who have not yet abandoned their goals of world conquest."[12] The thesis of Chinese proxy war has been wholly discredited, if not by the abundant evidence of North Vietnamese nationalism and independence, then surely by the pertinent fact that, so far as is known, no Chinese combat forces of any kind have ever participated in the fighting in Vietnam. If President Nixon's visit to China signified anything, it signified the recognition of the Chinese People's Republic as an established government and of China as a more or less "normal" great power with whom we were prepared to have normal dealings. Implicit in these acknowledgments was the recognition that China was not engaged in a campaign of aggression or subversion aimed at the conquest of Asia but indeed was engaged in no more than conventional great-power maneuverings in a region which the Chinese have always considered to be their natural "sphere of influence."

Despite all this, the view of the Vietnamese Communists as spear bearers for a global conspiracy still lingers, like the light of an extinct star, in the minds of our policy makers. In his speech of April 26, 1972, President Nixon spoke repeatedly, and with that special intonation one uses to refer to something evil and conspiratorial, of "Communist aggression"—not North Vietnamese but "Communist aggression"—as if to suggest that, in a secret and sinister way, the whole Communist world from China to Poland and Yugoslavia were engaged in a campaign to conquer Indochina. In that peculiar, idiosyncratic, human way in which people believe two different, inconsistent things at the same time, or acknowledge what they see and hear without quite being able really to believe it, our leaders claim to have repudiated the myth of the Communist conspiracy but at the same time give evidence that it retains a certain hold upon their hearts. Like half-convinced converts to monotheism, in secrecy and darkness they still worship the old pagan gods. Once it is clear that the war in Vietnam is neither a valid global testing of the liberation-war doctrine nor a proxy war in a grand Chinese strategy for the conquest of Asia, it follows inescapably that the United States has been fighting a war without need or justification—a war based on demonstrably false premises. The master myth of Vietnam is the greatly inflated importance which has been attached to it. From the standpoint of American security and interests, the central fact about

Indochina is that it does not matter very much who rules in those small and undeveloped lands. We have preferences, to be sure, but they are a product of sentiment and habit. One might add humanitarian feeling, except that it is hard to see what human purpose is advanced by inflicting the Saigon regime on anybody. What it all comes down to is that if all other things were equal—as indeed they are not—it might be a convenience to the United States to have the countries of Indochina ruled by non-Communist leaders. For this hypothetical advantage we have already spent more than 55,000 lives, 300,000 mutilated bodies, and a great deal more than $150 billion.

We are fighting a double shadow in Indochina—the shadow of the international Communist conspiracy and the shadow of the old, mindless game of power politics. Armed with weapons that have given war a new dimension of horror, and adorned with the sham morality of ideological conflict, the struggle for power and influence has taken on a deadly, new intensity at exactly the time when it has lost much of the meaning it once had. All the old power-politics bromides—about "stability," "order" and "spheres of influence"— are largely without meaning to a global super power armed with nuclear weapons. The world balance of power on which our security depends is a nuclear balance involving Russia, China, Western Europe, Japan and the United States. The preservation of a non-Communist—as against a Communist—dictatorship in South Vietnam is not going to protect us, or anybody else, from Soviet or Chinese missiles. It simply does not matter very much for the United States, in cold, unadorned strategic terms, which faction controls the governments in Saigon or Phnom Penh or Vientiane.

Nor does it matter all that terribly to the inhabitants. At the risk of being accused of every sin from racism to communism, I stress the irrelevance of ideology to poor, peasant populations. Someday, perhaps, it will matter, in what one hopes will be a constructive and utilitarian way. But in the meantime, what earthly difference does it make to nomadic tribes or uneducated subsistence farmers, in Vietnam or Cambodia or Laos, whether they have a military dictator, a royal prince or a socialist commissar in some distant capital that they have never seen and may never even have heard of?

At their current stage of undevelopment these populations have more basic requirements. They need governments which will provide medical services, education, birth control programs, fertilizer, high-yield seeds and instruction in how to use them. They need governments which are honest enough to refrain from robbing and exploiting them, purposeful enough to want to modernize their societies, and efficient enough to have some ideas about how to do it. Whether such governments are capitalist or socialist can be of little interest to the people involved, or to anyone except their incumbent rulers, whose perquisites are at stake, and their great-power mentors, fretting in their distant capitals about ideology and "spheres of interest."

So much for the myth that it matters to our security who rules the states of Indochina. Another myth, well-established after five years of futile warfare, is that we could do anything about it if it did matter—anything worth doing, that is. We could certainly "win" the war in Vietnam, Cambodia and Laos today if we wanted to bomb those little countries back into the stone age, as one of our generals once suggested. Perhaps we will do that before it is over; the bombing campaign initiated in the spring of 1972 was a step in that direction. We have, however, been reluctant to pull out the stops and apply the full weight of our power; and, because of the domestic uproar that would follow, it has become politically impractical to escalate beyond the present war of piecemeal extermination—which simply is not doing the trick.

The plain fact that comes out of our war in Indochina is that, puny as it is by great-power standards, North Vietnam is the strongest power in Indochina. In unadorned geopolitical terms, it is "their" part of the world in exactly the same way—except on a much more modest scale—that Eastern Europe is Russia's part of the world and Latin America is ours.

We may think this an immoral and obsolete way of running the world's affairs—I certainly do—but no one is showing much inclination to change it by trying, say, to breathe some life into the United Nations. As long as we are going to continue to play the old game of power politics, we might as well play it intelligently, and it is just not intelligent to expect to be able to poach on somebody else's territory without encountering serious resistance, while at the same time you fiercely defend the inviolability of your own. The Russians ran into a buzz saw when they tried poaching on our preserve in the western hemisphere, whereupon they prudently retreated from the field. What reason have we ever had to suppose that the North Vietnamese, within the limits of their resources, would react any differently from the way we react? Perhaps if our minds were less cluttered with ideology, the sham morality it fosters, and great-power pride, we could see that the only real differences are of scale—ours is a big sphere of influence; theirs is a small one—and in the weapons employed—we scared off the Russians with the threat of our H-bombs; the North Vietnamese and Vietcong challenge us with conventional and guerrilla warfare. It is not, as a late member of the Senate once suggested, that when we intervene, it is "for their own good."

We ought in a way to welcome North Vietnam's

preeminence in Indochina because, although North Vietnam has shown itself strong enough to dominate Indochina if left alone by outside powers, it has also shown itself determined and able to resist Chinese domination. At the same time North Vietnam is far too small a power to have any serious hope of conquering all of Southeast Asia, much less posing any kind of a threat to the United States. Suppose, by way of analogy, that Yugoslavia, instead of emerging from World War II as a strong, independent, unified Communist country, had reverted to political units coinciding with its component nationality groups—Serbian, Slovenian, Croatian, Montenegrin and Macedonian. Suppose too that all of these states had adopted some kind of Western parliamentary institutions, making themselves members—as the term is commonly used—of the "free world." Recalling also their Balkan tradition of mutual hostility and political instability, is it possible to believe that such a congeries of mini-states could have resisted Stalin's regional imperialism with anything approaching the success of Tito's Communist Yugoslavia? It seems unlikely. Perhaps if France and then the United States had refrained from intervening on each of the occasions when Ho Chi Minh was on the verge of unifying Vietnam under his rule—in 1946, in the mid-fifties and again in 1965—we might now be dealing with a stable, independent, unified Communist country—no more hostile to the United States than Yugoslavia itself. Perhaps, someday, that is exactly what we will be confronted with, when—and if—American military power is removed from Indochina.

It should not be necessary to add—although I suppose it is—that I do not advocate a Communist-dominated Indochina. I merely propose to accept it, if it arises from the local power situation, as tolerable from the standpoint of American interests, and most emphatically not worth the extravagant costs of a war like the one we are now fighting. By their own choice our leaders are playing the spheres-of-influence game in a world of power politics. It was their choice to do it this way rather than to pursue a policy of authentic internationalism through the United Nations. Having made their choice of the game they wish to play, they ought at least to play by its rules. Mr. Kissinger once wrote an admiring book about Metternich, the great Austrian diplomat whose name is a symbol for the old politics of the balance of power. In some respects, as previously noted, the Nixon Administration has improved upon the old cold-war outlook by implementing traditional geopolitical principles, notably in their partial rapprochement with the Soviet Union and China. Of all recent Administrations, the Nixon Administration ought to have known that if you are going to be a successful Metternichian, you have to be a consistent one.

That, however, is something which the Nixon Administration has unaccountably refused to do with respect to Indochina. Like President Johnson before him, President Nixon has seemed persuaded that he can preserve the American sphere inviolate while contesting somebody else's in the name of saving the world from communism. In this respect, Vietnamization represents a change in tactics from the Johnson policy—inescapable because of domestic opposition to the war—but not a change in the objective, which is to preserve some kind of American military foothold, either directly or by proxy, in an alien sphere of influence.

At first the change was welcome: Vietnamization was better than escalation, but only in the sense that it is preferable to be riding in a car heading for a precipice at thirty miles an hour than at eighty miles an hour. If I really had had my choice, I never would have been in that car at all. By 1972 it appeared that Mr. Nixon had arrived at the precipice of ultimate failure in Indochina. It is to his credit in a sense that Mr. Johnson might have gotten there sooner, but I am still unwilling to adorn the lesser folly with the name of wisdom. Like the escalation which preceded it, Vietnamization was an unsound policy from the start, aimed at an unnecessary and unattainable objective.

Having failed to beat the Communists with a well-led, well-trained and superbly equipped American army of over half a million men, we could hardly have expected the ARVN on its own to do the job—even with American air and logistic support, without which, indeed, it would have collapsed long ago. We have managed—and may still manage a while longer—to keep our punchy protégés staggering around the ring. That has served Mr. Thieu's purposes well enough—it has kept him and his friends in power, however precariously—and it has enabled the Nixon Administration to delay the political settlement which it has insisted upon calling our "defeat and humiliation." For these worthy ends the Vietnamese people have paid the price of an indefinite continuation of terror and death, and the American people have paid the price of reduced but continuing casualties, burgeoning expense, and the social and economic fallout which has been causing the fabric of our own society to begin coming unstuck.

The interest of the United States in southeast Asia is something less than a "vital interest": nothing much that happens—or is likely to happen—in that part of the world is a matter of life and death for the American people. We do have an "interest" in the region, but in the less cataclysmic sense of advantage or preference. In this sense we have an interest in the continued freedom of the countries of Southeast Asia from domination by China or any other great power. The prevalent view among Southeast Asia specialists outside of government is that the Chinese challenge to south Asia is more political and cultural than military, that a strong, independent Communist regime is a more effective barrier to Chinese power than a weak non-Communist regime, that the Hanoi government is nationalist and independent, and that accordingly, once peace is restored—if ever it is—North Vietnam will serve as a barrier rather than as an avenue to Chinese domination. Dr. Kissinger said, in a briefing for Senators and Congressmen before President Nixon departed for China, that the opening of communications between China and the United States would pose a cultural challenge not only in Southeast Asia but to American society as well.

Instead of deterring Chinese involvement in Southeast Asia, American military involvement is a powerful magnet for it. Some years ago in an interview with an American reporter, the Laotian leader, Prince Souvanna Phouma, recalled a warning he had been given back in 1956 by Chinese Premier Chou En-lai: "We don't care how much United States aid you take, but we cannot tolerate American military bases so close to our borders."[13] Similarly, Chou En-lai assured the Burmese leaders in a visit to Peking in 1954 that as long as Burma permitted no foreign bases or foreign military on her teritory, China would not interfere in Burma. Reporting on this meeting at which he had been present, United Nations Secretary General U Thant said in 1967 that since Burma had obtained its independence in 1948, there had not been "one single instance" of Chinese Communist support or provision of arms for the Burmese Communists despite a common border of 1400 miles.[14]

It stands to reason—or it should have. How much chance would the Mexicans have of keeping the Americans out of their country if they were so insane as to invite the Chinese to establish a base on Mexican territory? Metternich at least was prepared to abide uniformly by the rules of his game. His modern American admirers appear to believe that they can enforce Metternich's rules in the American sphere of influence but something closer to Napoleon's in somebody else's. The Nixon visit to China signified, if anything, a repudiation of the old, discredited policy of global anti-communism, which was the only real basis and rationale for the Vietnam war. Without it the war has no more basis than the fact that it has become an addiction, because the United States has no vital security interest in the preservation of South Vietnam as an independent, non-Communist state.

On the basis of their grudging, minimal contributions to the fighting in Vietnam, it would appear that our Asian and Pacific allies either have not taken the ostensible threat to their own security very seriously or have been content to have the United States do their fighting for them. In the course of the war the United States has financed, equipped, transported and supported a small contingent of Thais, a sizable force of Koreans, and a noncombatant engineer battalion from the Philippines. Australia, which raised an army of 682,000 in the Second World War, has, at its own expense, provided a token force which at its maximum reached 7,600 men, more, it would appear, as an investment in Washington's gratitude than as a serious contribution to the war. New Zealand, which had raised an army of 157,000 men in World War II, provided a maximum token contribution of 550 men. Both Australia and New Zealand have been rewarded with lavish praise and gratitude from the United States.

Gratitude for what? For making a tiny contribution to what they themselves considered their own defense? For patting America on the back at a time when most of the world was pelting us with epithets? How did the United States, the greatest and strongest nation on the face of the earth, allow itself to be reduced to such pitiable gratitude for such small favors? The explanation, according to our policy makers, was that the United States had global responsibilities which compelled it to bear burdens which no one else would bear. Then the familiar image is invoked: of America, the martyred giant, manning the ramparts of freedom, humoring the recalcitrance and enduring the insults of those who are free from the "discipline of power," bearing without complaint the unfair burdens which destiny has thrust upon us. Diplomats have described this role as the "responsibility of power"; others have called it imperialism.

I call it nonsense. Power is a narcotic, a potent intoxicant, and America has been on a "trip." We soared for a while, gladly dispensing goods and services for the tribute which nourished our vanity. Then our unpiloted space ship came down in the swamps of Vietnam, and suddenly, instead of soaring, we found ourselves slogging in mud. The contrast could not have been greater and it has shocked and confused us. We must hope that it will also have sobered us, and that we will be able to find our way out of the swamp, not, let us hope, to take flight again, but just to get back on our feet, which is the posture that nature intended for us.

To get back on our feet we will have to shake off the lingering effects of the narcotic of power. For a start we might stop the prideful nonsense about "defeat and humiliation." Liquidating a mistake is neither a defeat nor a humiliation; it is a rational and mature way of accommodating to reality, and the ability to do it is something to be proud of. When President Johnson used to declare that he would not be the first American President to lose a war, and when President Nixon warned against the "collapse of confidence in American leadership" which would result from "this first defeat in American history,"[15] they were not talking about the national interest but about the national ego and their own standings in history. A war is not a football game which you try to win for its own sake, or in order to maintain an unblemished record of victories. A war is supposed to be fought for purposes external to itself, for substantive political purposes, not just for the glory of winning it. When its political purposes are recognized as unworthy, as most assuredly they have been in Vietnam, it is rank immorality to press on for a costly, destructive and probably unattainable victory.

As to their own personal roles, both Presidents Nixon and Johnson seem to have subscribed to an essentially military view of history's judgment. "History," as they have invoked it, is a kind of divine magistrate, lavish in its praise of victors and scornful of all losers. To some extent that is probably true—witness the glorification of despots like Caesar and Napoleon—but if it is true, all it shows is that historians, like laymen, employ some primitive standards in judging their fellow men. Everybody knows that we could "win" in Vietnam; we could wipe that poor country and every living thing within it off the face of the map. What would "history" have to say about that?

When all the grandiose "principles," geopolitical theories, learned conjectures, analogies, "game plans" and "scenarios" have been considered and found wanting, we are forced back upon the merits of the case, and in the case of Vietnam there are no merits and never have been. It has all been a tragic mistake in judgment, a miscarriage of our own good intentions, and nothing that we do can ever alter that. We can "play out the game" by sustaining a devastating air war and a proxy ground war, trading Asian lives for the phantom of

American prestige, but that will not retrieve our past mistakes; it will compound them and, if anything, accelerate the social corrosion which this war has brought upon American society. The other choice is to acknowledge and liquidate our mistake and, by that very act, initiate the process of social—and moral—reconstruction of which our country is in so great need.

IV. Ending It

Early in his term of office President Nixon commented that the withdrawal of all American forces from Indochina would have been a "popular and easy course to follow."[16] It would indeed have been "popular and easy"; it would also have been prudent, far-sighted and wise. The policy President Nixon inherited was a discredited failure, and the people had given him a mandate to end the war as he had explicitly and repeatedly promised to do in his 1968 campaign for the Presidency. By 1972, after 20,000 more American deaths and hundreds of thousands more of Asian deaths, the war which Nixon refused to dispose of as "Johnson's war" had indeed become "Nixon's war," a stalled, futile crusade for a discredited cause.

It does not matter a great deal *how* it is ended. It could be settled at Paris if the President would instruct his representatives at the peace talks to offer these terms: complete American withdrawal for the return of our prisoners and the safe, orderly departure of our remaining forces. Failing that, Congress can end the war, as it has the authority and, in my view, the responsibility to do, by cutting off funds for the war on condition that the North Vietnamese release our prisoners. I do not think they would refuse. Nor do I think it would be promising for the United States to go beyond the terms essential to its own interests and to involve itself in the tortuous details of arranging the conditions, composition, or method of constituting a new interim or coalition government for South Vietnam. As Henry Kissinger has written ". . . the subject of a coalition government is, in all accounts, the most thankless and tricky area for negotiation *by outsiders*."[17]

We have one great liability and one great asset for negotiating a political settlement. The liability is our peculiar devotion to the Saigon regime of President Thieu. Since this regime survives at our sufferance, the handicap could be removed by the simple expedient of putting Mr. Thieu and his associates on notice that they can join in negotiating a compromise peace, make some other direct arrangement with their enemies, or continue the war on their own. It is not a matter of intruding upon the sovereignty of our "ally." Of all the options open to the Thieu government, the only one we can and should remove is its present veto on American policy. As long as the Saigon government is allowed to believe that it can count on undiminished American military backing regardless of its refusal to make concessions to the National Liberation Front, there can be little prospect for the successful negotiation of a compromise settlement between the Vietnamese factions. The issue seems to be one not of what we may impose on the Saigon government but what we allow it to impose upon us. By the same logic that the United States ought not to impose a coalition government upon South Vietnam, neither ought it to shield the Saigon leadership from having to enter a coalition government should that be the result of the natural interplay of indigenous forces within Vietnam.

Our great asset, which neither the Johnson nor the Nixon Administration has been willing to acknowledge, is that this war is not now and never has been essential to our interests, essential, that is, to the freedom and safety of the American people. The exact terms of peace do not, therefore, matter very much from the standpoint of American interests, but the early restoration of peace matters enormously, because every day that this war goes on, the sickness of American society worsens. The only requirement is that the internal political regime of South Vietnam be determined by the unhampered interplay of indigenous forces. Whether this is accomplished by direct negotiations between the Saigon government and the National Liberation Front, by an internationally supervised election as called for by the Geneva Accords of 1954, or by some other means is not of critical importance. In extremity, should the two parties prove intransigent, we have the option simply to let them fight it out—without further American military participation.

It is short-sighted and self-destructive to keep the war going for the sake of technical, abstract, often spurious and always contested issues of "principle." The North Vietnamese have no doubt violated the terms of the Geneva settlement of 1954; and so have we. They have quite possibly as well violated the "understanding" of 1968, if indeed there was such an understanding—an issue on which the belligerents disagree. The North Vietnamese have unquestionably committed acts in violation of the law of war; and so, as at My Lai, have we. We may all regret very much that they have rejected President Nixon's proposals for a cease-fire and supervised free elections. But they *have* rejected these proposals. Is there nothing we can do about it except to sustain the war, blast them into submission if we can, and in the process, rend our society even more than it has been rent already? The North Vietnamese are not interested in our conception of a fair and reasonable settlement; they believe themselves to be fighting for the unity and national independence of *their own* country, for which purpose they have shown themselves willing and able to endure—and inflict—enormous losses. What a price to pay for the myth that Vietnam ever really mattered to the security of the United States.

In 1961 General de Gaulle warned President Kennedy that intervention in Indochina would be "an endless entanglement." "We French," he said, "have had experience of it. You Americans wanted to take our place in Indochina. Now you want to take over where we left off and revive a war which we brought to an end. I predict that you will sink step by step into a bottomless military and political quagmire, however much you spend in men and money. What you, we and others ought to do for unhappy Asia is not to take over the running of these states ourselves, but to provide them with the means to escape from the misery and humiliation which, there as elsewhere, are the causes of totalitarian regimes. I tell you this in the name of the West."[18]

America, in its power and dynamism and pride, rejected President de Gaulle's wise counsel. Now, looking back on the history of Vietnam since World War II, it seems likely that, if we had not intervened, first to support the French in their colonial war, then to create and sustain the Diem government, then, finally and fatally, to fight a full-scale war of our own, the Communists long ago would have achieved the independence of a unified Vietnam. It would have been achieved at infinitely less cost in blood and money under the only authentic nationalist leader in modern Vietnamese history, Ho Chi Minh, and we might well today be on as good terms with a unified Vietnam as we are with Yugoslavia.

After all this killing and destruction, and unless we

sustain indefinitely our futile, misbegotten crusade, the eventual outcome will probably be the same that it would have been if Americans had never gone to Vietnam. Our leaders may then suffer a momentary loss of prestige but our country will have recovered its self-respect. As for the Vietnamese, they are a nation of tough, resilient peasants who will make their own accommodations to reality. A young South Vietnamese army officer told an American reporter: "In thousands of years of our history we have seen the Chinese and the French and the Japanese come and we have forgotten them all. In time we will forget the Americans, too. Whether they did good or ill, they will only be a footnote to our history."[19]

I agree wholeheartedly with President Nixon on one point. He said in his speech of November 3, 1969: "North Vietnam cannot defeat or humiliate the United States. Only Americans can do that."

4

The Middle East—
Myths and Realities

The journalist I. F. Stone, who has been concerned long and sympathetically with the aspiration of the Jewish people for a secure national home, has written: "The Arab-Jewish struggle is a tragedy. The essence of tragedy is a struggle of right against right. Its catharsis is the cleansing pity of seeing how good men do evil despite themselves out of unavoidable circumstance and irresistible compulsion. When evil men do evil, their deeds belong to the realm of pathology. But when good men do evil, we confront the essence of human tragedy. In a tragic struggle, the victors become the guilty and must make amends to the defeated. For me the Arab problem is also the Number One Jewish problem. How we act toward the Arabs will determine what kind of people we become: either oppressors and racists in our turn like those from whom we have suffered, or a nobler race able to transcend the tribal xenophobias that afflict mankind."[1]

In the Middle East there is a chance—though only a small one—for Arabs and Jews, Russians, Americans and others to "transcend the tribal xenophobias that afflict mankind" by attempting something unprecedented in international affairs: the settlement of a major international controversy through the procedures of the United Nations. It need not—and preferably would not—be an "imposed" solution, although we should not shrink from applying certain sanctions as a last resort for the removal of a chronic threat to the peace. The United Nations Charter, to which every nation involved in the Middle East has voluntarily subscribed, spells out a graduated series of sanctions, from economic to military, for the enforcement of peace. It makes no sense at all for us to shrink in horror at the very notion of an "imposed" solution, not only because we are legally bound by the Charter to accept certain kinds of "imposed" solutions, but because the absolute sovereignty of nations is an outmoded principle; it is indeed a principle of international anarchy. No community can function without some capacity for coercion; as President Wilson said of the Covenant of the League of Nations, "Armed force is in the background . . . if the moral force of the world will not suffice, the physical force of the world shall."[2] The crucial distinction is not between coercion and voluntarism, but between duly constituted force, applied through law and as a last resort, and the arbitrary coercion of the weak by the strong.

Far from foreseeing a settlement of this kind, I think the chances for it, as of mid-1972, quite remote. At that time that Israelis were pressing ahead with the settlement and consolidation of their hold on the occupied Arab territories—pursuing the policy, as they call it, of "creating facts"—while President Sadat, frustrated by the cautious policy of the Soviet Union, expelled Soviet military personnel from Egypt and declared that Egypt would "stand alone on the battlefield if need be." "I would rather see our blood shed than live in the present no-war, no-peace deadlock," President Sadat declared.[3] The cease-fire of August 7, 1970, still held but the prospect was for a continuing arms race, periodic crises, and little if any progress in the desultory United Nations mediation effort.

Despite these unpromising prospects, there remains one basis of hope: the fact that no one of the great powers—which is to say, the permanent, veto-wielding members of the United Nations Security Council—has a direct, valid national interest in the perpetuation of the conflict in the Middle East. The Russians have allowed themselves to be caught up in a sterile, costly bid for "influence" in the Arab world; the Americans, for their part, have allowed themselves to be drawn to the Israeli side by bonds of sympathy and by the impact of the most powerful and efficient foreign policy lobby in American politics. Such hope as may be held for a United Nations settlement in the Middle East derives from the chance that the Russians and Americans may eventually decide to act upon their own valid interests, which are neither geopolitical nor sentimental. Their real interests are in a settlement which gives security to Israel, restores lost territories to the Arabs, removes the Middle East as an issue of contention between themselves, and breathes life into the United Nations.

I. The Myths

The myths that shape events in the Middle East are the oldest myths of all.

Some derive from religion. The contested land is a "holy" land; more than a place for raising crops and building cities, it is "sacred soil" for three great religions. Jerusalem contains the Wall of the Temple, which is sacred to Jews, the Dome of the Rock, which is sacred to Muslims, and the Church of the Holy Sepulcher, which is sacred to Christians. Neither Jews nor Arabs can hold exclusive title to the city without also owning the other faith's shrine. Now, as in the days of the Crusades, religion exacerbates the issue, because, now as then, the behavior of the belligerents is more affected by the zeal with which they hold their beliefs than by the humane ethics taught by their respective religions. Now as in the past it is hard to strike a bargain over sacred soil.

Then there are the myths of mutual victimization. Perhaps one should say the half-myths, because both Jews and Arabs *have* victimized each other, though surely not with the deliberate and malign intent that each attributes to the other.

The Jews are obsessed with the fear of a repetition of the Nazi holocaust, and the Arabs do nothing to allay this fear with extravagant talk about "holy wars" and about throwing the Jews into the sea. These threats have understandably alarmed the Israelis in much the same way that Khrushchev's talk of "burying" us agitated Americans a decade ago. Presidents Nasser and Sadat of Egypt and King Hussein of Jordan have repudiated such draconian threats, but the Israelis seem not to have noticed the disavowals. As survivors of genocide, they can hardly be expected to distinguish with perfect clarity between Nazi crimes and Arab rhetoric. All they know is that they came to Palestine in peace, settlers in an underpopulated land, but have been allowed no peace; they have fought three wars they never wished to fight and still their enemies remain implacable, refusing even to talk to them, contesting— until recently—their right to survive as a state.

Nonetheless, the Arab-Nazi analogy is a faulty one; it clouds the distinction between the myth and reality of Arab intent—whatever these may be.

The Arabs, for their part, perceive zionism as a new form of Western imperialism. Having lived on the land of Palestine for thousands of years, they can have little sympathy for the historic sentiments of the Jewish diaspora. It is all but impossible for them to put themselves in the place of the Jews, whose cultural attachment to their ancient homeland sustained them through centuries of dispersal and persecution. The Arabs are on a different wavelength: while the Jews prayed for Palestine—"next year in Jerusalem," they said in their prayer—the Arabs inhabited the land. They could not see the Jews as the Jews saw themselves: as refugees from genocide seeking safe haven. What did this have to do with the Arabs? They had done the Jews no harm and could see no reason why they should compensate the Jews for the crimes of Europeans. In fact, to Arab eyes, the Jews were Europeans, armed with European skills and technology, coming on the heels of other Europeans to drive them from their homes and steal away their lands.

In its way zionism has seemed to the Arabs even more threatening than the old European imperialism. The British and French after all were only establishing colonies and, bad as that was, colonies come and go. But the Jews were establishing a homeland, and homelands do not come and go. On the contrary, once established, they are likely to expand. The Jewish state actively encourages immigration from all over the world, especially from the Soviet Union, creating for Arabs the specter of a Jewish drive for *Lebensraum*, which could only mean the annexation of even more Arab lands. Some elements within Israel and the world Zionist movement openly proclaim the need of a policy of expansion, which must give rise to a fear among Arabs not unlike that felt by the Jews when the Arabs talk of throwing them into the sea. To the Arabs, in short, zionism is not a program of deliverance for a persecuted race but a foreign conquest bolstered by strong ties between the conquering people and the most powerful government of the West.

As if the Arab-Israeli problem were not enough, the great powers have made their own special contribution to the mythology of the Middle East by infusing the crisis with the hocus-pocus of geopolitics. The Middle East, in geopolitical terms, is something far more abstract than an oil-rich desert contested by feuding Semitic peoples. Beyond that, it is the "gateway to the East," the "hinge of NATO," and the crucial cockpit of the historic Russian drive toward warm water. By sending planes and missiles to Egypt the Russians are not merely bolstering a shaky client; to the X-ray eye of the geopolitician, they are embarked upon a drive to convert the Mediterranean into a "Soviet lake." The concept is admittedly vague: would the Russians close the Mediterranean to foreign shipping? prohibit fishing? use it as a vacation resort? No one really knows what a Russian *mare nostrum* would be like, but the concept serves the purpose of its users: it scares people; it imputes the "vital interests" of the great powers to a regional conflict, converting it into a battleground of the cold war. In this frame of reference one even suspects the Russians of an insidious design in wishing to reopen the Suez Canal—something which used to be considered a good thing, before the geopoliticians came along.

The "vital interests" of the great powers are, in fact, involved in the Middle East—primarily because those powers have chosen to become involved. The ultimate danger is that the Arab-Israeli conflict could draw the super powers and the world into a nuclear war—and that certainly is a matter of "vital interest"—but the danger is not inherent in the local situation, nor is it predestined by fate. It has arisen because the great powers have surrendered much of their own freedom of action to the bellicose whims of their respective clients. There is of course one way in which the great powers are *obligated* to intervene: as members of the United Nations Security Council charged by the Charter with the responsibility to "decide what measures shall be taken" in response to a "threat to the peace, breach of the peace or act of aggression." Instead, the Soviet Union and the United States have played the role of cobelligerents to their respective clients, arming and financing them, committing their own prestige to the issue and, in so doing, converting a local conflict into a potential world conflict. All that can be said in mitigation is that both great powers—the Soviet Union more than the United States—have shown a certain prudence by holding back at times on the arms supplied to the quarreling parties.

Finally there is the myth of militarism, and that affects all of the parties. Each flirts from time to time with the notion that another round may settle things— although three wars have failed to end the conflict—or that some new weapons system will stabilize the balance of power—as if either side would accept the other's notion of what it takes to establish a proper balance. Since the June war of 1967 the Egyptians have acquired vast arsenals of Soviet weapons, including air support and advanced ground-to-air missiles; from August 1968 until August 1970 they waged a "war of attrition" along the Suez Canal. What did it get them? The Israelis were compelled to stop their deep-penetration air raids into Egypt but they still hold the Sinai; they still receive a steady flow of military equipment from the United States; and they have every prospect of acquiring additional Phantom and Skyhawk jets, electronic devices and other modern weapons from the United States whenever they judge these necessary to reestablish *their* version of the balance of power. Nor has the Soviet-supplied Egyptian hardware wrung any political concessions from the Israelis: Prime Minister Meir explicitly rejects the borders of 1967 and, instead of offering concessions, Foreign Minister Eban contributes pithy ironies about recognizing the right of the United Arab Republic to exist.[4]

The Israelis, for their part, have hardly profited from their military successes. They have gained territory and they have established their military superiority, but they have failed to gain what they most want: security. In 1967 they felt desperately insecure along the Gaza Strip frontier; today they feel desperately insecure along the Suez Canal, so much so that they and their friends abroad seem almost to have forgotten that it is not their own but Egyptian territory that they are defending so tenaciously. One begins to understand the spheres-of-influence psychology, which causes a nation to believe that it can have no security at all until it has robbed its neighbors of all semblance of security. Surrounded by hostile neighbors, holding down occupied lands inhabited by a million Arabs, plagued from time to time by *fedayeen* attacks, and oppressed by the costs of armaments, Israel is a desperately insecure nation. That is clear, but it is anything but clear that her present policy of relying on military superiority is ever going to alter the situation. Even if the United States provides all the Phantom jets the Israelis want and electronic jamming gear to neutralize the Egyptian SAM-2 and SAM-3 missiles, it is unlikely that Israel will gain more than a respite; the Russians—or perhaps some other foreign arms supplier—will soon enough come up with something else.

A leading Egyptian journalist told a visiting member of the Senate Foreign Relations Committee staff in late 1970 that only generations could bring peace in the full sense but that a political settlement could be obtained —indeed must be obtained—because, in his view, neither Egypt nor Israel could win a military victory. If the Israelis should capture Cairo, they would still not have won the war; they could only extend their occupation of Egypt until they exhausted themselves. Similarly, if the Egyptians should occupy Tel Aviv, what would they do with two and one-half million Jews? Somehow they would have to be lived with. (He made no reference to throwing them into the sea.) If the Israelis should destroy the Egyptian army again, the Russians would reequip it with tanks and guns. Or if the Egyptians should destroy Israel's armed forces, the United States would reequip them. This conflict was not, therefore, a traditional European kind of war which could be won or lost. For that reason a political settlement had to be reached, although the journalist was far from optimistic about reaching one easily or soon.

After the First World War the French tried to gain security in somewhat the same way that Israel seeks it today. They too were confronted with a potentially powerful but momentarily weakened antagonist, and they tried to perpetuate that situation by occupying the German Rhineland, temporarily detaching the Saar, and compelling Germany to pay reparations. The effort to make France secure by keeping Germany weak was a failure. Now, almost three decades after the Second World War, France has nothing to fear from Germany although Germany is strong and in possession of all of the western territories France once wished to detach.

France is secure now not because Germany has lost the power to threaten her but because she has lost the wish to do so.

The analogy is imperfect and simplified but it holds: Israel will be secure when and if the Arabs lose the wish to threaten her. Eliminating that wish should be an object worth pursuing from Israel's point of view. As victors the Israelis are in a position to be magnanimous without being suspected of "weakness"—which is something nations worry about whenever they are thinking about behaving sensibly. But thus far they have shown little inclination to trade their conquests for peace. Instead, they cling to the advantages won by their military victory of 1967, which is a wasting asset. One insecure frontier has been traded for another and all that the future seems to hold is continuing hostility and recurrent conflict, as threatening to the outside world as it is to the Arabs and Israelis.

Because the conflict is a threat to the outside world, it cannot be left solely to the humors of the belligerents. Under the United Nations Charter the Security Council has full authority—possibly even the obligation—to *impose* a settlement upon warring parties who fail to make peace on their own. The very premise of the Charter is that warring nations can no longer be permitted immunity from a world police power. As far as the United States is concerned, it is worth recalling now and then that the United Nations Charter is a valid and binding obligation upon us, ratified as a treaty with the advice and consent of the Senate. As to the Arabs and Israelis, they too are signatories to the Charter and no one can say they have been denied a fair opportunity to settle their differences peacefully and on their own. They might now be reminded of their commitment under Article 25 of the Charter, which states that "The Members of the United Nations agree to accept and carry out the decisions of the Security Council in accordance with the present Charter."

I think it would be a fine thing—a useful step forward for civilization—if, in the absence of a voluntary settlement by the parties, the United Nations were to "impose" a peaceful settlement in the Middle East. It would be an equally fine thing if the United Nations could "impose" a settlement in Southeast Asia. Unfortunately, there is no such prospect for Indochina, but I would not pass up the opportunity in the Middle East for the sake of a baneful consistency.

II. Perspectives

There are four major perspectives on the Middle East conflict and need of a fifth. The needed one, as I have suggested, is that of the world community through its duly constituted organ, the United Nations. The development of such a perspective and its translation into action will require changes and adjustments in the long-frozen perspectives of Arabs and Israelis, Russians and Americans. It may be well to review the prevailing perspectives of those involved in the Middle East, with a view to detecting misconceptions, desirable directions of change, and opportunities for future agreement.

Starting with Israel, it is less than adequate to say that the Jewish state is preoccupied with its survival. Surrounded and outnumbered by seemingly implacable foes, the Israelis are obsessed with the fear of being destroyed. This fear is based on salient facts but it is reinforced by fear itself, and by a two thousand years' history which planted the fear of extermination deeply in Jewish minds. The result is a tendency on the part of the Israelis to exaggerate their own vulnerability, to credit their adversaries with more relentless hostility than in fact they may harbor, and to dismiss tentative gestures of conciliation as hypocritical tricks. A visitor who had never been to Israel wrote soon after he arrived: " '*Our existence*'—that is the theme here—at least with all but a very few of the people one talks to. The suspicion of Arab intentions—the certainty, or near certainty, that the Arabs will *never* give up on their hope of destroying Israel—permeates the thinking of both officials and non-officials, along with the menace, as one official put it, of the 'presence of the Russian bear.' "

Chronic suspicion and fear are ultimately unrewarding; they give rise to an outlook which causes myths to displace realities in the minds of statesmen who pride themselves on realism and hardheadedness. It has distorted American perceptions of China and the Soviet Union, and it has distorted the Israeli view of Arab intentions and capacities. When suspicion governs policy, it becomes impossible for adversaries to communicate or negotiate because neither side is receptive to even the bare possibility that the other may be telling the truth when he makes a conciliatory gesture, or that he may be amenable to compromise.

The Israeli conviction of Arab hostility is by no means invention, but there is a touch of paranoia about it—just as there is in the American attitude toward communism—and the worst of it is that the prophecy is self-fulfilling. It is a truism of modern psychology that we influence the behavior of others by our own expectations of how they are going to behave. The critical question for Israel is whether it is willing to risk taking the Arabs at their word when they offer to live in peace —as they have done in effect by accepting the Security Council resolution of November 1967, which calls, among other things, for Israeli withdrawal from occupied territories, the termination of belligerency, the right of Israel and Arab states to "live in peace within secure and recognized boundaries," and a just settlement of the refugee problem. This is not to say that Israel can or should gamble her survival on the hope of Arab good will; Israel has the unchallengeable right to survive as a state and, as I shall indicate later, I would be willing to support a significant new commitment by the United States to assure Israel's survival. Nonetheless, I think it is incumbent upon Israel to credit her Arab neighbors with good faith when they say—as they have said repeatedly—that they are willing to live in peace. Hitherto, the Israelis have had a tendency to demand specific reassurances of one kind and another from the Arabs and then, when these assurances have been forthcoming, to dismiss them as insincere.

A promising opportunity was lost in the spring of 1970 when the Israeli government refused to authorize the President of the World Jewish Congress, Dr. Nahum Goldmann, to hold talks in Cairo with President Nasser. The "torpedoing" of the Goldmann mission was surprising as well as unfortunate because, as *The New York Times* pointed out at the time, a meeting between a veteran Zionist leader and the Egyptian President would have represented a "significant breakthrough toward the direct contacts on which the Israeli Government has always insisted."[5]

In Dr. Goldmann's view the Zionist movement has suffered since its inception from a failure to grasp Arab psychology. Instead of seeking to minimize the injustices done the Arabs by the establishment of the Jewish homeland in Palestine, Israel, Dr. Goldmann has written, "counted on military force or the intervention of foreign powers to attain its goals." As a result, in Goldmann's view, Israel "has ceased to project the image of a small country threatened with destruction" and has become "an occupying power," which "exercises control over peoples who reject it and whom it has subjected." The result of Israeli policy since the Six-Day War of 1967, Dr. Goldmann believes, is a dangerous impasse which does not work to Israel's advantage, because time is not on Israel's side. Israel's present advantage, Dr. Goldmann pointed out, derives from the virtues, character and technological ability of its citizens, but the Arabs too have demonstrated energy and talent in the past and they greatly outnumber the Israelis. "No one," wrote Dr. Goldmann, "can predict how long it will take them to catch up with Israel technologically, especially in the field of weaponry. But sooner or later the balance of power will shift in their favor." Maintenance of the status quo, Dr. Goldmann concluded, "will lead to new wars, new Arab defeats and growing hatred of the Israelis"—a situation which "could have disastrous consequences for the Jewish state in the long run."[6]

I had a conversation in the summer of 1970 with a prominent Israeli journalist who had played a leading role in the struggle against British rule before 1948. Concerned that Israel has become a garrison state, he expressed fear for his country's survival as a democratic society. I said that I had the same fear for America, because we too have been chronically at war for over two decades. We agreed that both Israel and the United States would do well to recall Alexis de Tocqueville's warning of a century and a half ago, that war is the "surest and shortest means" to the destruction of democracy.[7] The Israeli journalist concluded by expressing the hope that Americans of moderate persuasion would speak out on the Middle East. If they did, he thought, Israeli moderates too would be encouraged to speak in favor of a policy of conciliation.

Israeli policy since the Six-Day War has been characterized by a lack of flexibility and foresight. The establishment of Israeli settlements on the occupied west bank of the Jordan River and in the Sinai can only be interpreted as steps toward foreclosing the return of these territories to their previous Arab owners. The insistence upon the "non-negotiability" of the status of Jerusalem and upon the retention of certain other occupied territories—notably the Golan Heights, the Gaza Strip and Sharm el Sheikh—lends unfortunate credence to the late President Nasser's pessimistic prediction, in accepting Secretary Rogers' peace proposal of 1970, that "While we inform the United States that we have accepted its proposals, we also tell them that our real belief is that whatever is taken by force cannot be returned except by force."[8] President Sadat has reiterated this prognosis in the wake of the failure of the United Nations mediation effort of Ambassador Jarring. Premier Meir's contemptuous rejection of King Hussein's proposal in early 1972 for a federation of the east and west banks of the Jordan River under his leadership provides further evidence of the extreme unlikelihood of a voluntary settlement among the parties; to the Israelis as to the Arabs the rule of force still holds sway. Premier Meir commented on King Hussein's proposed federation that "The King is treating as his own property territories which are not his and are not under his control. He crowns himself king of Jerusalem and envisions himself as the ruler of larger territories than were under his control prior to the rout of June, 1967."[9] Equally distressing although not entirely unprovoked is the Israeli view of the United Nations as what Foreign Minister Eban has called a "packed court" whose recommendations may be ignored. The insistence upon the "non-negotiability" of Israel's annexation of Arab East Jerusalem is in open contempt of the United

Nations General Assembly, which censured that unilateral act by a vote of 99 to 0.

I write critically of Israeli policy in part because of my belief that Israel, as the momentary victor, has both an obligation and an interest in a policy of magnanimity. The obligation arises from general considerations of world peace and from the specific injustice which has been done to the Palestinian Arabs, who, as Arnold Toynbee has written, "have been made to pay for the genocide of Jews in Europe, which was committed by Germans, not by Arabs."[10] Israel's self-interest in magnanimity is a matter of the only kind of security which really is security. In the words of a member of the Law Faculty of Hebrew University: "A border is secure when those living on the other side do not have sufficient motivation to infringe on it. . . . We have to remind ourselves that the roots of security are in the minds of men. . . ."[11]

For reasons which may warrant our sympathy, but not our support, Israel pursues a policy of antiquated—and to a great degree delusional—self-reliance. As Foreign Minister Eban expressed it, "a nation must be capable of tenacious solitude."[12] In fact, neither Israel nor any other nation is capable of so profound an isolationism in our time. Israel is heavily dependent on the United States for both arms and economic assistance. Since 1948 private American citizens have provided several billion dollars in tax-deductible contributions and regularly purchase between $300 million and $400 million a year in Israeli bonds. Included in the massive American military aid, which has increased greatly since the 1967 war, have been aircraft, missiles and electronic systems more advanced than those provided to the countries with whom we are allied in NATO or SEATO. I do not see how this can be reconciled with a policy on Israel's part of "tenacious solitude."

A different view is taken by Israel's elder statesman and first Prime Minister, David Ben-Gurion. "Peace," he has said, "real peace, is now the great necessity for us. It is worth almost any sacrifice. To get it, we must return to the borders before 1967." "As for security," Mr. Ben-Gurion continued, "militarily defensible borders, while desirable, cannot by themselves guarantee our future. Real peace with our Arab neighbors— mutual trust and friendship—that is the only true security."[13]

The Arabs too must face up to certain realities: that Israel has come to stay; that it is demagogic nonsense to talk—as some of the Palestinian guerrillas still do— of driving the Jews into the sea; that in any case the Arab states can have no realistic hope of doing that because they themselves cannot defeat Israel, the Russians are not likely to do it for them, and the United States would almost certainly intervene to save Israel from destruction. Once these facts are recognized—as in large measure they have been recognized by the governments of Egypt and Jordan—the Arab countries will be able to free themselves from their morbid preoccupation with past defeats, from futile dreams of revenge, and from the oppressive burden of armaments which slows their development and makes them dependent upon foreign powers.

Although Egypt and Jordan are still credited with the desire to destroy Israel, both in fact have repudiated any such ambition and have done so explicitly and repeatedly. They did it in the first instance by accepting the United Nations Security Council Resolution of November 22, 1967, which required them to give up positions to which they had held tenaciously for twenty years. By accepting that Resolution, Egypt and Jordan, as already noted, committed themselves to terminate their belligerency against Israel; to acknowledge Israel's sovereignty, territorial integrity and right "to live in peace within secure and recognized boundaries"; and to respect Israel's right to freedom of navigation through the Suez Canal and the Strait of Tiran. Having accepted these provisions of the Resolution—which in fact meet *all* of Israel's stated and legitimate aspirations—the Egyptians and Jordanians now emphasize the *other* provisions of the Resolution of 1967: the withdrawal of Israel from occupied territories; a just settlement of the refugee problem; and "the inadmissibility of the acquisition of territory by war." The last is a general principal which goes beyond the special interest of the Arab states. Its vindication—even in one instance—would represent a long step forward toward the establishment of the rule of law in international relations. That would serve everybody's interests—everybody, that is, who wishes to survive in the nuclear age and who still has some hope that the United Nations can be developed into an effective peace-keeping organization. It is natural enough for Israel to resist the honor of being the first modern military victor to be obliged to abide by the principles and specifications of the United Nations Charter, especially when the great powers who dominate the Security Council have set such a wretched example. Be that as it may, the principle involved is too important to be cast away because of the hypocrisy or self-interest of its proponents.

Returning to the Arab perspective, I think there has been insufficient recognition of the distance the Egyptian and Jordanian governments have come toward accommodating themselves to some form of coexistence with Israel. Presidents Nasser and Sadat and King Hussein have repudiated the contention that they will be satisfied with nothing less than "driving Israel into the sea" not only by subscribing to the Security Council's

Resolution of November 1967, but through repeated and explicit public statements. As early as 1969, in a speech in Washington, King Hussein reiterated his own and President Nasser's willingness to abide by each of the provisions of the 1967 Resolution, and he then added: "In return for these considerations, our sole demand upon Israel is the withdrawal of its armed forces from all territories occupied in the June, 1967, war, and the implementation of all the other provisions of the Security Council Resolution."[14]

To take another example: in an American television interview on June 14, 1970, President Nasser stated unequivocally his willingness to accept the boundaries of Israel as they existed before the 1967 war as final boundaries. Asked whether Egypt would promise that its territory would not be used for attacks on Israel once the Israelis withdrew from the occupied territories, President Nasser replied—several times—"Yes."[15]

Unless one is prepared to contend—and back the proposition—that President Sadat and King Hussein have simply not been telling the truth, it seems to me irresponsible to continue accusing either Egypt or Jordan of a policy aimed at "driving Israel into the sea." The Jordanians have long been known to be willing to come to terms with Israel—to end the state of war and recognize Israel's existence as a state in return for the restoration of occupied territory. The United Arab Republic, in its reply of February 16, 1971, to questions put by the United Nations mediator, Ambassador Jarring, stated unequivocally that if Israel would withdraw from occupied Egyptian territory, Egypt would be prepared to end the state of belligerency, ensure freedom of navigation through the Suez Canal and the Strait of Tiran, establish demilitarized zones, agree to the establishment of a United Nations peace-keeping force, and "enter into a peace agreement with Israel. . . ."

The Egyptian reply concedes to Israel all that she once desired, all that she claimed to be struggling for in three wars. Nonetheless, in its own reply to Ambassador Jarring of February 26, 1971, the Israeli government stated bluntly that "Israel will not withdraw to the pre-June 5, 1967 lines." Israel, Mrs. Meir subsequently explained, insists upon the retention of Sharm el Sheikh; the Gaza Strip; the Golan Heights—because, as the Premier explained, "We paid for it"; Jerusalem—considered not even negotiable; and certain undefined parts of the west bank of the Jordan River. In addition, said the Premier, Sinai must be demilitarized, and the demilitarization must be guaranteed by a mixed force including Israelis. The Egyptians too might participate in this force on their own territory. All this, Mrs. Meir conceded, would be painful for President Sadat of Egypt, but people must pay for their deeds.[16]

Withdrawal from the occupied territories is one of two concerns which dominate the Arab perspective; the other is the question of the Palestinian refugees. Whatever the political considerations which have led Israel to evade responsibility and the Arab states to exploit their plight, the unhappy Palestinian refugees remain preoccupied with the indisputable facts that, after almost twenty-five years in exile, they are not permitted to return to their homes and they have been denied compensation for their lost properties. Although, according to United Nations estimates, some 60 percent of the refugees have found new homes and jobs, many thousands—made up mostly of the elderly, the very poor, the sick and the least educated—are still interned in miserable camps, living hopeless lives as wards of the United Nations. Since the 1967 war approximately half of the two and one-half million Palestinian Arabs have been living under Israeli occupation. Despite annual United Nations resolutions recognizing

their right to choose between returning to their homes
and resettling elsewhere with compensation for lost
properties, the refugees remain neglected and embit-
tered pawns in the continuing Middle East conflict, the
original 750,000 refugees of 1948 having increased to
well over a million. In the words of a study prepared by
a working party on the Middle East of the American
Friends Service Committee, "the Arabs of Palestine see
themselves as a people in diaspora, just at the time
when the Jews have won their struggle for a national
home."[17]

A member of the staff of the Senate Foreign Relations
Committee visited a Palestinian refugee camp near
Beirut in November 1970 and reported on the human
meaning of the refugee problem:

> Accompanied by an UNWRA official, an
> Embassy control officer and two uniformed, rifle-
> carrying soldiers of the "Armed Struggle Com-
> mand," I visited this morning one of the stinking,
> festering Palestinian refugee camps on the out-
> skirts of Beirut. It was as hateful and ugly, squalid
> and degraded a place as the worst "favelas" in Bra-
> zil or even the slums of Calcutta. The houses were
> wretched shacks, the stores makeshift huts, the
> streets—if they can be called that—filthy alleyways
> lined with open sewers. The population is dense,
> especially with ragged children. One sees how the
> 750,000 refugees of 1948 have become 1,400,000.
> There are differences from the shanty towns of
> Lima and Recife. First of all there is law and order,
> enforced by the indigenous soldiery which calls
> itself the "Armed Struggle Command." Second,
> there is a semblance of social cohesion: we visited
> a school within the camp and the children seemed
> well-tended and were neatly uniformed, although

the schoolhouse was makeshift. There also appears
to be no hunger—at least not starvation—thanks in
part to the pittance—about ten cents per person a
day—provided by UNWRA, which also runs the
schools and hires and pays the teachers. The most
important difference between the refugee camp
amd the slums I have seen in Asia and Latin America is that these people are not submissive, hollow-
eyed sub-revolutionaries. They are political and
angry and sometimes violent: they are refugees
and their anger and hatred flourish in the fetid soil
of the camp. It is not judged wise for visitors—
American visitors at any rate—to enter the camp
unescorted by the armed guard. They accompanied us everywhere—they were friendly
enough themselves—and I would not have wanted
them to leave us. As we left the refugee camp, a
Palestinian employee of UNWRA called me aside.
"Tell the people in Washington," he said, "that we
are disappointed with the United States."

Since the June war of 1967 the Palestinians have
emerged as active, although militarily ineffective, participants in the Middle East conflict. The largest of the
guerrilla organizations, Al Fatah, demands the dissolu-
tion of the present state of Israel and the creation of a
secular multireligious state. They reject partition but
they also deny any wish to "throw the Jews into the
sea." Other Palestinian Arabs, more moderate, more
realistic and—prudently, under present circumstances
—more silent, acknowledge that Israel is here to stay
and say that they are prepared to make peace—provided that Israel withdraws from the territories occupied in 1967.

The status of the Palestinians and the question of the
occupied territories are the critical issues for peace in

the Middle East. The two issues are closely related because many Palestinian Arabs are haunted by the fear that there are no bounds to Israel's territorial aspirations—a fear which feeds upon classic Zionist ideology as well as upon the declarations of military-minded Israelis who press the claim for "strategic" frontiers. A declaration by the Israeli government of willingness to restore the occupied territories as part of a general peace settlement would go far to alleviate Arab fears of Zionist expansionism. Such a statement would meet the Egyptian-Jordanian condition for peace and would also improve the chances for a settlement in Palestine.

In the Arab perspective the central issues are the occupied territories and the Palestinians. In the Israeli perspective the issue is the survival and security of the Jewish state. The United Nations Resolution of 1967 recognizes the legitimacy of both parties' concerns. The question now is whether the two sides, and their great-power mentors, are ready to proceed, either through the renewed mediation of Dr. Jarring or by some other means, toward the translation of general principles into specific agreements.

More perhaps than either would care to acknowledge, the two super powers have played similar roles in the Middle East, both characterized by a certain ambivalence. On the one hand, they have played the traditional great-power role, arming their respective clients, committing their own prestige, building spheres of influence, fretting over geopolitical abstractions—all serving to elevate a regional conflict into a global one. On the other hand, both the Soviet Union and the United States have shown an appreciation of the dangers in the Middle East, and that appreciation has caused them to restrain the two sides at critical moments and to encourage some form of accommodation.

It was through Soviet and American mediation, in which the American Secretary of State, William Rogers, played a leading role, that the "war of attrition" along the Suez Canal was stopped in the summer of 1970. The indirect negotiations through Ambassador Jarring which ensued have, however, proven sterile; two years after the indirect negotiations began, the two sides had still failed to achieve even a limited agreement for the reopening of the Suez Canal. The great powers, accordingly, still must determine the kind of role they are to play in the Middle East, whether they are to play power politics or undertake to advance and, if need be, enforce a compromise peace through the United Nations. Heretofore the super powers have vacillated between the temptation to turn the Middle East into a cold war battleground and a caution induced by the well-founded fear of an uncontrollable conflict. The outcome in the Middle East will be determined as much by the great powers' conception of their own interests and of their own proper roles as by the attitudes of the Arabs and Israelis.

Like their czarist predecessors, the Soviet leaders have pursued a foreign policy aimed at the acquisition of "influence" in the Near East and the Mediterranean. What, if anything, they have hoped to gain in concrete terms is unclear—probably even to themselves. The Russians do not appear much inclined to try to communize the region—even if they could; they have overlooked the imprisonment of local Communists and the suppression of Communist parties in Egypt, Syria and Iraq, eagerly providing armaments to all three countries, both before and since the June war of 1967.

The Russians appear to be interested in the Middle East for reasons of security and trade as well as "influence." They would like to see American military power removed from the region, although it is hard to see how that would benefit Soviet security, since American bases would remain in Greece and Turkey. That, however, is the sort of thing big countries worry about, and I for one am inclined to take it at face value. The Russians would of course benefit commercially from the reopening of the Suez Canal, as would other countries, but that could be accomplished through a compromise peace and hardly requires a Soviet "drive for power" in the Middle East. Basically, one suspects, the Russians are motivated by the same vague geopolitical impulses that all great powers are susceptible to: they enjoy sailing their warships around the Mediterranean and would enjoy it even more if we felt constrained to keep our ships out; they would like in general to be "Number One" in the Middle East and would be delighted to see American "influence" reduced or eliminated. It appears to be in large part a matter of ego gratification, or of what the psychologists call "self-maximization," and it is by no means a unique Soviet susceptibility. It is in fact normal behavior for a great power—quite similar to our own. We too keep a fleet in the Mediterranean, which is a good deal farther from our shores than it is from the Soviet Union; and our main objection to Soviet "influence" in the Arab countries is that it detracts from our own.

For the advancement of its vague geopolitical ambitions, Israel is indispensable to the Soviet Union. Israel, in the view of "Kremlinologists," is the Soviet Union's admission ticket to the Middle East. If it did not exist, the Arab states would have little need of Soviet military and political support, and the Russians would have nothing with which to charm the Arabs except their communism, which does not seem to charm them at all. The Russians have had no more success in buying ideological converts with their aid and support than has the United States. Since the mid-fifties the United Arab

Republic has received more Soviet aid than any other country, but the Egyptian government has suppressed internal Communists—more indeed than has the Israeli government—and the Russians have been warned repeatedly against meddling in internal Arab affairs. In July 1971 the Russians asked the Egyptian government to apply pressure in Khartoum against a crackdown on Communists in the Sudan, and President Sadat responded with an angry speech before the Arab Socialist Union in which he declared that Egypt would never become Communist or recognize an Arab Communist government.[18] When he ordered the expulsion of Soviet military personnel from Egypt in July 1972, President Sadat said, "Egyptian nationalism and Arab nationalism must stand alone."[19] Without Israel the dream of paramount Russian "influence" in the Middle East and of the Mediterranean as a "Soviet lake" would go aglimmering. If Israel did not exist, say the "Kremlinologists," the Russians would have to invent it.

Israelis can be forgiven for an unwillingness to base their security on Soviet national egoism, but at least they—and their supporters in the United States—ought to take solace in the available evidence that the Russians have a stake in their survival. The Israeli leaders are not known for simple-mindedness or a lack of diplomatic skill, and that causes one to suspect that they may be somewhat less terrified of the Russians than they care to let on. After twenty-five years of the cold war the word has pretty well gotten around that invoking the Communist menace is a fairly reliable way of keeping the Americans in line. Picturing herself as the bastion of democracy in the Middle East, Israel professes to be defending American interests by holding the line against a surging tide of Communist imperialism. Recent visitors to the Middle East assure me that the Israelis are quite sincere in their fear of being "thrown into the sea" and in their conception of the Soviet Union as an insatiable imperialist power, bent, presumably, upon the conquest and communization of the Middle East. Nonetheless, I perceive in this some of the same old Communist-baiting humbuggery that certain other small countries have used to manipulate the United States for their own purposes. When it comes to anti-communism, as we have noted in Vietnam and elsewhere, the United States is highly susceptible, rather like a drug addict, and the world is full of ideological "pushers." It is a fine thing to respect a small country's independence and to abstain from interference in its internal affairs. It is quite another matter when, in the name of these worthy principles—but really because of our surviving obsession with communism—we permit client states to manipulate American policy toward purposes contrary to our interests, and probably to their own as well.

Although the Nixon Administration tended increasingly between 1969 and 1972 to comply with most of Israel's demands for arms, some of its officials, including Secretary of State Rogers, have made a cooler assessment of Soviet intentions in the Middle East. They have recognized that although the Soviet Union has made harsh verbal attacks on Israel, it has been consistent in its advocacy of a political settlement based on the Security Council Resolution of November 1967. It also seems evident that the introduction of Soviet pilots and of SAM-2 and SAM-3 missiles into Egypt in 1970 was something less than a bid for Soviet domination of the Middle East. The Israelis had been flying "deep penetration" raids over Egypt and had even bombed the suburbs of Cairo. The Egyptians at that time seemed unable to counter Israeli air power, and there was even talk that this situation might result in the fall of President Nasser. The steps taken by the Russians since then have been cautious measures designed to bolster a faltering client. From the Egyptian point of view Soviet support has been exceedingly cautious: the Russians have consistently refused to provide the Egyptians with offensive weapons such as long-range bombers and ground-to-ground missiles. Compared with the things we have done to shore up both Israel and our faltering client states in Asia, Soviet support of Egypt has been prudent indeed.

The weight of evidence indicates that the Russians do indeed want a compromise settlement in the Middle East. It seems probable that they would welcome the reopening of the Suez Canal, relief from the heavy costs of arming Egypt, and a reduction of great-power tensions. A solution acceptable to the Arabs, moreover, would earn gratitude for the Russians in the Arab world, would enhance Soviet prestige all over the world, and appease the Jewish population of the Soviet Union.[20] And, most enticing of all, in the Soviet perspective, would be the ego-gratifying prospect of a region-full of neutralist states more amenable to Soviet than to American "influence"—whatever that might mean in concrete terms.

When ideological and moral pronouncements are set aside—as every now and then honesty commends—the American perspective on the Middle East is in a number of important respects the mirror image of that of the Russians. We too attach great importance to our fleet plying Mediterranean waters; we too have an economic stake in the region—American oil companies have large and profitable investments, although the United States is not heavily dependent on Middle Eastern oil, as are some of our allies; we too derive ego-gratification from wielding "influence"—although, like the Russians, we prefer to dress up our egoism in unctuous pieties; and, like our Soviet rival, we are a pushover for geopolitical grandiosities, the Middle East being, in President Nixon's phrase, the "hinge of NATO."[21]

Only in one respect is our interest in the Middle East fundamentally different from that of other outside powers: we are tied to Israel by bonds of culture and sentiment and by the special attachment of our American Jewish population. These bonds represent a perfectly valid basis for the definition of a "national interest" and for the making of a valid commitment based on that interest—provided that the commitment is made in an appropriately constitutional manner, and provided too that it does not infringe upon or derogate from other valid interests. As matters now stand, our commitment to Israel is de facto and undefined: we do not really know the extent of our own obligation, which could be very great, while Israel does not know what in the way of American support she can rely on. This uncertainty in turn appears to have driven Israel to greater militancy and inflexibility in her attitude toward the Arabs. For our part, the lack of a constitutionally legitimate commitment, candidly based on the sentimental and cultural bonds which are the real source of our interest in Israel, drives us to rationalize our involvement in terms of geopolitical metaphors.

The assumption appears to be that there is something illegitimate about sentiment as the basis of a national interest and that we must therefore disguise it behind a facade of tough-sounding realpolitik. I cannot help suspecting that the authors of all that stuff we keep hearing about the Russians testing the "intentions of the free world" in the Middle East and challenging the "national will of the United States" do not really believe it any more than I do. The authors of these statements feel a cultural and religious attachment to Israel but apparently do not feel they can persuade the United

States government to pursue a policy designed to serve that attachment unless it can also be justified in terms of the grand strategy of the cold war. I regret this attitude very much because the introduction of cold-war rationalizations has the dangerous effect of expanding a local issue into a global one.

Both President Nixon and Mr. Kissinger have tended at times to speak in those terms. In a televised interview on July 1, 1970, for example, President Nixon spoke of the Middle East as being "terribly dangerous, like the Balkans before World War I, where the two super powers, the United States and the Soviet Union, could be drawn into a confrontation that neither of them wants. . . ." Five days earlier, Mr. Kissinger had said exactly the same thing: ". . . what makes the situation in the Middle East so potentially dangerous is the fact that it has many similarities with the Balkans before World War I." Pressing the analogy, Mr. Kissinger contended that "no one caused World War I"; that it came about as an accident; and that the situation in the Middle East is roughly analogous, Israel and the Arab states each being allied to a super power ". . . each of them to some extent not fully under the control of the major country concerned."[22]

This tough talk, it has been explained, was designed to scare the Russians, not to be taken literally. Whatever effect it had on the Russians, I must say that it scared me, because it reveals a dangerously outmoded way of thinking about international politics. The catastrophe of war is conceived as something fated, controlled by quarrelsome client states if not by the iron "laws" of power politics. Implicit in this outlook is the supposition that the coming of a great war is beyond the control of statesmen—even beyond the control of the Pentagon computers, or of Mr. Kissinger's staff of experts in the White House basement.

The outlook is faulty, and so is the analogy. World War I was not primarily an accident, and it was certainly not predestined. It came about, as recent German historians have shown, because Germany was willing for it to come about and aided and abetted the events which led to the explosion. It was within Germany's power at any time to restrain her Austrian client and, in so doing, to prevent war. The German leaders knew they had this power but consciously chose not to exercise it because they thought they could win a general European war and judged that it would derogate from German pride and grandeur if the great German Empire shrank from war. That is why general war came in 1914, and it is for that kind of reason that it will come again, if it does come again. It will be, as it was in 1914, the result of human choice, human pride and human folly on the part of the leaders of the great powers. Left to their own resources, the Arabs and Israelis have the power to bring on a local war but not a world war. Only the super powers have that option and —whatever the political usefulness of historical mis-analogies—they had better not forget it.

Mr. Kissinger has referred to the American interest in the Middle East as deriving from our allies' dependence on Middle Eastern oil. The Japanese, Mr. Kissinger pointed out in 1970, get 90 percent, and the Western Europeans 75 percent, of their oil from the Middle East—"which again is one reason why *we** can have an overwhelming interest in preventing this area from being dominated by the Soviet Union."[23] For those who are worried about "neo-isolationism" Mr. Kissinger's words should provide ample reassurance that the policeman-of-the-world spirit has survived as a living force in American foreign policy. Without explanation

*Italics supplied.

or elaboration it is taken for granted that because Japan and Western Europe need Middle Eastern oil, the United States has to protect the oil supplies from "the Soviets and their radical clients." What about the Japanese and the Europeans? Why do they not send their fleets to keep the Mediterranean from becoming a "Soviet lake"? And why do we not expect them to? The answer appears to derive from the "laws" of geopolitics. The "responsibilities of power" have imposed upon us the duty of serving as the Hessians of the "free world," with the lesser "free world" countries at liberty to provide a regiment or two, if they wish, to put a nice face on things.

What in the world is meant by the notion of a "Soviet lake" anyway? Does anyone really think that the Russians are going to employ their fleet—in the manner of the British in the nineteenth century—to blockade ports or intercept the flow of oil to Europe and Japan on the high seas? In the nuclear age that kind of naval diplomacy is not only obsolete but insane. If the Russians should ever undertake to interfere with Europe's oil supply, it is far more likely that they would try to buy it up or somehow bribe or induce the oil-producing countries to shut it off. This being the likelihood, the rational way for the Western countries to protect their sources of oil in the Arab world is not by practicing an irrelevant, antiquated naval diplomacy but by cultivating and maintaining friendly relations with the Arab countries.

I do not care much for this geopolitical hocus-pocus. Whatever the reasons of strategy or preference that have induced the Nixon Administration to employ it from time to time, there is far more to be said for the sensible, conciliatory approach which brought about the cease-fire along the Suez Canal and the Jarring peace mission, unsuccessful though it has been. The geopolitical formulations of America's interest in the Middle East are basically romantic, historically unsound and dangerous. There is no relevance in the Balkan analogy of 1914, which purports to show that we are helpless. Nor do we have an automatic, unilateral vital interest deriving from the oil requirements of Europe and Japan. There are, to be sure, important American political and economic stakes in the Middle East, but our major specific interest is a cultural and sentimental attachment to Israel, rooted in the strong preference of a great many of the American people and their elected representatives.

We also have a crucial stake in the avoidance of conflict with the Soviet Union. It takes no great feat of imagination to conjure up some new Arab-Israeli crisis in which the two sides manage to draw their respective patrons into a head-on conflict. Premier Meir has said that the United States ought not to press for Israeli withdrawal from the conquered Arab territories because as she put it, "This is not the border of the USA. . . ."[24] If indeed that were the whole of the matter, if Israel, as the Premier has said, really were prepared to "stand up for itself" without involving others, it might make sense to let the Arabs and Israelis work out their differences, or fight them out, and come to their own solution. We all know, however, that that is not the case, that although American economic and security interests are not directly involved in the Arab-Israeli conflict, the gratuitous intrusion of the great powers has created the possibility that another war in the Middle East might set us against the Russians. This being the case, we have not only the right but a positive responsibility to bring an influence to bear.

The Soviet Union and the United States by and large have recognized that they have a surpassing interest in the avoidance of a major confrontation with each other.

The Russians, for their part, have consistently coun-
seled their Arab associates against reckless action; they
are reported, for instance, to have warned the Egyptians that they would not support a military operation
across the Suez Canal. Nor have the Russians ever indicated any expectation of, or desire for, the destruction of Israel; they were indeed among the first to
recognize the state of Israel when it came into existence in 1948. The Soviet position is that Israel should
return to the borders of 1967; that is substantially the
American position as well—at least officially—and it is
consistent with the Security Council Resolution of
November 1967, which calls among other things for the
"termination of all claims or states of belligerency and
respect for and acknowledgment of the sovereignty,
territorial integrity and political independence of every state in the area."

We also have a nonspecific interest in the Middle
East, which we share with the Arabs, the Israelis, the
Soviet Union, and the rest of the world. That interest
is in the vindication of the United Nations as an instrument for the maintenance of peace. The Security
Council Resolution of November 22, 1967, which Secretary Rogers has said "will be the bedrock of our
policy,"[25] emphasizes "the inadmissibility of the acquisition of territory by war," and it reminds the Middle
Eastern parties of their obligations under Article 2 of
the United Nations Charter, of which paragraph 3
states that "All members shall settle their international
disputes by peaceful means in such a manner that international peace and security, and justice, are not endangered."

This is where a fifth perspective comes in, over and
above that of Arabs, Israelis, Russians and Americans. If
a United Nations perspective could be developed and
brought to bear, we might come out of the Middle East

crisis with something better than a peaceful settlement. We might come out with a precedent too, with processes to draw upon in the future.

III. Toward Peace

For most of the life span of both entities, the United Nations and the state of Israel have been intimately, if not always cordially, involved with each other. Israel was legally initiated by the United Nations; since then its status, borders and policies have been the subject of a series of United Nations resolutions. The United Nations Relief and Works Agency still has primary responsibility for the Arab refugees; a United Nations peace force was placed between Egyptian and Israeli forces after the 1956 war; and United Nations observers have been stationed along the Suez Canal since the June war of 1967. The Security Council Resolution of November 22, 1967, is still the most complete, impartial and generally accepted policy statement for a Middle East settlement, and is still the best hope for a viable peace. If there has ever been an issue which is ripe and appropriate for peaceful settlement under United Nations auspices, it is the conflict between Israel and the Arabs.

First and foremost, a just settlement must vindicate the principle, as spelled out in the Security Council Resolution, of "the inadmissibility of the acquisition of territory by war." This principle goes to the heart of the Charter; Article 2, paragraph 4, states that "All Members shall refrain in their international relations from the threat or use of force against the territorial integrity or political independence of any state. . . ." The return of the conquered territories is the major single requirement for peace as stated by both President Sadat and King Hussein. As King Hussein put it, ". . . Israel may have either peace or territory—but she can never have both."[26]

Restoration of the occupied territories is also official American policy. In his notable speech of December 9, 1969, Secretary Rogers said:

> We believe that while recognized political boundaries must be established and agreed upon by the parties, any changes in the preexisting lines should not reflect the weight of conquest and should be confined to insubstantial alterations required for mutual security. We do not support expansionism. We believe troops must be withdrawn as the resolution provides. . . .

In return for withdrawal from virtually all of the territories occupied in 1967, Israel should be entitled to firm and specific guarantees of her security. One such guarantee might be the stationing of sizable United Nations forces in militarily neutralized zones on *both* sides of the borders at all of the points which are critical to Israel's security. United Nations forces might also be stationed on what is now the occupied west bank of the Jordan River; in and around the Gaza Strip and the old border between Israel and Egyptian Sinai; and at Sharm el Sheikh to guarantee Israel's egress through the Strait of Tiran. In all cases, it should be specified that the United Nations force could be removed only by consent of both Israel and the Arab government concerned. Perhaps too the consent of a majority of the United Nations Security Council might be required, either to remove the United Nations forces or to terminate the neutralized status of the zones in question.

Israel has a right to security, but not to territorial and military arrangements which would rob her Arab neighbors of security. In keeping with the Rogers plan, which would allow of "insubstantial" territorial changes, Israel has a reasonable security claim with respect to the Golan Heights. It would be unreasonable to expect the Israelis to withdraw to the Jordan valley from these highlands from which the Syrians used to fire down on civilian communities—all the more so since the Syrians have refused to accept the Security Council Resolution of November 1967, and have refused to participate in the Jarring peace talks. At the same time, the Israelis have no good claim to the permanent occupation of the entire Syrian territory they now hold. A defensible frontier might be drawn along the high ridge line immediately east of the Jordan valley, giving Israel a small, uninhabited but militarily significant strip of previously Syrian territory.

In the case of the west bank there is everything to be said for the principle of self-determination. Israel might be permitted to retain the "Latrun salient," the narrow finger of land astride the main highway from Jerusalem to Tel Aviv which was part of Jordan before the 1967 war and from which Israeli traffic between the two cities was harassed, but preferably in return for an equivalent cession of territory. There is no justification for claims of land north and south of the west bank which would enable Israel to mount a "pincers" attack in the event of an Arab threat to Israel's narrow coastal strip. This would effectively rob the west bank, whether independent or federated with Jordan, of any semblance of security, and would place still more unwilling Arabs under Israeli rule.

Another necessary provision of an Arab-Israeli peace settlement would be a mutual disavowal of any further efforts by either side to alter the adjusted frontiers of 1967. The Security Council Resolution of November 1967 specifies the right of *every* state in the area to "live in peace within secure and recognized boundaries free from threats or acts of force." The Arabs, it must be remembered, are as frightened of the Zionist doctrine of unlimited Jewish immigration leading to a drive for *Lebensraum* as the Israelis are of an Arab "holy war" to destroy Israel. Both sides are entitled to explicit guarantees against these deeply rooted fears. This could be accomplished by writing into a peace treaty a more explicit and detailed version of that provision of the Security Council Resolution which would require "termination of all claims or states of belligerency and respect for and acknowledgment of the sovereignty, territorial integrity and political independence of every state in the area. . . ."

Israel is entitled to free access through the Suez Canal as well as the Gulf of Aqaba and the Strait of Tiran. That too is called for in the Security Council Resolution and should be guaranteed in the definitive instrument of peace.

As to Jerusalem, I have no specific recommendation. Israel's annexation of the old city is one of those "new facts" with which the world has been confronted. I think it well, nonetheless, to recall that the United Nations General Assembly unanimously condemned Israel's unilateral annexation of the city* and that its status cannot be considered "non-negotiable." Some form of international status would seem to be the appropriate solution. The Friends' study suggests the desirability of "some sort of federal condominium to govern an undivided and demilitarized Jerusalem" and makes the further contention, in which I concur, that Jerusalem "cannot peacefully become the sole possession of one religion or one national state."[27] There may also be merit in Dr. Nahum Goldmann's suggestion that the old Arab section of Jerusalem be constituted "an auton-

---

*On July 4, 1967, by vote of 99 to 0, the United States abstaining.

omous enclave with an international status administered by its inhabitants." Such an internationalized city, Dr. Goldmann has suggested, might become a "center for world organizations" as well as a center for three great religions.[28]

Probably the most difficult and intractable of the issues to be resolved is that of "achieving a just settlement of the refugee problem" as called for in the Security Council Resolution of 1967. In justice and law —the latter in the form of numerous United Nations resolutions—the Palestinian Arab refugees are entitled to one of two forms of restitution: either repatriation or compensation. As a practical solution it should be feasible to work out an agreement under which Israel would take back within its 1967 borders an agreed number of refugees who would be accepted as Israeli citizens and whose former properties would either be restored or compensated for. For the majority of refugees, repatriation would probably be neither feasible nor desired. A commitment by the Arab states to accept them and assist in their resettlement—as in part they have already done—should be accompanied by generous Israeli financial support, both to compensate these refugees for their losses and to facilitate their resettlement. With contributions from friends abroad, and with the relief from military costs which peace would make possible, Israel should have no great difficulty in meeting these costs, which in any case ought to be accepted as an elementary moral obligation.

In due course the Palestinian Arabs will find it necessary to accept the existence of the state of Israel and to recognize that further efforts to destroy the Jewish state will be futile and will only compound their own suffering. The Palestinians have been done a great historical injustice, but it cannot now be undone in the way they would have it undone. Israel has existed as an independent state since 1948, and it would now be as great an injustice to disrupt that society as it was for the Jews to drive the Arabs from their land in the first place. A certain rough justice accrues to any existing state of affairs, insofar as it affects people's lives and homes; once people are established and living in a place—regardless of how they got there—it becomes an injustice, even if it were a practical possibility, to disrupt and expel them.

This must be a bitter pill for the Palestinian Arabs to swallow, but they are going to have to do it if they want an end to futile guerrilla warfare. In any case, the Palestinians are entitled to some form of self-determination on the non-Israeli territory of Palestine. Whether they will wish to form an independent Palestinian state, or federate with the Kingdom of Jordan as proposed by King Hussein, is beyond the reach of a foreigner's judgment.

Central and indispensable to a peace settlement based on the Security Council Resolution of November 1967 would be the guarantee of the entire settlement by the United Nations. Such a guarantee would properly take the form of a specific commitment by the United Nations Security Council to enforce the peace and all of its specifications, including the "secure and recognized boundaries" of both Israel and her Arab neighbors and the neutralized status of designated border zones. The agreement should also specify strict limitations on the sale or provision of arms to Middle Eastern states by outside powers. As permanent members of the Security Council, the United States, the Soviet Union, the United Kingdom, France and China would have major responsibility for enforcement of the peace terms, but that obligation would fall upon them not in their capacity as "great powers" but as members of the Security Council, which is entrusted by Article 24 of the Charter with "primary responsibility for the maintenance of international peace and security."

It might also be appropriate and desirable for the Security Council's guarantee to be ratified formally by the legislative bodies of the signatory states. Such action would represent a mark of the seriousness attached to this new commitment by members of the Security Council, although it might not be regarded as juridically essential since, by ratifying the Charter in the first place, every member of the United Nations is already committed, under Article 25, to "accept and carry out the decisions of the Security Council." It would do no harm, however, to remind the members, by formal parliamentary act, of this frequently forgotten obligation.

For reasons of varying merit Israel has indicated on numerous occasions a lack of confidence in the United Nations. In order to accommodate this attitude and provide Israel with an added assurance of security, I for one would be willing to supplement a United Nations guarantee with a bilateral treaty—not an executive agreement but a treaty consented to by the Senate—under which the United States would guarantee the territory and independence of Israel within the adjusted borders of 1967. This guarantee should neither add to, nor detract from, nor in any way alter the multilateral guarantee of the United Nations—which would obligate us, as a member of the Security Council, to defend the "secure and recognized boundaries" of both Israel *and* her Arab neighbors. The supplementary, bilateral arrangement with Israel would obligate the United States to use force if necessary, in accordance with its constitutional processes, to assist Israel against any violation of its 1967 borders, as adjusted, which it could not repel itself, but the agreement would also obligate Israel, firmly and unequivocally, never to violate those borders herself.

I conceive of an American treaty of guarantee of Israel as an instrument which would come into effect after—and only after—the multilateral guarantee of the United Nations had been agreed upon and ratified by all parties. The bilateral treaty with Israel would represent no more than a repetition of, and an additional assurance of, our intent to honor the multilateral guarantee of the United Nations. It would reiterate a commitment which every member of the Security Council, including the Soviet Union, would also have made through their multilateral guarantee of the borders of *all* of the states concerned.

The situation in the Middle East presents the world community with an important, indeed an unprecedented, opportunity. At its present juncture the conflict between Israel and the Arabs is the most significant issue since the end of World War II in which the Soviet Union and the United States have identified enough in the way of common interests to allow even of the possibility of a peaceful settlement mediated and guaranteed by the United Nations Security Council. Hitherto the insuperable obstacle to effective Security Council action has been the paralysis of the Security Council by the great-power veto. China, newly admitted to the United Nations, is an unknown quantity as far as the Middle East is concerned, but if the Russians and Americans meant what they have said about a Middle East settlement, and if they were prepared to back it up by the application of sanctions as provided for in the United Nations Charter, they might not find it impossible to bring about a settlement implementing the Security Council Resolution of November 1967. The importance of the opportunity can hardly be exaggerated. A settlement mediated by the great powers in their capacity as great powers quite possibly could be a fair and durable one, but a settlement mediated by the United Nations could serve as a precedent for the settlement of other conflicts through the procedures of international organization. Perhaps, if the precedents accumulated, and with further advances in civilization, it might even be found possible to apply these procedures in conflicts involving the great powers themselves. That, after all, was why we created the United Nations in the first place—"to save succeeding generations from the scourge of war. . . ."

5

The Rules of the Game

From the Greek city-states to the twentieth century the foreign policy of great powers has been, in its essence, a game of "one-upmanship" in an unending struggle for power. Prior to the twentieth century, however, it was done for the most part with restraint and decorum: battles were fought for the pleasure of winning, usually in open fields where they would not bother anybody except the local inhabitants; provinces changed hands without much ado or inconvenience to the inhabitants; kings enjoyed subjecting each other to "defeat and humiliation" in arms but more or less remained friends for social purposes; they seldom sought to dethrone each other and, in their moral lexicon, the only truly heinous crime was the mercifully uncommon one of regicide. There were many wars of course, but winning them was fun and losing was not all that terrible if you managed not to be one of the small number of people that got killed. It was a sportsmen's game with the saving grace that, except for a few upstarts like Napoleon and Bismarck, the players were content to play it with sportsmen's weapons.

This is not to suggest that all international conflicts before the twentieth century were trivial; some were serious indeed and a few were enormously consequential, but for every war that mattered, a great many more were vanity: trivial quarrels for trivial stakes. In the twentieth century all conflicts are serious because of the unlimited destructiveness of new methods of warfare, although as far as their substantive stakes are concerned, the ratio of serious to superficial has not visibly altered. For every issue of importance there are many more which are vanity: we are still playing the same old game of one-upmanship in a mindless struggle for power and prestige. Unfortunately, however, the distinction between the conflicts that matter and the ones that do not is not easily made, because both have been adorned with the same bloated vocabulary. Both are drenched in portentous allusions to "freedom," "survival," "vital interest," and all the other familiar grandiosities of ideology and power politics. The old myth of international politics—that it was the private preserve of sovereigns and their ministers and none of the people's business—has given way to a new myth: that politics is life and everything political is highly consequential—not just for those who make their living by politics but for everybody, everywhere. Every issue is now a "critical" issue; every threat a "grave" one; and I doubt if there is a square inch left on the face of the earth that someone does not regard as "strategic."

Not everybody of course appreciates the supremacy of politics; there remains a benighted mass of bumpkins who live in the illusion that there is more to life than the next election, the balance of power or the triumph of somebody's "way of life" over somebody else's. The

number of these illiterates, however, is shrinking because of the astonishing success of the "professionals" in
persuading us that politics—especially international
politics—is indeed what life is all about. The experts
have mastered the media, and the result of their overkill is not only a greatly inflated notion of how much
foreign policy matters to the daily lives of people but
the effective drowning of any distinction between issues that matter and issues that do not. Thus at one time
we were all very nearly persuaded that Tonkin Gulf
was as fateful as Pearl Harbor, and that Vietnam was of
a piece with the German conquest of Europe.

Still, in the minds of some people, an ancient dream
persists—a dream that politics can be subordinated to
—perhaps even put to the service of—ordinary human
needs; a dream that we can find a way to free ourselves
from the oppressive, expensive and dangerous burden
of international conflict. If mankind somehow could be
liberated from the scourge of war and the mindless
pursuit of power, nations could divert their energies
and resources to the human needs of their own societies, and even to a measure of helpfulness toward others. It is the age-old dream of beating swords into plow-
shares, of changing the rules of the old, discredited
game by supplanting the anarchy of nations with an
effective international peace-keeping organization.

I. Our "Vital Interests"

Whether or not it is feasible to build some kind of international security community, and whether or not we
Americans would wish to do so, must depend upon
what we hope to accomplish in the world, what we
perceive as our role, what we value, what we regard as

vital and what we regard as secondary or irrelevant. More often than not references to the nation's "vital interests" are made for purposes of closing rather than opening discussion, as if the term were self-explanatory, as if it were a known quantity which can be used to explain or justify whatever action is taken in its name. The term "vital interests" has the ring of hard realism about it, connoting something material, certain, clear-cut, calculated and down-to-earth, as against the abstract visions of idealists. As commonly used, it purports to justify a policy—such as the Monroe Doctrine, the "open door," or the Vietnam war—in strategic terms, in terms, that is, which connote life or death for the nation.

This liturgy of "realism" warrants review. Teddy Roosevelt and his fellow imperialists explained the war with Spain, the acquisition of the Philippines and the "open door" policy for China in terms of the "vital" strategic and economic interests of the United States. Historians now generally agree, however, that the liberation of Cuba, which was the official ostensible objective of the war with Spain, could easily have been accomplished without war; and that the Philippines, far from being a strategic asset to the United States, were a liability, a hostage of Japan for whose protection repeated concessions had to be made to Japanese ambitions. They also agree that the "open door" was a gratuity, involving the United States in Chinese affairs despite the fact that we had no strategic interest in China and only marginal commercial interests. In retrospect, it seems clear that, far from being rooted in dispassionate and objective calculations of strategy and commerce, the Far Eastern policies of the United States in the early twentieth century were the product of the romantic dreams of imperial glory of such men as Theodore Roosevelt, Admiral Mahan, Senators Henry Cabot Lodge and Albert Beveridge, and other fervent believers in America's "manifest destiny."

Obscured by the concept of "vital interests" as generally used is the question of values. What is vital to us in our foreign relations is the by-product of what is valuable to us in our own society. Our national security has been or has not been at stake in Vietnam depending on what it is we have hoped to secure. Underlying the long debate about Vietnam has been a deep disagreement about values. That disagreement can be understood in terms of two quite different interpretations which can be put upon President Wilson's famous declaration that America's aim was to "make the world safe for democracy."

The prevailing interpretation of that statement—and the one which, in corrupted form, has governed our policy in Indochina—is that America, acting if need be entirely on its own, has an obligation to defend existing governments which, even though they may be dictatorships, are deemed to be defenders of democracy because of their opposition to communism. The late Minority Leader of the Senate Everett Dirksen said, when asked if he thought there was a free government in Greece, "Yes, I do. Just because they have a military junta for a specific purpose for a little while to shove back the Communist influence. . . . "[1] By this very liberal criterion the Saigon government would also seem to qualify as one of the democracies for whom the United States is resolved to make the world safe.

There is another interpretation of President Wilson's famous dictum, one which I believe to be much closer to Wilson's own understanding of it. That is that the security of American democracy requires the United States to be prepared to join in an international organization with other democracies for the *collective* defense of their political independence and territorial integrity against acts of overt foreign aggression. The emphasis is on international action—if not through a League of Nations or the United Nations then through an alliance of sovereign equals.

Implicit in this approach is the idea that the nation's vital interests are essentially domestic in character, that it is our own democracy that is to be defended, that our proper concern is not with what we can make of the world but what must be done in the world to create conditions under which we will be free to make what we want of ourselves. President Wilson's aim was not to democratize the world but to make the world safe, through international organization, for those who wish to practice democracy. That is a fundamentally different concept of vital interest from the one which now governs American strategy in Southeast Asia. It is a sounder and safer concept. It can be called "neo-isolationism" but no designation could be more inaccurate. Its essence is selectivity in our international commitments—selectivity according to our own needs, our own capacities, and a healthy respect for the right of others to make comparable judgments for themselves.

The indispensable first step toward the formulation of a valid conception of the national interest is a reformulation of attitudes—especially the cultivation of an attitude of friendly curiosity rather than fear and hostility toward social and political forms which are alien to our own. In this connection the concept of "vital interests" as essentially domestic in its *ultimate* aspirations is of the greatest operational consequence, for our efforts to secure peace in Asia and for all of our foreign relations. Only when we have made a clear, conscious decision that "vital interests" have to do with the kind of society *we* live in, and not with the kinds of society other people live in, will it be possible to be comfortable in the face of diversity and to distinguish clearly between that which is really menacing and that which is merely unfamiliar.

II. Returning to First Principles

Someday the war in Vietnam will be over and, like a dreamer awakening from a nightmare, Americans will be able to look around and see that the sun still rises and sets, that life has gone on in their country and the world, leaving a profusion of tasks and opportunities on the neglected American agenda. Some of the problems we will face then, such as the population explosion and the world's food supply, may seem almost hopeless, but at least we will be free to act upon them and, human ingenuity being what it is, perhaps it will prove possible to do things that now seem beyond us. One wonders what the world would be like if, say, half of the human inventiveness that goes for weapons and war—to say nothing of the resources—were being applied to human needs and satisfactions.

For Americans the first requirement is a return to first principles, from which we have strayed perilously far in these years of our misadventure in Vietnam. Damaging and futile though the war has been, however, it will not have been all in vain if we emerge from it in chastened awareness that a sound American foreign policy must always be conceived within the framework of two basic postulates: the inseparability of foreign and domestic activities and the dangerous obsoleteness of traditional power politics in the nuclear age.

Foreign relations is an activity of diplomats and soldiers—an activity that draws upon but for the most part does not replenish the resources of the nation. The real life of a nation is the life of its people as a society; it is in the diverse activities of individuals within a society that life acquires meaning and the nation acquires wealth and strength. These observations may be read as truisms but they point to an absolutely fundamental distinction—between the concept of the nation as essentially a *power*, defending or pursuing power for its own sake as if that pursuit were a law of life and the major reason for the state's existence, and the concept of the nation as essentially a *society*, organized not as an end in itself but as an instrument or arrangement for the advancement of the welfare of its citizens. Of necessity, every nation acts both as a society and as a power in its public policy, but in the last twenty-five years the United States has become unhealthily preoccupied with its functions as a power, to the increasing detriment of American society. This preoccupation is reflected in the priority—often approaching exclusivity —of time, energy and attention given to foreign policy by all recent Presidents and Congresses, and by writers and academics, and in the development of a powerful military-industrial-labor-university complex oriented to the conduct of war and cold war.

It is contended—with some accuracy—that none of this was by our choice and—with less accuracy—that we can well afford to do the things that need to be done at home while waging war and cold war abroad. Whether or not we can afford to, we are not in fact doing the things that need to be done at home. Even if the material resources were available, the political resources are not; that has been conclusively demonstrated during the years of war in Vietnam. As to the contention that our global role was thrust upon us, that is only partly true: Stalin's menacing stance in Europe after World War II necessitated an American response, as have certain other provocations, but most of our postwar "crises"—the intervention in Lebanon, the Bay of Pigs, the Dominican intervention, the Cuban missile crisis quite possibly, and the Vietnam war most definitely—could and should have been avoided with comparative ease.

We have some choice in the extent and character of our foreign commitments—a great deal more than recent Presidents have recognized. We had better exercise that choice soon for a major shift of emphasis from foreign to domestic activities for two essential reasons: first, because the nation has been weakened by the material and spiritual drain of an overly ambitious foreign policy and it is past time for us to renew our strength at its source; second, because chronic war and crisis, giving rise to increasing and unchecked executive power, have become a clear and present danger to American democracy. In the long run a democracy, if it is to remain one, cannot allow foreign policy to become its dominant activity. The very essence of democracy is the commitment of public policy to the service of individual, societal ends; a nation preoccupied with power politics over a long period of time cannot help but lose touch with its own democratic objectives, whereupon it will cease to be a democracy and become —against its own wishes and intentions—a dictatorship.

Preoccupied with foreign wars and crises for a generation, we have scarcely noticed the revolution wrought by undirected change here at home. In the twenty-five years after World War II our population grew by some 60 million; a mass migration from country to city has crowded over 70 percent of our population onto scarcely more than one percent of our land; vast numbers of rural blacks from the South have filled the slums of northern cities while affluent white families have fled to shapeless new suburbs, leaving the cities physically deteriorating and financially destitute, and creating a new and socially destructive form of racial isolation combined with degrading poverty. Poverty, which is a tragedy in a poor country, blights our affluent society with something more than tragedy; being unnecessary, it is deeply immoral as well.

Defining our priorities is more a matter of moral accounting than of cost accounting. The latter may help us determine what we are able to pay for, but it cannot help us to decide what we want and what we need and what we are willing to pay for. It cannot help the five-sixths of us who are affluent to decide whether we are willing to pay for programs which will create opportunity for the one-sixth who are poor; that is a matter of moral accounting. It cannot help us to decide whether winning a military victory over a poor and backward Asian nation is more important to us than rebuilding our cities and purifying our poisoned air and lakes and rivers; that too is a matter of moral accounting. Nor can it help us to decide where our "vital interests" lie and whether they will be better served by an American effort to manage the world or by an American effort to rebuild America, whether they require our country, in the name of freedom, to be the defender of every regime that swears its hostility to communism or instead, in John Quincy Adam's words, to be "the well wisher to the freedom and independence of all" but "the champion and vindicator only of her own."[2] These too are matters of moral accounting.

For these reasons my primary recommendation for American foreign policy after Vietnam is that we have very much less of it—not necessarily forever and certainly not to the extent of a wholesale abandonment of foreign commitments, but for long enough and to a sufficient extent to give us a chance to replenish our depleted resources, renew our neglected society, and restore our endangered democracy.

III. After Vietnam

History is filled with turning points, which are not easily identified until long after the event. It seems almost inevitable that Vietnam will prove to have been a watershed in American foreign policy, but it is by no means clear what kind. Before it can represent anything of a lasting historical nature, the war of course will have to be ended—not just scaled down but ended, and not just for Americans but for the tortured Vietnamese as well. One assumes that it will be ended, if not by our present leaders then by their successors, and when at last it is, the American people will once again in their history have the opportunity and the responsibility of deciding where they want to go in the world, of deciding what kind of country they want America to be.

The Truman Doctrine, which made limited sense for a limited time in a particular place, has led us in its universalized form to disaster in Southeast Asia and demoralization at home. In view of all that has happened it seems unlikely that we will wish to resume the anti-Communist crusade of the early postwar years, yet it is not impossible: memories will fade, controversies may recur, pride may once again be challenged and competitive instincts aroused. The Truman Doctrine is frayed and tattered, but still an influence upon our policy and outlook.

I do not think we are going to return to isolationism. I would go farther: I do not think there is or ever has been the slightest chance of the United States returning to the isolationism of the prewar years. It will not happen because it cannot happen: we are inextricably involved with the world politically, economically, militarily and—in case anyone cares—legally. We could not get loose if we wanted to—and no one wants to. The charge of "neo-isolationism" is an invention of people who confuse internationalism with an intrusive American interventionism, with a quasi-imperialism. Those of us who are called "neo-isolationists" are, I believe, the opposite: internationalists in the classical sense of that term, in the sense in which it was brought into American usage by Woodrow Wilson and Franklin Roosevelt. We believe in international cooperation through international institutions. We would like to try to keep the peace through the United Nations, and we would like to try to assist the poor countries through such institutions as the World Bank. We do not think the United Nations is a failure; we think it has never been tried.

In the aftermath of Vietnam we have the option of returning to the practical idealism of the United Nations Charter. It is, I believe, consistent with our national tradition and congenial to our national character, and is therefore the most natural course for us to follow. It is also in our interests and the interests of all other nations living in a diverse and crowded but interdependent world in the age of nuclear weapons.

The essence of any community—local, national or international—is some degree of acceptance of the principle that the good of the whole must take precedence over the good of the parts. I do not believe that the United States (or any of the other big countries) has ever accepted that principle with respect to the United Nations. Like the Soviet Union and other great powers, we have treated the United Nations as an instrument of our policy, to be used when it is helpful but otherwise ignored. Orphaned at birth by the passing from the political scene of those who understood its possibilities, the United Nations has never been treated as a potential world security community, as an institution to be developed and strengthened for the long-term purpose of protecting humanity from the destructiveness of unrestrained nationalism. The immediate, short-term advantage of the leading members has invariably been given precedence over the needs of the collectivity. That is why the United Nations has not worked. There is no mystery about it, no fatal shortcoming in the Charter. Our own federal government would soon collapse if the states and the people had no loyalty to it. The United Nations has not functioned as a peacekeeping organization because its members—including the United States—have not wished it to function; if they had wanted it to work, it could have—and it still can. Secretary of State Acheson and his colleagues of the early postwar years were wholly justified in their expectation of the United Nations' failure; their own cynicism, along with Stalin's cynicism, assured that failure.

Our short-sighted, self-serving and sanctimonious view of the United Nations was put on vivid display in the reaction of the Nixon Administration in October 1971 to the General Assembly's vote to take in mainland China and expel Nationalist China. Mr. Nixon expressed unctuous indignation not at the loss of the vote but at the "shocking demonstration" of "undisguised glee" shown by the winners, especially those among the winners to whom the United States had been "quite generous"—as the President's press secretary was at pains to add.[3] Mr. Agnew at least spared us the pomposities, denouncing the United Nations as a "paper tiger" and a "sounding board for the left" whose only value for the United States was that "It's good to be in the other guy's huddle."[4] The Senate Minority Leader was equally candid: "I think we are going to wipe off some of the smiles from the faces we saw on television during the United Nations voting."[5]

The revelations are striking. Having controlled the United Nations for many years as tightly and as easily as a big-city boss controls his party machine, we had gotten used to the idea that the United Nations was a place where we could work our will; Communists could delay and disrupt the proceedings and could exercise the Soviet veto in the Security Council, but they certainly were not supposed to be able to win votes. When they did, we were naturally shocked, all the more because, as one European diplomat commented, our unrestrained arm-twisting had turned the issue into "a worldwide plebiscite for or against the United States."[6] When the vote went against us nonetheless, cold-war ideologues among us saw it as proof of what they had always contended—that the United Nations was a nest of red vipers.

The test of devotion to the law is not how people behave when it goes their way but how they behave when it goes against them. During these years of internal dissension over the war in Vietnam our leaders have pointed out frequently—and correctly—that citizens, however little they may like it, have a duty to obey the law. The same principle applies on the international level: *"pacta sunt servanda,"* the international lawyers say—the law must be obeyed. The China vote in the General Assembly may have shown a certain vindictiveness toward the United States, but it was a *legal* vote, wholly consistent with the procedures spelled out in the Charter. The United States has long and quite properly condemned the refusal of France and the Soviet Union to contribute to the cost of United Nations peace-keeping operations of which they have disapproved. Now that the United States no longer dominates the United Nations as in its early years, it is we whose willingness to subordinate our own preferences to the decision of the corporate whole is being tested.

The entry of China into the United Nations offers the best opportunity since the Organization was formed in 1945 to make it an effective instrument for peace, because the United Nations has now, for the first time, become a universal organization of the large nations of the world, except for the two Germanys. Whether the opportunity will be realized will depend in large measure upon the cooperativeness of the great powers who make up the permanent membership of the Security Council. If the Chinese play a disruptive role, for example, by excessive and irresponsible use of their veto in the Security Council, the opportunity to strengthen the United Nations will be lost. There is nothing we can do about that, however; we can only wait and see. But there is something we can do about our own role—we can decide what it is going to be.

The old balance-of-power system has its merits, as we have noted, but it also has shortcomings, of which the most notable is its tendency to periodic breakdown, as in two world wars in the twentieth century. The human race managed to survive those conflicts; it is by no means certain it would survive another. At its best the old system was only fairly successful in preventing and limiting war, but in the age of nuclear weapons only one breakdown would result in a universal catastrophe, quite possibly in the destruction of civilized human life on earth. Sooner or later the law of averages is going to run out on us. We may celebrate triumphs of "crisis diplomacy" such as the Cuban missile crisis of 1962, or President Nixon's pretense of a triumph in "facing down" the Russians by mining the North Vietnamese ports in 1972. But what about the next "eyeball to eyeball" confrontation? and the one after that? What about the next fifty or a hundred years?

There is very little in international affairs about which I feel certain but there is one thing of which I am quite certain: the necessity of fundamental change in the way nations conduct their relations with each other. It is argued, I am well aware, that an international community to supplant the old system is a hopeless dream. That may be so, but if it is so, the human species has a limited life expectancy. Far therefore from being unrealistic, the dedication of our foreign policy to the single overriding objective of forging the bonds of an international community is not only the course of realism but the only available course of sanity. When the alternative to a long shot is no shot at all, trying for the long shot is the only practical course of action. There is no tried and true system to fall back on in international affairs, only a proven failure, handicapped as never before by the burden of man's most terrible invention. This being the case, it is myopic to dismiss the idea of an effective world peace-keeping organization as a visionary ideal, or as anything indeed but an immediate, practical necessity.

Given the will on the part of the most powerful members, the United Nations could become a reasonably effective peace-keeping organization. With the cooperation of the major powers—and there is no reason why they should not cooperate from the standpoint of their own national interests—the conflict in the Middle East, as suggested in the previous chapter, could be resolved on the basis of the Security Council Resolution of 1967. Similarly, I believe that the Security Council, which is entrusted by Article 24 of the Charter with "primary responsibility for the maintenance of international peace and security," should have interceded to prevent the war of the winter of 1971–1972 between India and Pakistan. This proved impossible largely because of the self-seeking of the great powers, each of whom perceived and acted upon the situation not on its merits, and certainly not in terms of human costs, but in terms of its own short-sighted geopolitical interests. Moreover, the Security Council waited until war had actually broken out and an Indian victory seemed certain before attempting to intervene. The time for the

United Nations to have acted on the crisis in Bangladesh—then East Pakistan—was many months earlier when the Bengalis were being brutally suppressed by the armed forces of their own Pakistani government. The United Nations, it is true, is proscribed by Article 2 of the Charter from intervention in "matters which are essentially within the domestic jurisdiction of any state," but Article 2 also states that "this principle shall not prejudice the application of enforcement measures" under the peace-enforcement provisions of the Charter. By any reasonable standard of judgment, the mass killing of East Bengalis and the flight of 10 million refugees across the Indian border constituted a "threat to the peace" as that term is used in the Charter, warranting United Nations intervention.

Nor does it seem likely under present circumstances that the United Nations could play a mediating role in the war in Indochina—the disabling circumstance being that the belligerents, including the United States, almost certainly would not permit it. But, looking ahead to the time when the Vietnam war is finally ended, it would be feasible for the United Nations to oversee and police a general peace settlement, through a revived International Control Commission, and perhaps through the assignment of peace-keeping forces.

When a conflict presents what Article 39 of the Charter calls a "threat to the peace, breach of the peace or act of aggression," it makes no sense to leave the issue to the caprice of the belligerents. As I said in the previous chapter, I do not understand why it is so widely regarded as outrageous or immoral for external parties to "impose" a solution to a dangerous conflict. Under the United Nations Charter the Security Council has full authority—possibly even the obligation—to impose a settlement upon warring parties who fail to make peace on their own. The very premise of the Charter is that warring nations can no longer be permitted immunity from a world police power. As far as the United States is concerned, it is worth recalling that the United Nations Charter is a valid and binding obligation upon us, ratified as a treaty with the advice and consent of the Senate. And as far as the parties to various conflicts are concerned—Arabs and Israelis, Indians and Pakistanis—it needs to be recognized that they too are signatories to the Charter and are therefore obligated, under Article 25, "to accept and carry out the decisions of the Security Council in accordance with the present Charter."

A community in its essence is a state of mind. Kenneth Boulding once commented that the American bombardier who dropped the atomic bomb on Hiroshima would almost certainly have refused if he had been ordered to drop it on Milwaukee. The difference, wrote Boulding, "is a 'we' difference. The people in Milwaukee, though we don't know any of them, are 'we,' and the people in Hiroshima are 'they,' and the great psychological problem is how to make everybody 'we,' at least in some small degree."[7]

By what practical means are we to proceed toward that end? What specific things can the United States do in the world as it is toward the formation of an international community? Clearly we cannot soon convert the United Nations into the effective security community contemplated by its Charter, nor is it likely to prove feasible in the near future to amend the Charter or otherwise reform the world organization in a fundamental way. There is, however, a good deal that can be done toward shaping the attitudes which in turn might open the way to a fundamental strengthening of the United Nations.

The United States could, for example, commit itself now to an expanded program of international aid and technical assistance through international organizations such as the World Bank, the International Development Association and the several international regional banks. We would of course hope that others, especially the Soviet Union, would join in the effort to create a kind of international fiscal system based on the idea that aid to the poor nations is neither a gratuity nor an instrument of national policy but a public responsibility comparable to the redistribution of wealth within societies by means of taxation and social services. Under an internationalized development program Russians, Americans and people from many other countries could begin to form the habit of working together as international civil servants. Out of such cooperation might arise new attitudes as well as material benefits, attitudes which could be built upon to take further practical steps toward the gradual creation of an international community. The agreements reached at Moscow in May 1972 for cooperative Soviet-American ventures in space, for joint research in science and medicine, and for the avoidance of incidents at sea are excellent examples of the kind of joint venture which is not only valuable in itself but useful in fostering new, favorable attitudes toward international cooperation; it is only regrettable that President Nixon and the Soviet leaders did not see fit to make these commendable arrangements under the aegis of the United Nations.

Difficult though it is to contemplate, I do not think we need rule out the idea of a standing United Nations police force in the foreseeable future. I have no doubt that it would be a long and arduous effort to persuade both large and small nations to allocate forces and place some degree of trust in an international peace force. Education, however, like charity, properly begins at home, and it seems to me that the United States could initiate the process of building trust in an international peace-keeping force by setting a persuasive example. This would mean something more than eloquent advocacy; it would require a clear demonstration of America's own willingness to rely on international peace-keeping procedures, or—to put it in a way that may be more pertinent—a clear repudiation by the United States of its present habit of unilateral intervention.

How might this work out in practical terms, in the case, say, of "another Vietnam"? For a start—and for a change—I would hope to see the United States evaluate the merits of a case—whether the conflict were or were not a civil war, whether or not it were a case of genuine international aggression. Then, but still prior to taking any action, I would hope that the United States government would make a clear, explicit evaluation of American security interests—involving such questions as whether the conflict was one which we could not under any circumstances allow our friends to lose, or whether their failure would be only unfortunate but not disastrous from the standpoint of American security, or whether it would not really matter much at all. It would also be of the greatest importance that we evaluate the viability of the government in question: if, for reasons of its own incompetence or lack of popular support, it could not be saved, it would be an academic question whether it ought to be saved. In this connection we might profitably take a leaf from the Chinese notebook, wherein the so-called Lin Piao doctrine states explicitly that "wars of national liberation" can only succeed on the basis of strong indigenous support, in the absence of which—and despite external support—"no victory can be won, or be consolidated even if it is won."[8] In broader terms, the doctrine might be stated that a nation which wishes to have its foreign policy projects succeed does well to abstain from impossible projects.

That is what we forgot in Vietnam, where we deceived ourselves from the beginning, telling ourselves that it was "their" war to win or to lose until each of the several occasions when "they" were about to lose, whereupon, in each case, we leaped into the fray.

To continue our hypothetical case: except in the case of an incontrovertible, vital national interest—not merely "vital" in the routinized sense in which that term is so often and so thoughtlessly employed—which might warrant direct unilateral action, and assuming that the situation was judged to be a genuine case of international aggression against a reasonably competent and popular government, the United States should then be prepared to act through the United Nations— but only through the United Nations. By what procedures we might do so—through the Security Council or the General Assembly—and with what kind of international force—permanent or ad hoc, with or without great-power participation—are questions that statesmen and students of international organization would do well to consider. The point to be made here is that the United States can and should encourage international peace enforcement first and foremost by demonstrating its own willingness to act in this way—and *in no other*. Through its interventions in Vietnam, the Dominican Republic and elsewhere, the United States has earned itself the title of "policeman of the world"; only when we have purged ourselves of chronic unilateralism and demonstrated that we mean it by our deeds —or nondeeds if you will—can we hope to divest ourselves of a dubious and dangerous role. In our role as the world's policeman, we have found that some nations will oppose us, a few will criticize us, but most will simply let us do the dirty work, abjuring any costs and responsibilities for themselves. Unilateralism feeds on itself; having gotten into the habit of acting on our own because others seemed unwilling to act cooperatively, we now find that they are all the more unwilling to accept international responsibilities because they believe they can rely on us. It would do no harm, I think, to remind some of our friends, politely but clearly, that the United States, though willing to share the responsibility for peace enforcement, is, after all, capable of defending itself, and that it is they, being less powerful, who have the greater need of international security arrangements. Only when we have made it clear that we cannot and will not carry the burden alone can we seriously expect other nations to join in making the United Nations into something resembling the peace enforcement agency it was meant to be.

In this century of conflict the United States led in the conception and formulation of plans for an international peace-keeping organization. We did not invent the idea, nor have we been its only proponents, but without our leadership the ideal embodied in the Covenant of the League of Nations and the United Nations Charter would not have attained even the meager degree of realization it has attained. It is this idea of world organization—rather than our democratic ideology, or our capitalist economy, or our power and the "responsibilities" it is supposed to have thrust upon us—which entitles the United States to the claim of having made a valuable and unique contribution to the progress of international relations. Coming as we did on the international scene as a new and inexperienced participant, and with a special historical experience which had sheltered us from the normal pressures of world politics, we Americans pursued our conception of a rational world order with uncritical optimism and excessive fervor. As a consequence, the first encounter with disappointment, in the form of Stalin and his ambitions in eastern Europe, sent us reeling back from Wilsonian idealism.

And from the practical idealism of the United Nations
Charter we reverted to the unrealistic "realism" of the
Truman Doctrine in its universalized application. We
made the conversion from Wilson to Machiavelli in the
same zealous spirit with which a repentant Communist
may become a devout believer in a religion or a repentant hawk may offer himself as a martyr for peace.

At no point, of course, did the leading architects of
Vietnam, or of the Bay of Pigs or of the Cuban missile
crisis, conceive of themselves as power brokers pure
and simple. Having themselves been reared in the ten-
ets of Wilson-Roosevelt internationalism, and having
lived through the disaster of appeasement in the interwar years, they came to regard themselves as "tough-
minded idealists," as "realists with vision," and, above
all, as practitioners of collective security against aggression. What the United Nations could not do, the United
States could and would do, with allies if possible, alone
if necessary. It was up to us, if all else failed, to curb
"aggression" at its outset, to bear whatever burdens
had to be borne, to accept whatever sacrifices had to be
made, in order to defend the "free world" against the
new, Communist predator. We, in effect, were the
successors to an enfeebled United Nations, and were
forced by fate and circumstance to endure the glory
and agony of power. In this way the policy makers of
the nineteen-sixties combined what they took to be a
hard-headed realism with Wilsonian idealism, ideological anti-communism, and an intoxicatingly romantic
notion of power to form one of the more extraordinary
—and capricious—intellectual muddles of the modern
age.

In this heady frame of reference Vietnam and its
consequences might be conceived of as the ripe harvest
of the American era of romantic "realism." Primarily,
no doubt, because of its military failures, the war in

Vietnam has brought many Americans to an awareness of the sham idealism of the "responsibilities of power," and of the inadequacies of the new "realism" once it is stripped of its romantic facade. Many young Americans, and some older ones, are appalled not only by the horrors of the Vietnam war but by the deterministic philosophy, espoused by the intellectuals who came into government in the sixties, of a permanent, purposeless struggle for power and advantage. We seem to be discovering, once again, that, without a moral purpose or frame of reference, there can be no such thing as "advantage."

America may be coming near to the closing of a circle. Having begun the postwar period with the idealism of the United Nations Charter, we retreated in disillusion to the cold war, to the Truman Doctrine and its consummation in Vietnam, easing the transition by telling ourselves that we were not really abandoning the old values at all but simply applying them in more practical ways. Now, having failed most shockingly and dismally, we are beginning to cast about for a new set of values. The American people, if not their leaders, have come near to recognizing the failure of romantic, aggressive "realism," although a new idealism has yet to take its place. Perhaps we will settle for an old idealism—the one we conceived and commended to the world but have never tried.

PART II

The Domestic
Consequences

All those who seek to destroy the freedom of the democratic nations must know that war is the surest and shortest means to accomplish this. That is the very first axiom of their science.

Alexis de Tocqueville
Democracy in America

6

Congress
and the War

The American Constitution was never meant to operate in a condition of permanent warfare and crisis. Rooted as it was in the rationalist values of the eighteenth century, our political system depended from the beginning upon the ability of rational men to resolve their political problems in good faith through carefully balanced representative institutions. War was considered to be an abnormal state of affairs, antithetical by its very nature to democracy, and to the conditions in which a democracy can function. Democracy thrives on open discussion and humane enterprises; war by its very nature compels secrecy, deceit and the suspension of humanitarian policies at home and abroad. Even when a war is of limited duration, when its objectives are clear and defensible, when the people are united in support of it, and when the nation is led by men of integrity and vision—as was the case in both World War I and World War II—there is a legacy of lasting damage to democracy. Wars are invariably followed by periods of reaction and repressiveness, and the emergency powers yielded to the executive in wartime are never subsequently restored in their entirety to the people or the legislature.

When a war is of long duration, when its objectives are unascertainable, when the people are bitterly divided and their leaders lacking in both vision and candor, then the process of democratic erosion is greatly accelerated. Beset by criticism and doubt, the nation's leaders resort increasingly to secrecy and deception. The people in turn—and especially the young, who have no memory of better days—thereupon begin to lose trust, first in the government in power, then in the institutions of government. That is what is happening in America today, and it ought not to surprise us. When truth becomes the first casualty, belief in truth, and in the very possibility of honest dealings, cannot fail to become the second. And when mutual trust goes, so in time will democracy itself, the ultimate casualty of war.

The extraordinary thing is that in this free democracy we do not really know what we are fighting for. It is as if our war aims were the President's personal secret. What does President Nixon really intend? we ask one another. Does he really mean to get out of Indochina? or does he plan, through the use of surrogate armies—backed by American money and air power—to fight on indefinitely? The rest of us can debate and speculate if we like—especially if we do not mind being accused of giving aid and comfort to the enemy—but the answers to these questions lie locked away in the inner recesses of the White House. Instead of providing answers, the remote, regal personage in the White House stages periodic television spectaculars consisting of discredited homilies about America's "commitments," the hypothetical horrors that would ensue if we failed to keep them, and jingoist bromides about "respect" for the office of the Presidency.

In addition, it is suggested—slyly by the President, crudely by his retainers—that the failure of the President's war policy is not really his fault at all but rather the fault of his critics. The "one remaining hope" of the Communists in Vietnam, said President Nixon on April, 26, 1972, "is to win in the Congress of the United States, and among the people of the United States, the victory they cannot win among the people of South Vietnam or on the battlefield in South Vietnam." The Vice President, as usual, put it more directly, accusing a long list of dissenters of "vicious attacks" on America and, in one instance, singling out Senator Muskie of Maine for what Mr. Agnew described as "a singular lack of enthusiasm for his native land."[1] In the weeks after the President made his sly accusation of treason in Congress, North Vietnamese military successes made it seem quite possible that they could win a military victory, and the President struck back with the desperation measure of mining the North Vietnamese ports. Then, in an equally futile effort to fend off domestic criticism, the President unleashed his principal lieutenants to demand silence in the name of patriotism. The Secretary of State called upon members of Congress to rally around the President and defer criticism "until the campaign begins."[2] The Secretary of the Treasury accused Democratic Senators who deplored the President's recklessness as "putting party above country."[3] In the seventeenth century Louis XIV was able to identify himself with the state: "L'état, c'est moi." When an American President equates criticism of his policies with an "attack on America," he is invoking the same dangerous autocratic principle.

Americans may well ask how this state of affairs came about. Did our Constitution really intend the demo-

cratic process to "stop at the water's edge?" Did the
framers really intend the President to be a remote,
secretive and all-powerful leader in matters of foreign
policy and a virtual dictator when it comes to starting
wars and ending them? Historians have noted that in
the great summit conferences of World War II Prime
Minister Churchill used to make only provisional commitments, because he had to consult with his Cabinet,
while President Roosevelt made final decisions on the
spot. Even Premier Kosygin of the Soviet Union deferred matters for his colleagues when he met with
President Johnson at Glassboro, New Jersey, in 1967,
while the President felt himself to be under no such
restraint. Was that the kind of official the Founding
Fathers had in mind as the successor to George III?

Senators who serve on the Foreign Relations Committee are permitted from time to time to hear
briefings on the war by the Secretary of State and other
Administration officials. At the insistence of the executive these briefings are almost always held in secret;
recent Administrations have shown a keen dislike of
having to explain their foreign policies in public. This
is usually explained on the ground that sensitive matters of national security will be discussed; in fact I can
hardly recall hearing anything of consequence in these
secret briefings that I had not already seen in my morn-
ing paper. Quite obviously, the secrecy has little to do
with protecting our country from a foreign enemy; its
purpose is to protect the Administration from scrutiny
and criticism at home.

Even if these briefings and hearings had real substance, they would still not provide Senators and Congressmen with the opportunity to discuss matters directly and candidly with the principal authors of our
foreign policy. Occasionally the President will hold an
audience at the White House for senior members of

Congress or for members of his own party, but these are ceremonial occasions, upon which the legislators dutifully demonstrate their awe and deference toward the Presidential office. Anyone who has the temerity to ask a direct question or express a candid opinion is frowned upon, like a child misbehaving in church. Occasionally, too, the President's Assistant for National Security Affairs holds briefing sessions for selected members of Congress, or what are called "background" sessions for the press. Under no circumstances, however, will Mr. Kissinger or any of his staff accept an invitation to testify before a Congressional committee, in public or in private. When invited, these close advisers of the President invariably decline, invoking what they call "executive privilege."

In every sense the war in Indochina is a Presidential war. Congress, the body vested by the framers of the Constitution with almost exclusive authority to initiate war, has been reduced to a near nullity in matters affecting this longest and most divisive of our foreign wars. How this inversion of the Constitution came about in the case of Vietnam will be examined in the remainder of this chapter; its broader context will be explored in the following chapter.

I. A Presidential War

One of the most unheralded events of recent American constitutional history occurred on January 12, 1971, when President Nixon signed into law a bill which, among other things, repealed the Gulf of Tonkin Resolution. The repealer went unnoticed because it was generally thought to be inconsequential. To the Administration and its Congressional supporters the repeal of Tonkin was unobjectionable because, in their view, the President has full authority to make war in his capacity as Commander-in-Chief. To others of us—"strict constructionists"—the repeal of the Tonkin resolution represented the withdrawal of Congressional sanction from the one legislative instrument which, contested and corrupted though it was, provided some façade of constitutional legitimacy for the war in Indochina. The President signed the repealer because he thought it did not matter, because he thought he could conduct the war without it. I voted for repeal because I thought it did matter, because I wanted a disastrous and unnecessary war ended and I believed that Congress has the authority to end it.

The two Administrations which have conducted the war in Indochina have been equally insistent upon their authority to conduct a Presidential war. The Johnson Administration contended that it did not really need Congressional sanction but had it nonetheless. In testimony before the Senate Foreign Relations Committee on August 17, 1967, Under Secretary of State Katzenbach said that the SEATO Treaty and the Gulf of Tonkin Resolution, taken together, were the "functional equivalent" of a declaration of war. The Gulf of Tonkin Resolution, he said, was "as broad an authorization for the use of armed forces for a purpose as any declaration of war so-called could be in terms of our internal constitutional process."[4] The Nixon Administration has maintained that it did not need Congressional authority to conduct the war because it was merely engaged in the "protection" of American troops placed in Indochina by the preceding Administration. The Nixon Administration did not even oppose repeal of the Tonkin Resolution, explaining that it "has not relied on or referred to the Tonkin Gulf Resolution of August 10, 1964, as support for its Vietnam policy."[5] The general thesis of the Nixon Administration was reiterated by Secretary of Defense Laird in April 1972. I asked him at that time on what authority the President relied in ordering the renewal after four years of sustained heavy bombing of North Vietnam. The Secretary answered: "It is the protection of the American personnel. . . . You don't need any more authority than that. . . . that is sufficient, complete and total. . . . "[6]

Claiming only to be "protecting" American forces by waging protracted, devastating warfare, President Nixon's position in its essence is that if President Johnson's war was constitutional, so is his. It is worthwhile, accordingly, to review the alleged constitutional bases of the war in Indochina.

The SEATO treaty contains two operative provisions. Article IV, paragraph 1, states that each party will, in the event of an armed attack in the treaty area, "act to meet the common danger in accordance with its constitutional processes." Article IV, paragraph 2, states that in the event of a threat by means other than armed attack, which is to say, by internal subversion, the parties "shall consult immediately in order to agree on the measures which shall be taken for the common defense."

It is clear from the language of the treaty that there is no automatic obligation to go to war in southeast Asia, and it is very clear that the treaty does not give the President the authority to go to war without the consent of Congress—unless the "constitutional processes" referred to are regarded as something not involving Congress and its war powers. All that the treaty obligates us to do is to "consult" with our allies in the event of internal subversion such as has taken place in South Vietnam and, in the event of an act of international aggression, to act to meet the "common danger" in accordance with our constitutional processes. The latter clearly require affirmative action by Congress, since

Congress, and Congress alone, has the constitutional power to initiate war. In any case the Vietnamese war, legally and in political fact, is a civil war and not the result of international aggression as the Nixon Administration has insisted. The Final Declaration of the Geneva Conference of 1954, which ended the first Indochina war and drew the demarcation line between northern and southern Vietnam, stated explicitly that "the military demarcation line is provisional and should not in any way be interpreted as constituting a political or territorial boundary."

This interpretation of the SEATO treaty is upheld by the legislative record, which also makes it clear that the framers of the treaty did not contemplate large-scale land warfare in Asia. In his testimony on the SEATO treaty before the Foreign Relations Committee on November 11, 1954, Secretary of State John Foster Dulles said that the treaty was not intended to form a full-fledged counterpart to NATO. "We do not intend," he said, "to dedicate any major elements of the United States military establishment to form an army of defense in this area." And, Mr. Dulles added:

> I believe that if there should be open armed attack in that area the most effective step would be to strike at the source of aggression rather than to try to rush American manpower into the area to try to fight a ground war.[7]

In response to a question by Senator Margaret Chase Smith of Maine, Secretary Dulles commented as follows on the meaning of the treaty's provision pertaining to subversion:

> Well, Article IV, paragraph 2, contemplates that if that situation arises or threatens, that we should

consult together immediately in order to agree on measures which should be taken. That is an obligation for consultation. It is not an obligation for action.[8]

Again, asked by Senator Green of Rhode Island whether the SEATO treaty committed the United States to help Southeast Asian governments put down revolution, Secretary Dulles replied:

No. If there is a revolutionary movement in Vietnam or Thailand, we would consult together as to what to do about it, because if that were a subversive movement that was in fact propagated by communism, it would be a very grave threat to us. But we have no undertaking to put it down; all we have is an undertaking to consult together as to what to do about it.[9]

As now interpreted to justify the war in Vietnam, SEATO is an entirely different instrument from the treaty consented to by the Senate in 1954. As it was then understood, the treaty was a conditional commitment to act under certain possible circumstances and to act in accordance with our constitutional procedures. Even Secretary of State Rusk said in 1964 that, although he thought the SEATO treaty was a "substantiating basis" for the American presence in Vietnam, "we are not acting specifically under the SEATO treaty."[10] He was later to change his view and invoke the treaty *ex post facto* as authorizing the President to engage in war in Indochina. That, however, was not the intent of the Senate, either when it approved the treaty in 1954 or at any subsequent time.

So much then for SEATO. What of the second part of

the Johnson Administration's "functional equivalent" of a declaration of war?

Often referred to loosely as an act of Congressional *authorization* for the President to commit the United States to full-scale war in Vietnam if he saw fit, the Gulf of Tonkin Resolution is in fact not an authorization at all. The Resolution says nothing about authorizing or empowering anybody to do anything. The critical language, from a legal and constitutional viewpoint, is the statement that Congress "approves and supports the determination of the President, as Commander in Chief," to take military measures to repel attack and "prevent further aggression." Being already *determined* to take the action referred to, the President could not have regarded the Resolution as a necessary conferral of authority; and, as already noted, the Johnson Administration did not in fact regard the Resolution as a necessary grant of authority. In the Administration's view, it was more in the nature of a courtesy extended to Congress, permitting it, as President Johnson explained in a press conference on August 18, 1967, to "be there on the takeoff" as well as on the "landing," although, the President emphasized, "we did not think the resolution was necessary to do what we did and what we're doing."

In retrospect, it appears that the major significance of the wording of the Tonkin Resolution was not the executive's claim of authority to initiate hostilities but rather Congress's acknowledgment and approval of that claim. Resolutions such as the Gulf of Tonkin Resolution amount to Congressional acquiescence in the exercise by the executive of a power which the Constitution vested in Congress and which the Congress has no authority to give away. In this respect, the distinction between an expression of *approval* and a grant of *authority* would seem to be of critical importance.

The Gulf of Tonkin Resolution was adopted by Congress on August 10, 1964, after only two days' debate, including Committee proceedings in both Houses. The reasons for the Congress's hasty enactment of the Tonkin Resolution have been recounted many times. I review them here only briefly:

First, Congress was confronted in August 1964 with a situation that was described to it as urgent, requiring prompt acquiescence in an expedient that seemed likely to meet the needs of the moment, of which the foremost need—so we allowed ourselves to be persuaded—was a resounding expression of national unity at a moment when it was believed that the country had been attacked.

Second, in the course of two decades of cold war and chronic foreign-policy crisis, we had grown so preoccupied with threats to our national security and with measures for dealing with each such threat that arose, that we had become neglectful of legal and constitutional matters. Owing to the newness of America's role as a world power, historical guidelines for the exercise of Congressional authority in a real or seeming emergency were lacking, and Congress felt itself at a loss to do anything but acquiesce in measures urged upon it by the executive.

This was all the more the case because of what might be called the tyranny of the experts. Armed with computers and an opaque jargon, a veritable army of foreign policy experts, employed by the executive, have successfully perpetrated the myth in recent years that foreign policy is an exact science which only they can truly understand. A rather uncritical acceptance of this myth added to Congress's willingness to submit to executive direction.

Still another factor, brought to light in early 1968, is the fact that the Gulf of Tonkin Resolution was enacted on the basis of what may be described charitably as incomplete information. Adoption of the Resolution was based on the firm conviction of Congress—spelled out in the first two "whereas" clauses—that the naval units of North Vietnam had deliberately and repeatedly attacked United States vessels in international waters in violation of international law and that these attacks were, in the words of the Resolution itself, "part of a deliberate and systematic campaign of aggression" on the part of North Vietnam. It has since been established that the two ships involved, the *Maddox* and the *Turner Joy,* were engaged in intelligence activities in the Gulf of Tonkin, a fact that was not vouchsafed to Congress when it considered the Resolution. In addition, considerable doubt has been raised as to the exact circumstances of the alleged second attack on the two vessels, most particularly as to whether the Administration had proof of it at the time that it ordered its retaliatory air strike on August 4, 1964, or whether it occurred at all.

A final and extremely important factor in the concession of sweeping powers to the executive was the existence of a major discrepancy between the language of the Resolution and the intentions and expectations of Congress. The Resolution said in effect that the President could use force as he saw fit in Southeast Asia; the nonpartisan expectation of Congress, clearly expressed even in the attenuated Senate debate of August 6 and 7, 1964, was that the President had no intention of engaging in large-scale war in Asia, that, indeed, by adopting the Resolution, Congress was helping to *prevent* a large-scale war.

During debate I was asked, in my capacity as manager of the bill, whether the Resolution would authorize or approve the landing of large American armies in Vietnam or China. I replied that "there is nothing in the Resolution, as I read it, that contemplates it," although, I conceded, "the language of the Resolution would not prevent it." "Speaking for my own Committee," I continued, "everyone I have heard has said that the last thing we want to do is to become involved in a land war in Asia; that our power is sea and air, and that this is what we hope will deter the Chinese Communists and the North Vietnamese from spreading the war. That is what is contemplated. . . . "[11]

In an exchange with Senator Nelson of Wisconsin, I said: "I personally feel it would be very unwise under any circumstances to put a large land army on the Asian continent." I said also that I would "deplore" the landing of a large army on the Asian mainland.[12] A little later in the debate I added: "I have no doubt that the President will consult with Congress in case a major change in present policy becomes necessary."[13]

Other Senators also expressed the general expectation that the Resolution would help to prevent a large-scale war, as the President had assured us it would. The Chairman of the Armed Services Committee, Senator Russell of Georgia, said: "I am sure that all of us who intend to vote for the joint resolution pray that the adoption of the resolution, and the action that may be taken pursuant to it, will achieve the same purpose and avoid any broadening of war, or any escalation of danger."[14] Senator Church of Idaho expressed his general understanding that it was not the President's purpose to expand the war.[15] Senator Keating of New York expressed his understanding that the Resolution was not a "blank check" for expanded hostilities to be undertaken without the consent of Congress.[16]

Senator Nelson offered an amendment to the Gulf of Tonkin Resolution which would have expressed the sense of Congress that the United States sought no extension of the war and would continue to attempt to

avoid a direct military involvement. In my capacity as
floor manager—and to my regret—I said that I could
not accept the amendment, but only because it would
necessitate a conference with the House of Representatives, which would have delayed final adoption. I made
it clear, however, that I thought that Senator Nelson's
amendment was not contrary to the Resolution but an
"enlargement" of it. I also expressed my belief that
Senator Nelson's amendment was "an accurate reflec-
tion of what I believe is the President's policy, judging
from his own statements. . . ."[17]

What the foregoing illustrates is that, in adopting the
Gulf of Tonkin Resolution, Congress had no intention
whatever of authorizing the commitment of the armed
forces to full-scale war in Asia. The language of the
Resolution, it is true, lends itself to that interpretation,
but as the executive well knew, that unfortunate language was accepted only in response to its urgent
pleadings and assurances that the Administration had
no intention whatever of plunging into an Asian land
war.

These expectations were by no means without foundation. The country, it will be recalled, was engaged in
an election campaign in which President Johnson repeatedly expressed his determination not to involve
the United States in a large-scale war in Asia. To cite
just a few of the many Presidential statements to that
effect:

On August 12, 1964, the President said in New York:

Some others are eager to enlarge the conflict.
They call upon us to supply American boys to do
the job that Asian boys should do. They ask us to
take reckless action which might risk the lives of
millions and engulf much of Asia and certainly

threaten the peace of the entire world. Moreover, such action would offer no solution at all to the real problem of Vietnam.

In a speech in Texas on August 29, President Johnson said:

> I have had advice to load our planes with bombs and to drop them on certain areas that I think would enlarge the war and escalate the war, and result in our committing a good many American boys to fighting a war that I think ought to be fought by the boys of Asia to help protect their own land. And for that reason, I haven't chosen to enlarge the war.

And in Akron, Ohio, on October 21, he declared:

> . . . we are not about to send American boys 9,000 or 10,000 miles away from home to do what Asian boys ought to be doing for themselves.

The Senate debate of August 6 and 7, 1964, shows clearly that, in adopting the Gulf of Tonkin Resolution, the Senate thought that it was acting to prevent a large-scale war, not to authorize one. The Resolution was, however, as much as there has ever been of Congressional authorization for the war in Indochina. Its repeal has not resolved the great issues relating either to the war or to the constitutional division of foreign policy powers between the President and Congress. It has served only to remove the frayed façade of constitutional legitimacy from the war, dispelling a legacy of confusion and illegitimacy, and leaving it to Congress to determine how the constitutional vacuum should be filled.

II. The Inert Congress

There is no great mystery in the inclination of executives to override legislatures whenever they can get away with it. The real puzzle is the frequency with which legislative bodies acquiesce tamely in the loss of their own authority. All over the world constitutional government is in decline. Experiments in democratic government have been abandoned in much of Asia, Africa and Latin America, and even in Europe. Dictatorship is now the dominant form of government in the world, not only in Communist countries but in a very large part of what we call the "free world." In most of these countries parliamentary bodies of one kind or another have been retained for decorative and ceremonial purposes, but they are without power or real influence; their function is to "cooperate." In many cases, their loss of authority came about with their own cooperation, enlisted as a seeming necessity in time of national emergency.

The genius of the American Constitution is that it does not compel us to rely on the conscience and principles of our Presidents to protect us from dictatorship. Through the separation of powers and the federal system, our Constitution provided countervailing institutions with countervailing powers to protect us against the danger of executive usurpation. If our Presidents are men of conscience and principle, as most of them have been, that is all to the good, but it is not something you can count on; as Vice President Agnew has pointed out—in a different context—every barrel is bound to contain a "rotten apple" or two. Under our Constitution we do not have to rely on such good fortune for the protection of our liberties—*as long as* the countervailing institutions, which is to say, Congress, the courts and the state governments, exercise their countervailing powers. The contingency that the Founding Fathers could not have foreseen—and could not have done anything about if they had—was that one or more of the other institutions of government would cease to exercise and cease to defend their own authority against executive incursions.

That, however, is exactly what Congress has let happen in the field of foreign relations, most especially in the tame acceptance of the Presidential war in Indochina. Out of a well-intended but misconceived notion of what patriotism and responsibility require in a time of world crisis, Congress has permitted the President to take over the two vital foreign policy powers which the Constitution vested in Congress: the power to initiate war and the Senate's power to consent or withhold consent from significant foreign commitments. So completely have these two powers been taken over by the President that it is no exaggeration to say that, as far as foreign policy is concerned, the United States has joined the global mainstream; we have become, for purposes of foreign policy—and especially for purposes of making war—a Presidential dictatorship.

It has been apparent for some time that a majority of members of Congress are convinced that our involvement in Indochina has been a disastrous mistake and that it should be liquidated. It is also apparent that despite the erosion of its war and treaty powers, Congress has the means, through its control of appropriations, to compel an early or immediate end to the war. Nonetheless, Congress has acquiesced in every major Presidential action in the long war. A majority may wish to end the war, but less than a majority of the two Houses have been willing to take the responsibility for ending it. The legislature, which does not hesitate to defeat or override the executive on domestic legislation or to reject a Supreme Court nominee, reverts to a kind of tribal loyalty to the "chief" when war is involved, even though, in our system, of all functions of state war is the one which the framers of our Constitution were most determined to place under the control of the legislature. It is not a lack of power which has prevented the Congress from ending the war in Indochina but a lack of will.

Such initiatives as Congress has taken toward ending the war have been either unsuccessful or too limited to be of decisive consequence. The most significant legislative achievements have been the two Church-Cooper amendments, the first prohibiting the use of American ground combat forces in Laos and Thailand, the other prohibiting the use of American ground combat troops or military advisers in Cambodia. An amendment to the Defense Appropriation Act for fiscal year 1971, which I sponsored, prohibited the use of American money to support other foreign forces in Cambodia or Laos; but the Administration has continued to finance Thai units operating in Laos, evading the law by pretending that the Thai soldiers involved are "volunteers." The first binding legislative proposal for ending the war to be voted on by the Senate, the McGovern-Hatfield amendment, would have cut off funds for the war after December 31, 1971, subject to provisions for the recovery of our prisoners. In somewhat different forms the McGovern-Hatfield amendment was defeated in the Senate on September 1, 1970, by a vote of 55 to 39, and again on June 16, 1971, by a vote of 55 to 42. Had this amendment been adopted, the United States would now be at peace, and so, quite probably, would the countries of Indochina.

In allowing the President to wage war as he sees fit, Congress has been peculiarly insensitive to public opinion, in a manner and to a degree that would be inconceivable in domestic affairs. A poll taken in August 1971 in the districts of ten Democratic and Republican leaders of the House of Representatives showed that absolute majorities in nine of the districts and a plurality in the tenth wanted their Congressmen to vote in favor of legislation to bring all American forces home from Indochina before the end of 1971; but only one of these Congressional leaders, Representative O'Neill of Massachusetts, the Majority Whip, voted with his constituency in favor of withdrawal. Taking note of this discrepancy, Representative Bella S. Abzug of New York was moved to make reference to the "House of Semi-Representatives."[18]

At the end of 1971 the two Houses of Congress finally succeeded in enacting a measure for ending the war, although it did not specify a date like McGovern-Hatfield: the Mansfield amendment to the Military Procurement Authorization Act for fiscal year 1972 declared it to be "the policy of the United States to terminate at the earliest possible date all military operations of the United States in Indochina"; the amendment provided further for the withdrawal of all American forces by a "date certain" subject to the release of American prisoners of war. Confronted at last with a binding provision of law, President Nixon announced that he would defy it. The amendment, he said while signing the Military Procurement Act, was "without binding force or effects and it does not reflect my judgment about the way in which the war should be brought to a conclusion."

Congress took no official action or position regarding the President's declaration of intent to violate the law. Following upon the North Vietnamese offensive in 1972, the consequent discrediting of the Vietnamization policy, and the President's desperate re-escalation of the war, the Senate again refused to compel a change of the bankrupt policy. On May 16, 1972, by a vote of 47 to 43 the Senate emasculated the Church-Case amendment to the State Department authorization bill, which would have cut off funds for the war four months after an agreement on prisoner return, by adding the unrealistic requirement of a cease-fire prior to a political settlement as proposed by the President and consistently and adamantly rejected by the North Vietnamese and the Vietcong. A week earlier, for what it was worth, the Senate Democratic caucus voted its "disapproval" of the President's escalation of the war.

By midsummer of 1972 there were signs that Congress at long last might be prepared to mandate an end to the war. On July 24, by a vote of 50 to 45, the Senate adopted an amendment to the military assistance authorization bill requiring the withdrawal of all American ground, naval and air forces from Indochina within four months and prohibiting the use of further funds for any military purpose in Indochina except the protection of our forces during withdrawal, subject only to release of the American prisoners of war. This first binding Senate vote against the war was nullified when the Senate went on to defeat the entire military assistance bill, but it was reenacted on August 2 by a vote of 49 to 47, this time as an amendment to the military procurement bill for fiscal 1973. At the same time the House of Representatives, which for so long had accepted executive supremacy in matters of the Vietnam war, also took a step toward exercising an independent judgment when its Foreign Affairs Committee, on July 25, by a vote of 18 to 17, adopted an amendment to the military assistance bill requiring the withdrawal of American forces and an end to all hostilities in Indochina by October 1, 1972, contingent upon the release of American prisoners and a limited cease-fire to permit safe withdrawal. It seems unlikely, as of this writing in the summer of 1972, that binding legislation to end the war will be adopted by the two Houses of Congress and then, if vetoed by the President, win the necessary two-thirds majorities to override a Presidential veto and so be enacted into law. Nonetheless, by its votes for binding legislation to end the war, the Senate had at long last registered its lack of confidence in the Nixon war policy.

For reasons with which one may sympathize—although I confess to growing impatience—many Senators and Congressmen have found it extremely difficult to cast their votes against military appropriations, even though, had they been given the chance, they would have opposed the initial involvement. A few Senators believe that, even though it may have been a mistake to get into a war, and even though the President may have done it without constitutional authority, once you are in it is your duty to go all out and win. Closely related is the belief that in foreign affairs, and certainly in war, the President must be backed, no matter how unsuccessful his policies. A larger number of Senators and Congressmen find themselves confronted with a Hobson's choice in the matter of appropriations for a war: it becomes a question not of whether you approve or disapprove of the war, but of whether you wish to support or abandon our boys out there on the firing line and in the prisoner-of-war camps. Lost to view in such agitated circumstances is the fact that, in our system, withholding funds is a legitimate, appropriate—and, all too often, the only effective—means of restraining the executive from initiating, continuing or extending an unauthorized war, or from taking steps which might lead to war.

The Johnson and Nixon administrations both contended that the Congress has shown its approval of the Indochina war by continuing to provide funds for it. The "approval" they have given is like the "approval"

Congress gave to President Theodore Roosevelt's action in sending the fleet halfway around the world by providing the funds demanded by the President to bring the fleet home. Providing funds for a military operation already under way is certainly a different form of "consent" from that involved when Congress is given the opportunity, as required by the Constitution, to decide in advance whether or not American forces will be committed to battle in some specific place for some specific purpose.

Even the enactment of binding prohibitions has disturbing connotations. The enactment by Congress of *restrictions* on the use of the armed forces, unaccompanied by any form of *authorization* for their use, seems to acknowledge that in the absence of explicit restrictions, the President can do whatever he pleases. Recent Presidents have claimed this unlimited right to use the armed forces under an inflated interpretation of their powers as Commander-in-Chief. But under the Constitution, on the other hand, as written and as interpreted by the framers, Congress alone has the authority to initiate military action for any purpose beyond repelling a sudden attack. This being the case, it should not be necessary to pass a law to stop the President from doing something he does not have legal authority to do anyway, except insofar as he is authorized to do it by Congress. It should not be necessary, but after years of usurpation, it obviously is. As far as the President's use of the armed forces is concerned, the logic of the Constitution is that nothing goes unless it is authorized by Congress; current practice—indeed the practice of the last three decades—has been that anything goes unless it is prohibited.

The difficulties of this approach have become increasingly apparent. Regarding itself as being at liberty to do anything that is not specifically forbidden by law, a willful executive has only to redefine its activities in terms that fit the letter—as sharply distinguished from the spirit—of the law. In Cambodia, for example, instead of "advisers," who are forbidden by the law, we now have a "military equipment delivery team" (MEDT) to travel around the Cambodian countryside checking on the deployment of American military equipment. Pentagon spokesmen acknowledge that the "team" members might just possibly drop some hints to Cambodians on how the American equipment works—showing them, for example, where the on-and-off buttons are—but under no circumstances are they to give the Cambodians any "advice." Senate investigators have confirmed that, although MEDT personnel in Cambodia "seem to be acutely aware of the prohibition against their acting as advisers or participants in the planning and execution of tactical operations, they are nevertheless deeply involved as advisers or organizers in activities such as force planning, military budgeting, logistics and training."[19] There has even been at least one instance in which a helicopter retrieval team jumped briefly into civilian clothes for a quick foray into Phnom Penh airport, thereby converting themselves, for the moment, from the "combat troops" prohibited by the Cooper-Church amendment into "tourists" or "sightseers." Such fine distinctions—between "advisers" and "military equipment delivery teams," between foreign "forces" and "volunteers"—bring to mind an old story, probably apocryphal, about the invention of the mace, which was said to have been devised for the convenience of warlike medieval clerics, who were forbidden by ecclesiastical law to shed blood but found it quite satisfactory to deal with their enemies by inflicting fatal—but bloodless—concussions. One is driven to conclude that these limited, legislative restraints have not only proven insufficient to the task;

they have provided the Administration with excuses for doing anything and everything that is not explicitly forbidden—and, as we have seen, all it takes to transfer some contemplated military action from the prohibited category to the permissible is a certain agility in semantics and an extraordinary contempt for the constitutional authority of Congress. The Nixon Administration, like its predecessor, has shown itself to be richly endowed with both of these attributes.

The violations of trust, and indeed of the Constitution, which currently agitate the Congress are reflections of the deep division in our country and in our government over the war in Indochina. I do not think these differences between the executive and some of us in Congress can be eliminated by briefing sessions, Congressional hearings, or even by artfully worded legislative prohibitions. If we as legislators are to have any effect in bringing our own best judgment to bear in those areas where the Constitution has given us definite responsibilities, we are going to have to make full use of the legislative instrumentalities which are properly at our disposal: the power to pass or reject legislation, including military appropriations bills; the power to consent to or withhold consent from proposed foreign commitments; and, above all, the power to authorize, or refuse to authorize, the initiation of war.

Congress not only has to start using these powers again; it also has to reestablish its right to use them. After three decades of atrophy due to Congressional passivity, people in general—and Presidents in particular—have forgotten that it is Congress which is supposed to initiate wars, if wars are to be initiated, and the Senate which is supposed to approve treaties, if commitments are to be made at all. Congress has the job not only of reasserting its powers but of reestablishing its good name.

There is no denying that the institution has fallen into disrepute. Ridiculing Congress is quite respectable, like shouting catcalls in a vaudeville house, while words of irreverence for the Presidency are severely frowned upon, like cutting up in church. I regret this attitude very much, not only because I believe that the Presidency has become a dangerously powerful office, more urgently in need for reform than any other institution of American government, but even more because, for all its failures and frailties, Congress remains the institutional centerpiece of our democracy. Whatever may be said against Congress—that it is slow, obstreperous, inefficient or behind the times—there is one thing to be said for it: it poses no threat to the liberties of the American people. The size and diversity of legislative bodies in general prevent them from working their unchecked will; indeed they have no single will to enforce. To the best of my knowledge, no elected legislative body has ever established its *own* dictatorship over a population.

The major virtue of legislatures is neither wisdom nor prescience—and certainly not "charisma"—but the basic inability to threaten the liberties of the people. The ancient Egyptians spent themselves into penury to give their mummified Pharaohs glorious send-offs to heaven; humble folk were rewarded by vicarious participation in the ascent. We in turn build great monuments to revered departed Presidents, perhaps for similar reasons. But who would dream of "mummifying" or deifying a legislature? The plodding, workaday character of Congress, its lack of glamour and mystery, its closeness to ordinary people with ordinary problems, even its much-reviled "parochialism," make of our national legislature an object entirely unsuitable for deification. That is why Congress is incapable of threatening our democratic liberties; that too is why an asser-

tive, independent Congress is the first line of defense
against an expanding executive, which can and does
threaten our liberties.

The conventional view holds that in time of emergency, patriotism demands that we set aside our differences and unite behind our President. And so, I agree,
we should, in those uncommon instances, such as the
Japanese attack on Pearl Harbor, when the emergency
is great and immediate. But when the emergency has
abated, or when, as in the years since World War II, it
is chronic and recurrent but less than overwhelming,
when the country is in a condition of permanent, low-
grade emergency—then it is the legislator's duty to do
everything he can to defend the authority of the legislature against executive usurpation. At best it is a holding
action, because a condition of permanent crisis must
almost certainly lead any society to eventual dictatorship. In the long run, I have little doubt, the preservation of democracy in America will turn on questions of
value—the values which guide us in the conduct of our
foreign relations and in the running of our own society.
Until those questions are resolved, however, and with
a view toward resolving them in a manner consistent
with the preservation of our liberties, the most important service a legislator can perform is to let nothing of
consequence go unquestioned or unexamined. The
legislator's job is to analyze, scrutinize and criticize,
responsibly and lawfully, but vigorously, candidly and
publicly. He may in certain instances be mistaken, or
inadvertently unfair—legislators after all are no more
immune from error than executives—but, from the
standpoint of preserving our liberties, an occasional excess of criticism is less harmful than a habit of automatic
praise.

As far as the war in Indochina is concerned, a great
many of us in the Senate—and a sizable majority of the

American people—are now convinced that our involvement in that conflict has been a disastrous mistake. Some of us are no less convinced that the policies of the Nixon Administration have led not to an end of the war but to its indefinite perpetuation in an altered form. Feeling as we do about the matter, we are impelled to defend and use the established procedures of Congressional democracy, in the hope that, by so doing, we may help to save our country from the disasters of continuing war and eventual dictatorship.

7

The Decline— and Possible Fall— of Constitutional Democracy in America

There is no better measure of a country's belief in its own professed values than the ease or difficulty with which it betrays them. America is having an exceedingly difficult time in repudiating the ideals of Jefferson, Lincoln and Wilson in favor of the new militarism which our leaders have said is our destiny and responsibility. This shows the authenticity of our attachment to democracy, but it does not guarantee democracy's survival. The outcome of the present crisis in our affairs— whether we are to remain a constitutional democracy or degenerate into an imperial dictatorship—is beyond our present range of vision. All that we know for certain is that, if we do give up on democracy, if we do turn our backs on the humane, rationalist values of our tradition, we will not have done it easily, or gladly—or, most ironically, with any real knowledge of what we were doing.

I. The Jurisprudence of Crisis

Perspective is easily lost in time of crisis: you do what you think you have to do to meet a threat or an imagined threat or seize an opportunity—with little regard for procedure or precedent. Ends give way to means, law is subordinated to policy, in an atmosphere of urgency, real or contrived. In 1940 and 1941 President Roosevelt took over both the treaty power of the Senate and the war power of the Congress, not because he wished to set himself up as a dictator but because he judged the nation to be endangered by Germany and Japan—as indeed it was—and he needed to act in a hurry. In 1950 President Truman committed the country, for the first time in its history, to a full-scale war without the benefit of Congressional authorization; he did not do that because he wished to usurp the authority of Congress but because he perceived a clear and present danger in Korea and he needed to act in a hurry. In 1964 President Johnson subverted the Congress by persuading it, on the basis of erroneous information, to adopt the Gulf of Tonkin Resolution, which he invoked later to justify his massive intervention in Vietnam. President Johnson too was in a hurry; he said that he needed an immediate and overwhelming expression of Congressional support and, to our own subsequent regret, we gave it to him.

These occurrences have one common attribute: the subordination of constitutional process to political expediency in an atmosphere of urgency and seeming danger, resulting in each case in an expansion of Presidential power at the expense of Congress. The fact that Roosevelt and Truman were substantially correct in their assessment of the national interest in no way diminishes the banefulness of the precedents they set. FDR's deviousness in a worthy cause made it much easier for LBJ to practice the same kind of deviousness in an unworthy cause.

The favored euphemism for executive usurpation is "flexibility." Mr. Katzenbach, as Under Secretary of State, argued for an "essentially political approach to the conduct of our foreign affairs,"[1] leaving controversies over the division of authority between the executive and legislative branches of government to be resolved by "the instinct of the nation and its leaders for political responsibility."[2] If the rule of law must depend on a President's "instinct for political responsibility"—especially when he goes into his vainglorious role as Commander-in-Chief—then we are all about as secure as gazelles in a tiger cage; our only hope is that the tiger may not be hungry at the moment. Secretary of State Acheson pretty well summed up the "jurisprudence" of crisis when he told the Senate in 1951 that it ought not to quibble over President Truman's claim of authority to station American troops in Europe, because, as Acheson put it, "We are in a position in the world today where the argument as to who has the power to do this, that, or the other thing, is not exactly what is called for from America in this very critical hour."[3]

More than twenty years—and many a critical hour—have passed since President Truman sent the troops to Europe, and arguments about "who has the power to do this, that, or the other thing" still arouse intense distaste in the executive branch of our government. It is best—so we are still told—to leave matters of decision-making in foreign policy to be resolved according to the requirements of the moment, and who can doubt what the requirements of any given moment are going to be: the President must be left unencumbered to make war or commitments abroad essentially as he sees fit, drawing Congress into the decision-making insofar as he finds it useful and convenient. Besides, in this time of crisis—permanent, institutionalized crisis, as it has developed—appeasing Congress would surely be interpreted as a dangerous sign of Presidential "weakness," which could only lead to further demands for power and participation. Is this after all not the lesson of Munich? Burdened as he is with weighty responsibilities in a dangerous world, a President simply cannot afford to appear as a "pitiful, helpless giant"—no more to the Senate than to the North Vietnamese themselves.

Only if one subscribes to the cult of the "strong" Presidency which mesmerized American political science in the fifties and early sixties can one look with complacency on the growth of Presidential dictatorship in foreign affairs. In those days, when the magic glow of FDR still flickered in our memories, when Eisenhower reigned with paternal benignancy and the Kennedys appeared on white chargers with promises of Camelot, it was possible to forget the wisdom of the Founding Fathers, who had taught us to mistrust power, to check it and balance it, and never to yield up the means of thwarting it. Now, after bitter experience, we are having to learn all over again what those pre-Freudian students of human nature who framed the American Constitution understood well: that no single man or institution can ever be counted upon as a reliable or predictable repository of wisdom and benevolence; that the possession of great power can impair a man's judgment and cloud his perception of reality; and that our only protection against the misuse of power is the institutionalized interaction of a diversity of politically independent opinions. In this constitutional frame of reference, a good executive is not one who strengthens his own office by exercising his powers to the legal utmost and beyond, but one who, by respecting the limits of his own authority, contributes to the vitality of the constitutional system as a whole.

When, as in recent years, the conduct of foreign policy is thought to necessitate the steady attrition of established constitutional processes, that foreign policy has become subversive of the very ends it is meant to serve. Why after all do we engage in foreign relations if not for the purpose of securing certain values, including the preservation of our constitutional democracy? The values of democracy are in large part the processes of democracy—the way in which we pass laws, the way in which we administer justice, the way in which government deals with individuals. When the exigencies of foreign policy are thought to necessitate the suspension of these processes, repeatedly and over a long period of time, such a foreign policy is not only inefficient but utterly irrational and self-defeating. I am willing to predict with reasonable confidence that if democracy is destroyed in America in the lifetime of the present younger generation, it will not be the work of the Russians, or of the Chinese, and certainly not of the Vietnamese Communists; the totalitarianism toward which we are heading will be a home-grown product. Like the American major in Vietnam who found it necessary to "destroy Ben Tre in order to save it," we may find some day, without quite knowing when or how or why it happened, that we have destroyed our own constitutional democracy—in order to save it.

Executive incursions upon Congress's foreign-policy powers have had three main results. First, the authority to initiate war, which the Constitution vested solely in Congress, has passed into the hands of the executive. Second, the treaty power, which was meant to give the Senate final authority over significant foreign commitments, has been reduced to a near nullity by resort to executive agreements and simple declarations as means of contracting foreign obligations; by the reinterpretation of treaties in such a way as to impute to them meanings which were unintended or disavowed at the time they were contracted; and even by the actual alteration of treaties through subsequent executive agreements. Finally, the "advise and consent" function, which once served to bring the Senate's judgment to bear on the broad range of foreign-policy decisions and directions, has been so diminished that little or no cognizance is now taken of the Senate's counsel, while "consultation" is commonly used to refer to ceremonial briefings regarding decisions which have already been made.

II. The War Power

The notion that the authority to commit the United States to war is an executive prerogative, or even a divided or uncertain one, has grown up only in recent decades. The framers of the Constitution were neither uncertain nor ambiguous in their determination to vest the war power exclusively in the Congress. As Thomas Jefferson wrote in a letter to Madison in 1789:

> We have already given in example one effectual check to the dog of war by transferring the power of letting him loose from the executive to the legislative body, from those who are to spend to those who are to pay.[4]

As to the powers of the President as Commander-in-Chief, Alexander Hamilton, an advocate of strong executive power, wrote in Federalist Number 69:

> The President is to be Commander-in-Chief of the Army and Navy of the United States. In this respect his authority would be nominally the same

with that of the King of Great Britain, but in substance much inferior to it. It would amount to nothing more than the supreme command and direction of the military and naval forces, as first general and admiral of the confederacy, while that of the British King extends to the declaring of war and to the raising and regulating of fleets and armies—all which, by the Constitution under consideration, would appertain to the legislature.[5]

Presidents of recent decades have not only committed the country to war without Congressional authorization but openly asserted their right to do so. A number of their predecessors, especially in the late nineteenth and early twentieth centuries, usurped the war powers of the Congress on certain occasions, but did so on a small scale and without openly asserting the right to do so. Earlier Presidents explicitly acknowledged the exclusive war powers of Congress. President Madison, for example, who had been one of the principal framers of the Constitution, sent a message to Congress on June 1, 1812, in which he recounted the depredations of British ships on American commerce on the Atlantic but then referred the matter to Congress, acknowledging that the question of war or peace was "a solemn question which the Constitution wisely confides to the legislative department of the government."[6] The Monroe Doctrine is frequently cited as an early precedent for the commitment of the armed forces by the President acting on his own authority. In fact, President Monroe made a critical distinction between a statement of policy and the authority to implement it. In 1824 the government of Colombia inquired as to what action the United States might take under the Monroe Doctrine to repel possible European intervention in the Latin American republics, and Secretary of State John Quincy Adams replied that "by the Constitution of the United States, the ultimate decision of this question belongs to the legislative department of the government."[7] Daniel Webster, one of our greatest constitutional lawyers, wrote in 1851, during his tenure as Secretary of State: ". . . I have to say that the warmaking power in this government rests entirely in Congress; and that the President can authorize belligerent operations only in the cases expressly provided for the Constitution and the laws."[8]

The Supreme Court has also declared unequivocally that the power to initiate war is an exclusively Congressional one. In the "Prize Cases" of 1862 the Supreme Court said:

> By the Constitution, Congress alone has the power to declare a national or foreign war. . . . The Constitution confers on the President the whole executive power. . . . He is Commander-in-Chief of the Army and Navy of the United States. . . . He has no power to initiate or declare a war either against a foreign nation or a domestic state.[9]

Another, more recent example is noteworthy. In his concurring opinion in the case of *Youngstown v. Sawyer*, Justice Jackson, replying to the assertion of Solicitor General Perlman that the American troops in Korea "were sent into the field by an exercise of the President's constitutional powers," said: "I cannot foresee all that it might entail if the Court should endorse the argument. Nothing in our Constitution is plainer than that declaration of war is entrusted to Congress."[10]

The passing of the actual means to initiate war—as distinguished from the legal authority—out of the hands of the Congress into the hands of the executive has been one of the most remarkable, and unnoticed, developments in the constitutional history of the United States. If this drastic imbalance is to be corrected, it is essential that we understand how and why it came about.

The most important cause, as already noted, has been three decades of war and crisis. Lacking historical guidelines for the accommodation of our constitutional system to our new role as a world power, we have tended since our initial involvement in World War II to respond to seeming emergencies with an anxious disregard for normal constitutional procedure. Time after time, from the undeclared naval war in the Atlantic with Germany and Italy in 1941 to the Korean War to the invasion of Cambodia, the executive has undertaken large-scale military enterprises without even informing, much less seeking the necessary authority from, Congress. Until recently the Congress supinely concurred, setting aside whatever apprehensions its members might have felt, lest they cause some critical delay or omission. Without protest or question, Congress has repeatedly acquiesced in the executive's accounting of the facts of a situation and in its judgment as to whether the case at hand constituted a genuine national emergency.

Another factor in Congress's passivity was the success of the executive, aided and abetted by legions of eminent political scientists, in persuading Congress and the country that foreign policy was an esoteric science which ordinary mortals, including Congressmen and Senators, were too stupid to grasp, and which, therefore, was best left to the experts with their computers and their scientific methods of analysis and prediction. One might say that we permitted ourselves to be "brainwashed." Only as the results of the experts' techniques have begun to unfold—in such places as Vietnam and the Middle East—has the thought gained currency among legislators that perhaps foreign policy is not so exact a science as the political scientists have claimed. Perhaps too, in the words of a leading diplomatic historian, ". . . there are no experts in wisdom concerning human affairs or in determining the national interest, and there is nothing in the realm of foreign policy that cannot be understood by the average American citizen."[11] Or, as George Reedy, who was President Johnson's Press Secretary and Special Assistant, has written: "On sweeping policy decisions, which are, after all, relatively few, a President makes up his mind on the basis of the same *kind* of information that is available to the average citizen."[12]

Corollary to the cult of the experts has been the tyranny of secret information. On numerous occasions the Senate Foreign Relations Committee has been told in effect that we would be well advised to mind our own business—which is to say, refrain from meddling in foreign policy—because we do not have the detailed and secret information on which certain delicate and clandestine policies are based. There is some truth in this contention, but it is true only because of the diligent and dedicated efforts of the executive to withhold information from the Congress.

Since 1969 a special subcommittee headed by Senator Symington has conducted a study of American military commitments abroad, as a result of which Congress and the country have become aware for the first time of certain startling and far-reaching American military involvements. Early in its period of operation the Symington subcommittee discovered, for example, that without the knowledge of the American people and Congress, the United States had been conducting a secret war in northern Laos, far away from the Vietnamese infiltration routes along the Ho Chi Minh Trail, at the cost of many American lives and billions of dollars. When the Ambassador to Laos, William Sullivan, was asked in an appearance before the Symington subcommittee why at an earlier hearing he had withheld information about the critical role the United States Air Force was playing in northern Laos, he replied that he had not been asked any *direct* questions about United States air operations in northern Laos. My own comment at the time was that "There is no way for us to ask you questions about things we don't know you are doing."[13]

Another possible explanation for Congressional acceptance of executive predominance in foreign policy may derive from the isolationist experience of the years between the two world wars. It has long been accepted that the Senate acted with disastrous irresponsibility in rejecting the Covenant of the League of Nations in 1919 and that the Congress was shortsighted and ignorant in its isolationist attitude during the 1930's. Perhaps it was in part out of a sense of guilt and regret for its earlier shortsightedness that the Congress became so loyal and uncritical a supporter of the President during and after the Second World War. The real lesson of the interwar years is not, however, that Congress ought to be compliant and uncritical in matters of foreign policy but that it ought to be responsible and constructive in the discharge of its constitutional responsibilities. To contend, as was popular in the years after World War II, that "politics properly stops at the water's edge" is virtually the same as saying that democracy should stop at the water's edge.

Many professionals in the field of foreign policy have welcomed the trend toward executive predominance as a necessity for dealing with the fast-moving events of our time, and many citizens have concurred in that judgment, reluctantly or otherwise. My own view is that unrestricted Presidential power in questions of war and peace is neither necessary to current circumstances nor tolerable in a democratic society. Established constitutional procedures make ample allowance for responding to a genuine emergency with whatever speed is required. No responsible person contests the right—indeed the duty—of the President to take action to repel an attack upon the United States or its armed forces. What many of us do contest is the right of the President to act entirely on his own authority in situations which fall far short of questions of life and death for the nation. I refer to such instances as the intervention in Lebanon in 1958, the Bay of Pigs in 1961, the Gulf of Tonkin episode in 1964, the Dominican intervention of 1965, and the blockade of the North Vietnamese ports in 1972, no one of which involved anything resembling a clear and present danger to our national safety.

Far from having been rendered obsolete by the realities of the nuclear age, the checks and balances of our Constitution have become more essential than ever. Nuclear weapons, ballistic missiles, and a vast arsenal of lesser weapons have vested in the single person of the President of the United States something approaching absolute power over the lives of millions of people all over the world. It is something of an understatement to say that that is too much power to be entrusted to any individual. In the early days of the Republic, the separation of powers was thought essential to protect our liberty; now it has become essential for the protection of our lives as well.

Among the steps to be taken toward the restoration of Congress's proper constitutional role in the making of foreign policy, none is more urgent and necessary than the reassertion of the war power. It may be granted that "declarations" of war are obsolete, but this is to say no more than that the *form* in which Congress has exercised its constitutional war power in the past is no longer appropriate. To infer from this change in international usage that the entire authority to initiate war ought to be transferred from the Congress to the executive is illogical and disingenuous. A leading student of the war power has written:

> It was not a special license to use the words "declare war" that the Founding Fathers gave to Congress. Rather it was the full, red-blooded reality of deciding that another country is our enemy and that war—any form of war—should be levied upon it. The power is not basically changed or diminished because current circumstances call for a different method of using it when necessary.[14]

On April 13, 1972, the Senate adopted a war powers bill. The bill, sponsored principally by Senator Javits of New York, purports to reassert the Constitution by confining unauthorized use of the armed forces by the President to specified conditions of emergency. Even in a designated emergency, however—and this is the bill's major provision—the President would not be permitted to continue hostilities beyond thirty days unless within that time Congress authorized him to do so. In its report on the war powers bill the Foreign Relations Committee commented that it was "necessary legislation" which, however, "would not have been necessary if Congress had defended and exercised its responsibility in matters of war and peace. . . ."[15]

III. The Treaty Power

During the same years that the war power has been passing out of the hands of Congress, there has also been a steady attrition of the status and significance of treaties submitted to the Senate. The constitutionally and historically sanctioned distinction between the treaty as the proper instrument for contracting important, substantive agreements and the executive agreement as an instrument for the conduct of routine and essentially nonpolitical business with foreign countries has now all but disappeared. The term "commitment" has come to be used to refer to engagements with foreign countries ranging from those contracted by treaties to those resulting from executive agreements, simple declarations and mere suppositions deriving from repeated, casual assertions. Simply by repeating again and again that we have an obligation to someone or other, we have come in a number of instances to suppose that our word and even our national honor are involved, as completely as they would be by duly ratified treaties.

Such has been the case with both Israel and South Vietnam, to take the two most conspicuous recent examples. Except for SEATO's requirement of consultation, no *treaty* obligates us to take any action, military or otherwise, on behalf of either of these nations. This seems to me a cogent fact, although most Americans would probably be astonished to hear it. Presidents and their various subordinates have gotten so in the habit over the years of saying that we are "committed" to Vietnam or to Israel that they and virtually everyone else have come to accept these presumed obligations as articles of faith. Without benefit of treaties consented to by the Senate, our commitments to these two countries have been elevated over the years from factuality to solemnity to sanctity. The suggestion (in Chapter 4) that the United States conclude a security treaty with Israel on certain specified conditions is made not in the belief that we would be contracting a new obligation but, quite frankly, for the purpose of codifying and limiting a de-facto obligation.

The denigration of the Senate's treaty power has taken three forms: the contracting of significant obligations by executive agreements as well as through less formal processes of simple declaration; the interpretation of existing treaties in extravagant and unwarranted ways; and, on occasion, the revision of treaties approved by the Senate by subsequent executive agreements.

One of the more blatant examples of military commitment made by executive agreement—or, to give the executive the benefit of a small doubt, a virtual or potential military commitment—is the series of agreements providing for the maintenance of American military forces in Spain. The original executive agreement, concluded in 1953, stated that an attack on the joint Spanish-American facilities in Spain would be regarded as a "matter of common concern." The scope of the agreement was substantially expanded in 1963, when Secretary of State Rusk and the Spanish Foreign Minister signed a joint declaration asserting, among other things, that "A threat to either country, and to the joint facilities that each provides for the common defense, would be a matter of common concern to both countries, and each country would take such action as it may consider appropriate within the framework of its constitutional processes." The real significance of the arrangement with Spain was summed up accurately if indiscreetly in a memorandum written in late 1968 by General Wheeler, then Chairman of the Joint Chiefs of Staff. He pointed out that "By the presence of the United States forces in Spain the United States gives Spain a far more visible and credible security guarantee than any written document."

When the agreement came up for renewal in 1968, the negotiations became protracted because of Spanish insistence upon a greatly increased American payment for base rights. The Senate Foreign Relations Committee made known to the executive on several occasions its objections to the renewal of the arrangement with Spain by executive agreement. In a report issued in the spring of 1969 the committee advised the executive that, in its view, "a military commitment to Spain could only be binding on the United States if it were the result of a treaty approved by the Senate."[16] Again, in a hearing held on July 24, 1970, the Foreign Relations Committee strongly urged Under Secretary of State U. Alexis Johnson and Deputy Secretary of Defense David Packard to send the new agreement with Spain to the Senate in the form of a treaty or, in any event, to make its terms known to the country through a public hearing of the Foreign Relations Committee. The Administration responded to the committee's request by stepping up its schedule for the conclusion of the new agreement with Spain by executive agreement. The Spanish Foreign Minister was hastily summoned to Washington to sign the agreement before the committee could press the matter further. The renewed agreement, signed on August 6, 1970, committed each country, among other things, to ". . . support the defense system of the other and make such contributions as are deemed necessary and appropriate to achieve the greatest possible effectiveness of those systems to meet possible contingencies. . . ." The agreement also established a Spanish-American "joint committee" on defense matters.

The Nixon Administration insisted that the Spanish arrangement was not a commitment, and in December 1970 the Senate adopted a resolution expressing the sense of the Senate that nothing in the Spanish agreement "should be construed as a national commitment by the United States to defend Spain." All this is a kind of word game, in which it is affirmed, in effect, either that the President does not intend to do what he has said he would do, or that words do not mean what they say. The language of the agreement is vague, but regardless of disavowals, it is difficult to interpret it as anything but a military commitment to Spain.

The Spanish themselves seemed to be in little doubt as to the meaning of the agreement. According to press reports, Foreign Minister Lopez Bravo assured the Cortes, Spain's legislative body, that the 1970 agreement was to Spain's advantage, representing an increased American commitment. It is of interest too that the Spanish government, which is considered a dictatorship, found it necessary to explain the agreement to its legislative body while the American Administration took a different view of its accountability to the Senate.

The most pertinent current example of treaty revision through extravagant interpretation is provided by SEATO. The SEATO treaty, according to the State Department, "establishes as a matter of law that a Communist armed attack against South Vietnam endangers the peace and safety of the United States" and that the President has "the constitutional responsibility for determining what measures of defense are required when the peace and safety of the United States are endangered."[17] The executive branch has thus asserted, in effect, that the treaty obligated us to make war in Vietnam and further gave the President full authority to initiate and conduct that war. As was shown in the preceding chapter, this interpretation of SEATO is an extravagant reinterpretation of the treaty as it was contracted and ratified in 1954—so much so, in fact, as to make it a new and different commitment. In the view of the authority on the war power cited earlier, the

State Department "transformed the treaty with a stiff injection of sophistry."[18]

If indeed SEATO *had* authorized the President to make war at his discretion, as indeed it did not, the treaty could properly have been regarded as unconstitutional. The treaty-making power has been held by the Supreme Court not to extend "so far as to authorize what the Constitution forbids."[19] In its report on the war powers the Foreign Relations Committee commented that this limitation was properly construed "as preventing the President and the Senate from exercising by treaty a power vested elsewhere by the Constitution. The President and the Senate could not, for instance, use the treaty power to abridge the Bill of Rights; nor, in the Committee's view, can a treaty be used to abridge the war-declaring power, which is vested not in the Senate alone but in both Houses of Congress. The framers of the Constitution considered and rejected the possibility of vesting in the Senate alone the power to declare war. That power was deliberately vested in the Congress as a whole; a decision to initiate war must be made by both the Senate and the House of Representatives and cannot, therefore, be made by treaty."[20]

In addition to altering treaties by reinterpretation, the executive has on certain occasions gone so far as to alter treaties consented to by the Senate by subsequent executive agreement. If this can be done, it reduces the Senate's treaty power to a nullity. Of what significance is the Senate's authority to pass upon the terms of a treaty if the executive may subsequently alter those terms at will? A President who presumed to repeal a domestic law would be regarded as having executed a coup d'état and might even be impeached, but in foreign affairs the practice is not only accepted but scarcely noted. In recent years there have been two particularly notable instances of this patently unconstitutional practice. Specific terms of both the Italian and Japanese peace treaties have been altered by executive agreements. In one case, the return of the Bonin Islands to Japan, the agreement was not submitted to the United States Senate, although it was made subject to approval by the Japanese Diet.

The provisions of the Italian peace treaty altered by executive agreement pertained to the limitations on Italy's armed forces and to the status of the city of Trieste. Italy was released from the military clauses of the treaty, as far as the United States was concerned, by the simple means of a communication from Secretary of State Dean Acheson to the Italian government on December 21, 1951. As to Trieste, Article 21 of the peace treaty terminated Italian sovereignty over the Free Territory of Trieste until such time as the United Nations Security Council established a permanent regime. When agreement on a permanent regime could not be reached, the United States joined with Italy, Yugoslavia and the United Kingdom in a "memorandum of understanding"—an executive agreement, that is—which divided the Free Territory of Trieste between Italy and Yugoslavia.

Article 3 of the Japanese peace treaty obligated Japan to "concur" in any proposal by the United States to place certain specified islands, including the Bonins and the Ryukyus (which include Okinawa), under a United Nations trusteeship with the United States as sole administering authority. Pending such arrangements, the treaty stated that "the United States will have the right to exercise all and any powers of administration, legislation and jurisdiction over the territory and inhabitants of these islands, including their territorial waters." The treaty made no provision for the return of these islands to Japan. It seems quite clear that any initiatives to restore the designated islands to Japan, constituting as they did changes in the terms of the peace treaty as approved by the Senate, should have been submitted to the Senate as additional treaties. Nonetheless, on December 24, 1953, the Eisenhower Administration concluded an executive agreement with Japan relinquishing to Japan all rights of the United States with respect to the Amami Islands. The Bonin Islands were returned to Japan by another executive agreement, signed on April 5, 1968. This agreement, as already noted, specified that it would come into effect only after Japan had advised the United States that Japan "has approved the agreement in accordance with its legal procedures." No comparable reference was made to the legal procedures of the United States.

There have been other instances in which treaties have been altered or supplemented through agreements requiring legislative ratification by the other party but not by the United States. In August 1959, for example, the United States and other NATO countries concluded certain agreements supplementing the North Atlantic Treaty Status of Forces Agreement, which itself had been approved by the Senate. These supplementary agreements required "ratification or approval"; the other parties ratified but the United States simply approved. Similarly, an agreement of April 27, 1951, between the United States and Denmark, made "pursuant to the North Atlantic Treaty," and having to do with the defense of Greenland, was made subject to parliamentary approval by Denmark but not by the United States. A defense agreement "pursuant to the North Atlantic Treaty," concluded between the United States and Iceland on May 5, 1951, provided that the arrangement would come into force upon notification from Iceland of its ratification of the agreement, but ratification by the United States was not specified.

By ironic contrast, here are a few examples of the kinds of treaty revisions which *have* been submitted to the Senate for its advice and consent, as shown by a review of the Senate Foreign Relations Committee calendar: In 1951, the year the United States released Italy by executive agreement from the military restrictions of the Italian peace treaty, the Truman Administration did submit to the Senate a protocol prolonging the International Agreement Regarding the Regulation of Production and Marketing of Sugar. In 1953, the year in which the Eisenhower Administration by executive agreement relinquished to Japan American rights over the Amami Islands, the executive did submit to the Senate a convention modifying and supplementing a 1948 convention between the United States and Belgium for the avoidance of double taxation. In 1954, the year in which the Free Territory of Trieste was divided between Italy and Yugoslavia by a "memorandum of understanding," the executive did submit as treaties a protocol amending the slavery convention and a proposal to extend the double-taxation agreement with the Netherlands to the Netherlands Antilles. In 1968, the year in which the Bonin Islands were returned to Japan by executive agreement, the Johnson Administration submitted to the Senate for its advice and consent: a protocol with Mexico modifying an agreement between the two countries concerning radio broadcasting; six amendments to the International Convention for the Safety of Life at Sea; and a revision of certain international radio regulations adopted at Geneva in 1959. Instances such as the foregoing underlay the assertion of the Senate Foreign Relations Committee in the spring of 1969 that ". . . we have come close to reversing the traditional distinction between the treaty as the instrument of a major commitment and the executive agreement as the instrument of a minor one."[21]

As far as their substance is concerned, I personally approved of each of the revisions which were made in the Italian and Japanese peace treaties, and I favored, most strongly, the restoration of Okinawa to Japan, which was accomplished by a treaty, approved by the Senate in November 1971. The executive had hesitated for some time before making the decision to submit the Okinawa agreement as a treaty, apparently for fear of a controversy in the Senate over Japanese textile exports to the United States and possible defeat of the treaty, and also because the Japanese government expressed fear that a debate in the Diet on ratification would touch off violent anti-American riots. In order to spare ourselves and the Japanese these inconveniences, serious consideration was given to a procedure violating our own Constitution, the apparent underlying assumption being that whenever government officials are in more or less general agreement that some provision of the Constitution is obsolete, inconvenient, or detrimental to the smooth conduct of foreign policy, that provision of the Constitution can simply be set aside without benefit of a constitutional amendment.

The implications of the matter are enormous. What is at stake is nothing less than the treaty power of the Senate as that power is defined in the Constitution and in long-established constitutional usage. If the executive is to be conceded the right to alter the terms of treaties by his own declaration or by executive agreement, then the treaty power of the Senate will have been reduced to a nullity. It will be an exercise in futility for the Senate to study and debate the provisions of treaties before giving its consent if it knows that those provisions can be altered subsequently at the option of the executive. In the past it has been the practice of the Senate to consider the provisions and implications of treaties with care and deliberation; it has done so in the belief that a treaty consented to by the Senate was, as the Constitution itself provides, part of the "supreme law of the land." It is obvious that any law which can be altered or nullified at the will of the executive is not only not "the supreme law of the land"; it is no law at all.

We are, we have long assumed, a society committed to the rule of law. It is presumably for the purpose of defending and preserving that kind of society that we have a foreign policy. When, as has so often been the case in recent years, considerations of the smooth and efficient conduct of foreign policy are permitted to take precedence over the constitutional rules that foreign policy is designed to uphold, even to the extent of fostering the evasion or violation of those rules, clearly there has been an inversion of ends with means. A foreign policy conducted in such a way as to undermine or defeat its own objectives is, no matter how skillfully executed, a bankrupt policy. As I have said, I favored the restoration of Okinawa to Japan and I voted with enthusiasm for the treaty which accomplished that. At the same time, I should rather have not achieved that highly desirable objective if it could only have been achieved by unconstitutional means.

It may be sufficient—it may have to be sufficient—for the time being for the Senate to maintain vigilance as to its prerogatives and responsibilities and to keep a close watch on the misuse of executive agreements and declarations. The Senate has passed a bill, sponsored by Senator Case of New Jersey, calling for the submission of all executive agreements to Congress at least for its information if not its approval, but even this limited, seemingly innocuous measure was opposed by the Nixon Administration, which claims the right not only to make foreign commitments on its own executive authority, but the right as well to keep those commitments secret from Congress and the American people. In March 1972 the Senate adopted a non-binding resolution calling on the executive to submit pending agreements for bases in the Azores and Bahrain to the Senate for its advice and consent. In June 1972 the Senate adopted a binding amendment to the military assistance authorization bill prohibiting the expenditure of any funds to implement the Azores base agreement until that agreement was submitted to the Senate as a treaty and another amendment prohibiting the expenditure of funds for the implementation of any new agreements for the establishment of American military installations in foreign countries unless such agreements first received the advice and consent of the Senate. The fate of these constitutionally significant prohibitions was cast in doubt, however, when the Senate rejected the entire bill of which they formed a part.

I do not think it likely that the Senate would be receptive in the near future to a constitutional amendment like the Bricker proposal of 1954 to limit the President's power to make foreign commitments. If, however, as in the case of the Spanish bases, the executive continues to ignore appeals for compliance with constitutional procedure, Congress will eventually have to devise one method or another of enforcing its authority, or else simply submit to the de-facto dictatorship of the President over the conduct of foreign relations.

IV. The Imperial Presidency

The gradual usurpation by the executive of the war and treaty powers of the Congress is part of a broader process of expanding Presidential authority in the conduct of foreign relations and in those areas of domestic life which are closely related to foreign policy, especially in its military aspects. It may not be too much to say that as far as foreign policy is concerned, our governmental system is no longer one of separated powers but rather one of elected, executive dictatorship.

The potentiality for this, now being realized, was probably inherent in the Presidential office from the beginning. Alexander Hamilton, known as an advocate of strong executive power, nonetheless warned in Federalist Number 75:

> The history of human conduct does not warrant that exalted opinion of human virtue which would make it wise in a nation to commit interests of so delicate and momentous a kind as those which concern its intercourse with the rest of the world to the sole disposal of a magistrate created and circumstanced as would be the President of the United States.[22]

As long as the President's capacity to dominate foreign policy remained an unrealized potentiality, as was the case until the twentieth century, and as long as that power, once it did begin to take form, was exercised in a way that won the approval of progressive-minded scholars and politicians, criticism of the Presidential office was confined to a handful of conservative Senators and academics who were dismissed as reactionary mossbacks. Hardly anyone, for example, took serious notice in 1950 when Senator Watkins of Utah questioned the authority of President Truman to commit the country to war in Korea without consulting Congress, and said that, if he were President, he ". . . would have sent a message to the Congress of the United States setting forth the situation and asking for authority to go ahead and do whatever was necessary to protect the situation."[23] In retrospect, the so-called mossbacks seem like prescient constitutionalists.

In the wake of the Roosevelt era, a whole school of political science developed around the cult of the Presidency as the fountainhead of wisdom, creativity and humanitarianism in politics. Even as late as the mid-sixties, one of our most influential political scientists, Professor James MacGregor Burns, wrote that:

> As a general proposition the Presidency has become the chief protector of our procedural and substantive liberties; as a general proposition, the stronger we make the Presidency, the more we strengthen democratic procedures and can hope to realize modern liberal democratic goals.[24]

Only in the last five years have the celebrants of the Presidency found it appropriate to reconsider their position. This reconsideration has not of course taken place in an intellectual vacuum but rather has been precipitated by a series of foreign-policy disasters wrought in large part by the unencumbered working of the Presidential will. I do not say this with any personal pleasure or pride, because I myself was among those who took an ingenuous view of Presidential power until the disaster of Vietnam compelled me to reevaluate my position. Whatever the cause or catalyst, that reconsideration is now in full swing, and I think it a healthy development in American political thinking. Whatever may be wrong with Congress, it is beginning to be recognized that the Presidency has serious, even dangerous, shortcomings of its own.

Of these, the most important appears to be the unique capacity of the office to isolate and mislead its occupant. So, at least, writes George Reedy, who served as President Johnson's press secretary and special assistant, in one of the most thoughtful and disturbing books on the Presidency of recent years. Encased from the day he takes office in an atmosphere of privilege and deference that amounts to royalty, the President is steadily divested of a politician's primary requirement, the maintenance of contact with reality; so much so, in fact, that, in Reedy's view, ". . . the White House is an institution which dulls the sensitivity of political men and ultimately reduces them to bungling amateurs in their basic craft—the art of politics."[25]

The essential cause of the difficulty is the isolation of the President at the apex of power. No one speaks to him unless spoken to; no one, as Reedy points out, ever invites him to "go soak his head"; no one in his presence ever addresses himself to anyone except the President, and always in terms of reverential respect. No one is his peer, certainly not his White House assistants, nor the Cabinet members who are his political servants, nor even Senators and Congressmen when they meet the President on his home ground. Even the most independent-minded Senator, says Reedy, ". . . enters cautiously, dressed in his Sunday best and with a respectful, almost pious, look on his face," because "The aura of reverence that surrounds the President when he is in the Mansion is so universal that the slightest hint of criticism automatically labels a man as a colossal lout."[26]

Perhaps the single most important difference between an American President and a Prime Minister in a parliamentary system is that the latter is compelled to meet his critics face to face, giving him a lever on reality that the American President is denied. "Under the American system," as one political scientist, Professor Alexander Groth, points out, "the executive is virtually *prevented* from engaging in public debate on policy by the institutional setting of his office; under the British system he is expected and, in fact, *compelled* to engage continually in it."²⁷ In parliamentary systems the Prime Minister is obliged to descend into the arena of the House or Chamber, where he has to answer questions, respond to criticisms, and endure whatever barbs and insults the Opposition chooses to throw at him. His appearance in the House is not a state occasion like the President's infrequent visits to the Congress, which are steeped in pomp and ceremony but usually quite lacking in political substance. The Prime Minister cannot barricade himself behind a phalanx of assistants and advisers; he is obliged to think and speak for himself. As Professor Groth points out, it is not the power to vote no confidence and compel the Prime Minister's resignation which gives the British House of Commons its decisive influence, but rather its ability to compel the Prime Minister and his Cabinet colleagues continually to explain and justify their policies to an informed and critical body of colleagues. It is not "confidence" in its technical sense that a British Prime Minister must retain but confidence in its ordinary sense—confidence in his judgment, competence and responsibility.

The President, by contrast, is more nearly in the position of the British Monarch, except for the crucial fact that he has power and the Queen does not. When he speaks, it is always on his own terms and never on someone else's. Whether it be a national television address, a Rose Garden ceremony, or even a Presidential press conference, it is one form or another of a "speech from the throne." No American President is ever required to answer criticism head-on; no President ever has to explain his assertions in detail, or reconcile them with criticisms and objections offered by others. Much as they may imagine themselves to be tough-minded and independent, White House journalists have a vested interest in not giving offense to the President, and have no special interest, as does an opposition politician, in exposing his mistakes and misjudgments. In addition, newspapermen share the impulse of so many of the inhabitants of the capital city to help shape history, to the extent that some of the more influential among them seem to write columns more for their impact on the President than for the enlightenment of the rest of us.

When the President speaks, it is from a pedestal. His annual State of the Union message is seldom a serious analysis of the nation's problems and prospects; more commonly, it is a self-serving catalogue of his Administration's alleged triumphs, interlarded with a lot of vacuous eloquence about "driving dreams," or a "second American revolution" which turns out to be a plan for some bureaucratic reshuffling. On other occasions—when, for instance, his standing in the polls sinks low—the President is likely to use his near-monopoly of the television to speak "directly" to the American people; on these occasions, it is usually not a new policy that the President wishes to convey but a new "image"—an image of honesty or strength or sincerity, or even an image of indifference to "images." The total effect of all this indirect and inauthentic sham "communication" is to defraud the people of one of their most basic rights and the President of one of his most basic needs: the knowledge of each other's thinking.

Congress is at a great disadvantage in discussing issues, because the executive has a near-monopoly on effective access to the public attention. The President can command a national television audience to hear his views on controversial matters at prime time, on short notice, at whatever length he chooses, and at no expense to the federal government or to his party. Other constitutional officeholders are compelled to rely on highly selective newspaper articles and television news spots, which at most will convey bits and snatches of their points of view, usually selected in such a way as to create an impression of cranky carping at an heroic and beleaguered President. The problem for a Senator or Senate committee is not simply one of being heard. Anything that has the color of scandal, sensation, accusation or prediction will command eager attention from the media. What you cannot easily interest them in is an idea, or a carefully exposited point of view, or an unfamiliar perspective, or a reasoned rebuttal to a highly controversial Presidential statement. During the years of the Vietnam war, the Foreign Relations Committee has heard thoughtful and significant statements on the war by scholars, professors, journalists, businessmen, theologians, and political and military leaders, but owing to the lack of interest of the media, many of the most enlightening of these proceedings have remained a well-kept secret between the witnesses and the members of the committee. Why this is so is beyond my understanding. All I do know is that the only reliable way of getting the media to swallow an idea is by candy-coating it with a prediction or accusation or by drowning it in the spectacle of a "head-to-head confrontation" with some prominent executive-branch official.

Take for example the issue of the war powers of the Congress as against the President's authority as Commander-in-Chief. The whole country has heard the President hold forth on many occasions about how *he alone* as Commander-in-Chief is responsible for the conduct of the war and the safety of our fighting men. The very words "Commander-in-Chief" are intoned with a reverential awe appropriate to eighteenth-century courtiers speaking of "His Most Christian" or "Britannic" or "Imperial and Apostolic Majesty." Millions of people have heard recent Presidents expound their inflated concept of their role as Commander-in-Chief, but virtually no one outside of the Senate has heard the thoughtful and learned expositions of Senators on constitutional doctrine and the intent of the framers. The result is that the country has been suffused with the constitutional theories of Lyndon Johnson and Richard Nixon, while the contrasting views of Jefferson, Hamilton and Madison remain buried in history. As fast as they are called up by members of the Senate, they are laid again to rest in the pages of the *Congressional Record*.

There is nothing in the Constitution which says that of all elected officials the President alone shall have the right to communicate with the American people. That privilege was a gift of modern technology, coming in an age when chronic war and crisis were already inflating the powers of the Presidency. We all remember FDR's fireside chats on radio and his use of these to win the people to his viewpoints. I am not sure anyone ever did find out whether that battleship really was sent up to Alaska to pick up the President's "little dog Fala." No one cared after the President's skillful use of radio to ridicule the allegation. Communication is power and exclusive access to it is a dangerous, unchecked power. If Roosevelt had had television, he might have been proclaimed emperor by acclamation. None of FDR's successors have matched his genius for mass communication, but each one has found television to be a powerful tool in the service of Presidential policies and opinions. Television has done as much to expand the powers of the President as would a constitutional amendment formally abolishing the coequality of the three branches of government.

Without quite acknowledging it to ourselves, we have perceived the Presidency with something of the awe and reverence accorded to monarchs of an earlier age. Even in the American Republic, there seem to be atavistic longings for a king who can "do no wrong." When we are most dissatisfied with a President, it is not for essentially human failings, like a lack of competence or foresight; more commonly it is for superhuman failings, for a lack of "charisma," for his failure as a "father figure," for a failure to measure up as a suitable object of worship. In constitutional monarchies people can get the instinct for emperor worship out of their systems by lavishing affection upon a powerless king or queen. In Presidential republics, all the inflated esteem is directed toward the most powerful man in the country, giving rise to a permanent, residual danger of dictatorship—a danger which becomes concrete in time of emergency, and acute when the emergency is of long duration. That is the condition of America today, and it is precisely for this reason that now, more even than in ordinary times, the Congress must defend and assert its independence.

V. Doing Something About It

With a view to restoring a degree of constitutional balance to the making of American foreign policy a number of legislative proposals have been put forth. Reference has already been made to the war powers bill, the legislative proposals relative to executive agreements, and the various proposals for ending the Vietnam war. In 1970, to cite another example, I proposed legislation designed to break the President's monopoly of television access to the American people by requiring the networks to provide as a public service a reasonable amount of broadcast time to authorized representatives of the Senate and House of Representatives to present Congressional views on major issues.

I have also submitted legislation, in 1971, to breach
the wall of executive secrecy in matters of foreign
policy by limiting the practice known as "executive
privilege," through which officials of the executive
branch claim the right to withhold information from
Congress when, in their own judgment, disclosure
"would be incompatible with the public interest."[28] As
between the executive and legislative branches of our
government, the effect of "executive privilege" is
rather like a suspension of diplomatic relations between nations. No direct communications take place
between those who make foreign policy in the executive branch and those in Congress who are supposed to
participate in the making of policy and to oversee its
execution. Like the Arabs and Israelis, they communicate through intermediaries, with the Secretary of
State cast in the role of the United Nations mediator.
"Executive privilege" is not a legal or constitutional
principle but simply a custom, a survival of the royalist
principle that "the King can do no wrong." Legal scholars regard the claim to an absolute executive discretion
in matters of providing or withholding information as
an anachronistic survival of monarchical privilege, an
extension from King to President of the doctrine of
sovereign immunity. As currently invoked and prac-
ticed in our country, executive privilege represents a
gap in the rule of law, placing the government—or,
more exactly, its executive branch—in a position of immunity from principles of law which are binding upon
ordinary people.

In the case of officials who are considered personal
assistants to the President—such as Mr. Kissinger,
President Nixon's Assistant on National Security Affairs,
and his staff—as distinguished from Department heads
—such as the Secretary of State—the claim of "executive privilege" is extended beyond the withholding of

information to the withholding of the person himself, to his refusal even to apppear before a Congressional committee, either in public or in closed session. The Secretary of State has repeatedly refused invitations from the Senate Foreign Relations Committee to testify in public, but he has usually acceded to invitations to testify in closed session. On these occasions the Secretary of State has all too often withheld information from the committee, but at least he has withheld it in person, giving Senators the opportunity to make their own views known and also to see if they can gauge the intentions of the Administration by listening to the Secretary's tone, so to speak, as well as his words.

It is, needless to say, even more difficult to ask questions of and make recommendations to people who refuse to talk to you, as has been the case, for example, with President Nixon's principal foreign-policy adviser, Mr. Kissinger. Although Mr. Kissinger has appeared on television, provided "background" briefings for the press and occasionally provided special briefings for selected Congressmen and Senators, he has steadfastly refused to appear before any Congressional committee, either in public or in private. The result has been that the people's representatives in Congress have been denied direct access not only to the President himself but to the President's chief foreign-policy adviser.

No one questions the propriety or desirability of allowing the President to have confidential personal advisers. President Wilson relied heavily on the advice and friendship of Colonel House, and President Roosevelt relied similarly on Harry Hopkins. President Nixon has certainly been entitled to the private and personal counsel of Mr. Kissinger, but Mr. Kissinger in fact has been a great deal more than a personal adviser to the President. Unlike Colonel House and Harry Hopkins, who had no staffs of their own, and even unlike Walt

Rostow under President Johnson, who at the end of 1968 had a substantive staff of no more than twelve persons, Mr. Kissinger has presided over a staff of over fifty "substantive officers" and a total staff of about a hundred forty employees. In addition, Mr. Kissinger has served as chairman of six interagency committees dealing with the entire range of foreign policy and national security issues and has also been in charge of "working groups" which prepare the staff studies on which high-level policy discussions are based. The National Security Council staff budget, which includes funds for outside consultants, stood at $2.2 million in fiscal year 1971, which was more than triple Mr. Rostow's budget in 1968. Mr. Kissinger's role is comparable to that of Colonel House in about the same way that a moon rocket is comparable to the Wright brothers' airplane. None of this is meant to suggest that Mr. Kissinger's influence, or that of his new foreign-policy bureau, has been in any way sinister, illegitimate or even inappropriate—except in one respect: their immunity from accountability to Congress and the country behind a barricade of executive privilege.

The legislation which I have proposed would lay down specific guidelines for the invocation of executive privilege, in effect requiring the President to take personal responsibility for every decision to withhold information from Congress. The bill would also require employees of the executive branch to appear in person before Congress or appropriate Congressional committees when they are duly summoned, even if, upon their arrival, they did nothing more than invoke executive privilege. The purpose of this bill is to make a small breach in the wall of secrecy which now separates Congress from the executive in matters of foreign policy and particularly in matters pertaining to the war in Indochina. The specific change of procedure that would be required is a limited one, perhaps even a minor one, but its intent goes to the core of the democratic process by reaffirming the principle of accountability to Congress in the conduct of foreign policy.

Reviewing the various legislative proposals for the restoration of constitutional balance in the making of American foreign policy, one is bound to take due notice of the crucial and pertinent fact that no one of these bills—for restricting executive privilege, regulating executive agreements, limiting the President's war powers, or ending the war in Vietnam—has been enacted into law. Nor, as of the middle of 1972, does any major bill seem likely to be enacted into law. The reason, as noted earlier, is not a lack of power on the part of Congress but a lack of will. There remains a disabling gap between Congress's wishes in foreign policy and the actions for which it is prepared to accept responsibility. The disabling factor is that tribal anachronism, the impulse to rally behind the "chief" in time of foreign conflict, even when the chief seems fixed upon a course for disaster. Only when we consider the way in which, throughout the ages, ordinary people have sacrificed life and treasure without complaint to the martial pretensions of their leaders does it seem less surprising that legislators too are susceptible to Caesarism.

It is disillusioning nonetheless because a strong and independent Congress is essential for keeping the regal figure in the White House in contact with the world of unpleasant realities. When all considerations of organizational discipline, expertise and the occasional need for speedy action are taken into account, Congressmen and Senators have the one essential qualification for an effective role in the making of policy which cannot be found within the executive branch: the power to speak and act freely from an independent political base, the power to tell the President to "go soak his head." The experts and executive advisers lack independent political authority; Congressmen and Senators have it. That is their essential qualification for a role in the making of foreign policy.

Early in my Senate career I made a speech called "The Legislator" in which I attempted to define the proper role of a Senator. One passage seems pertinent here:

> The legislator may not often give us the inspired leadership which is necessary in the crises of human affairs, but he does institutionalize, in the form of law, those measures which mark the slow lifting of mankind up from the rule of the tooth and the claw. Like the stop on a jack, the legislator may not elevate our civilization, but he does prevent our slipping back into the tyranny of rule by brute force.[29]

Increasingly over the years I have become convinced that a legislature serves a society as much by what it delays or prevents as by what it expedites or enacts. If efficiency were the sole criterion of a good legislature, there would be everything to be said for dismantling the Congress, or at least for revamping its procedures and introducing a system of strict party discipline. That is what many reformers say they want to do in the apparent belief that decision is always better than delay and action better than inaction—a dubious assumption indeed, rooted in a Panglossian view of human nature. To those of us who have developed an appreciation of the capacity of people in high places for doing stupid things, there is much to be said for institutional processes which compel people to think things over before plunging into action. Justice Brandeis pointed out: "The doctrine of the separation of powers was adopted by the convention of 1787, not to promote efficiency but to preclude the exercise of arbitrary power. The purpose was not to avoid friction, but, by means of the inevitable friction incident to the distribution of the governmental powers among three departments, to save the people from autocracy."[30]

In the long run, even the most energetic and ingenious means of reasserting Congressional prerogative will of themselves prove insufficient to the maintenance of constitutional government. As Tocqueville pointed out, war breeds dictatorship. I for one am fairly well convinced that neither constitutional government nor democratic freedoms can survive indefinitely in a country chronically at war, as America has been for the last three decades. Sooner or later, war will lead to dictatorship. Important though it is for Congress to assert its prerogatives and to devise new means of enforcing them, the issue ultimately will turn on questions outside of the legislative process, on questions of the allocation of resources between domestic needs and foreign involvements, questions of our willingness, whenever possible, to rely on the United Nations rather than our own military power, questions having to do with the kind of society we build at home.

The worst single consequence for our society of this long era of crisis and war has been the steady undermining of the rule of law. From the White House to the university campuses legal inhibitions have been giving way to faith and fervor, to that terrible irrational certainty of one's own rightness which leads men to break through the barriers of civilized restraint. Outraged as they have had every right to be by dishonesty, deviousness, and lack of restraint on the part of those in high office, many of our young people have seen fit, most regrettably, to imitate rather than repudiate the example. Supposing themselves able, in their purity of mo-

tive and intent, to right the injustices wrought by unworthy leaders, they have seemed unwilling to recognize that it has not been conscious malice or greed or
hunger for power that has led the leaders of this country to make the terrible mistakes that have been made
in these unhappy times, but rather that very same qual-
ity of mind which many young people themselves ex-
hibit—a supreme, arrogant confidence in the rightness
of their own opinions.

That has been the worst of it: the breakdown of law
—not really of law itself but of the state of mind in
which people value and respect law. We seem to be
casting aside the insights of Freud and of the framers
of the American Constitution: that nothing can more
surely deceive a man than his own uninhibited conscience; that the human mind is limited and imperfect
in its perceptions of morality; that law is the closest
approximation of morality of which a human community is capable.

The founders of our country understood these human disabilities, and that is why they mistrusted power.
"Confidence," said Jefferson, "is everywhere the par-
ent of despotism—free government is founded in jealousy; . . . it is jealousy and not confidence which pre-
scribes limited constitutions, to bind down those we are
obliged to trust with power. . . . In questions of power,
then, let no more be heard of confidence in man, but
bind him down from mischief by the chains of the Constitution. . . ."[31]

To arrest and reverse the decline of democratic government in America, we are going to have to recover
our mistrust of power—in the Presidency and wherever else it is found.

8

State of the Society

Perhaps I attribute too much to the war in Vietnam—
I have certainly been accused of that—but I have the
feeling nonetheless that if we could but extricate ourselves from that futile crusade, it should not be too
difficult to get the country back on a healthy and decent
course. The nation's capital, to be sure, is a place of
anxiety and agitation, but in the towns and countryside
of my home state of Arkansas—and I would guess, in
much of the rest of the country—America does not
seem like a profoundly or incurably sick society. People
are dismayed, to be sure, by the war, by extravagant
military costs and the paucity of social services, by poverty and unemployment, by the busing controversy
and the social and racial issues of which it is symp-
tomatic. But these are not insoluble problems; still less
are they the kind of problems that cause a society to
disintegrate, provided they are given proper attention.

That is precisely what they have not been given, and

the reason they have not is the preoccupation of our national leadership with war and crisis abroad. A President preoccupied with summits and confrontations has little time or energy to spare for the workaday tasks of tending to the needs of our society. Obsessed with the politics of the war and morbidly fearful of a loss of "respect" by foreigners for the Presidential office, and presumably for himself, President Nixon has allowed otherwise soluble domestic problems to fester and grow worse. Failing as well to speak plainly and directly to the American people, the Nixon Administration, like its predecessor, has acquired a reputation for secrecy, lack of candor and manipulation. At least as much as the war itself, this failure of moral leadership has frightened and alienated a great many Americans, older as well as younger, who used to regard the Presidential office as preeminently a place of moral leadership.

The result has been profound disillusion with a government that seems incapable of response to the real and neglected needs of our society. Among many young people, who have no memory in their lifetime of a government that was responsive and responsible, the sense of outrage and impotence has extended beyond our recent leaders to the political system itself. In the last few years serious voices have been raised contesting the hitherto uncontested premise of a basically healthy society, contending, indeed, that, far from being a miscarriage of the American system, war and social injustice are indigenous to it and insurmountable by means short of radical alteration of the system itself. My own view is that our society *is* basically healthy and capable of self-renewal and that a new, more responsive leadership could demonstrate this capacity in fairly short order, but until and unless we acquire such leadership, the ills of our society can only grow, compounded by the steady loss of confidence in the justice and decency of the American political system.

I. Money and Priorities

Far from being a dry accounting of bookkeepers, a nation's budget is full of moral implications; it tells what a society cares about and what it does not care about; it tells what its values are. Since the end of World War II the United States has spent more than one trillion, 400 billion dollars for military purposes, an unimaginable sum that perhaps takes on meaning when it is pointed out that it is an amount greater than the total bank deposits of the entire population of the United States. As a result of having allocated a predominant portion of our tax money, as well as our human resources, for military purposes, we have had parasitic rather than productive growth. Every nation, as suggested in Chapter 5, has a double identity: it is both a *power* engaged in foreign relations and a *society* serving the interests of its citizens. As a power the nation draws upon but does not replenish its people's economic, political and moral resources. The replenishment of wealth—in this broader than economic sense—is a function of domestic life, of the nation as a society. In the last three decades the United States has been heavily preoccupied with its role as the world's greatest power, to the neglect of its responsibilities at home, and the state of our society reflects this distortion.

Despite imposing rhetoric to the contrary, the emphasis has not significantly changed during the Nixon years. Although in his budgets for fiscal years 1972 and 1973 President Nixon stressed that more would be spent for "human resources" than for military purposes, the military budget in fact was increasing, from $77.1 billion in total obligation authority in fiscal 1972 to a requested $85.7 billion for fiscal 1973. The proposed fiscal 1973 expenditure was in fact the largest since World War II, and the cost trend was "clearly upward," according to an analysis of federal spending by the Brookings Institution. Brookings has forecast an increase in defense spending of from $10 billion to $18 billion by 1977 over the amount projected for fiscal 1973 and estimates that the defense budget, in 1972 dollars, could reach about $100 billion in 1977.[2] Although President Nixon claimed that "only" thirty-two cents of every budget dollar for fiscal 1973 would go for military purposes, the figure in fact was almost twice that. The Joint Economic Committee of Congress has calculated the true fiscal 1973 request for military and related expenditures, which must include veterans' benefits and most of the interest on the national debt, at well over $110 billion.[3] Trust fund expenditures in the budget—for such purposes as social security—account for $72.5 billion; well over half the government expenditures not covered by trust funds go to the military. By my calculations, about sixty-two cents of every tax dollar, therefore, goes for military or military-related expenditures or for the space program.

The Nixon Administration originally pledged a balanced budget and has consistently underestimated the massive deficits it has incurred, while trying to minimize—or obfuscate—them with talk of a "full employment" concept. The record indicates a deficit in the "administrative" budget of about $125 billion during the four Nixon years—roughly one-fourth the total outstanding federal debt. Under the "unified" budget adopted in fiscal 1969, which counts the surplus from trust funds—social security, Medicare, highways—against the deficit, the deficit would be $88 billion.

Whatever accounting method is used, the deficits add up to the largest in history except for the World War II years.

One standard by which the nation's economic well-being is usually measured is the gross national product. Although little consideration seems to be given to what constitutes the GNP and what it really means, it has become a sort of national totem or idol; as long as it grows higher, the belief apparently is that we have nothing to worry about. A kind of national celebration has been drummed up over the fact that the GNP has passed the trillion-dollar mark. A trillion dollars sounds impressive—especially when we are told that the United States GNP is greater than the combined GNP's of Japan, West Germany, France, the United Kingdom, Italy and Canada; or that our GNP has more than doubled in the last dozen years. But I am afraid all the talk of a trillion-dollar economy and our ever-growing GNP has deluded us about the true status of our economy. Although we have great resources and unprecedented economic capacity, it does not take an erudite economist to determine that the economy is not in sound condition. Inflation has been a prime contributor to the GNP and an expected federal budget deficit approaching, perhaps exceeding, $40 billion in fiscal 1972 also distorts the GNP: the greater the deficit, the greater our GNP. Nor does the GNP take account of an international balance-of-payments deficit of more than $30 billion in 1972.

Frequently when I have expressed doubt about our ability to undertake certain expenditures—for example, the foreign-military aid program—I have been met with replies citing the trillion-dollar GNP as evidence of our ability to afford whatever might be in question. It is asserted that our military spending is not really so significant because it accounts for only 7 to 10 percent of the GNP; but annual military budgets approaching or exceeding $80 billion, plus $25 billion in related costs, also represent more than 60 percent of that portion of the federal budget which can be controlled. Some have even made the assertion that our involvement in Vietnam has had no detrimental impact on the economy. Professor Walt Rostow, special assistant to former President Johnson, has said of the war: "It has never been an economic problem at home. The peak cost was $25 billion—that out of a near trillion-dollar economy."[4] My own view is that the war's real cost has been immeasurable, going far beyond the $200 billion estimated by the Library of Congress to be the cost accrued by the end of 1971.[5] No one indeed has been able to quantify the effects of this experience on the American people. Nor has anyone really been able to measure the economic costs incurred through inflation, high interest rates and balance-of-payments deficits, or through the loss of vital domestic programs which have gone unfunded while we poured billions into Vietnam. A number of economists have concluded that the war has brought about an inflationary psychology which has made it all the more difficult to bring prices under control. These consequences cannot be dismissed by glib reference to a trillion-dollar economy.

Far from measuring the true productivity or social welfare or economic health of our society, the gross national product is no more than a crude measure of goods and services ranging from gambling to garbage disposal. The cost of bullets used in a gangster's or assassin's gun goes into the national accounts with the same weight as the price of computers, a loaf of bread or medical equipment. It could even be claimed that increased crime is a stimulus to the GNP, since we have to spend more on law enforcement. In computing the GNP nothing is subtracted from the value of gasoline or automobiles because they contribute to atmospheric pollution, or from agricultural output because some fertilizers or agri-chemicals may pollute the air or water. In fact, the cost of producing pollutants, as well as the expenditures for attempts at cleaning up the pollution they cause, are included in the GNP. On the other hand, the costs of poor health and deteriorated environments which are often the by-products of wasteful affluence are not reflected in the GNP. The National Urban Coalition estimates air-pollution costs at $13.5 billion annually just in property damage from soiling, corrosion and abrasion of materials; water pollution costs the country at least an additional $12 billion annually.[6] These are included in the GNP only insofar as we try to correct them, and then they appear as part of the vaunted trillion-dollar economy.

Coming back to earth from the stratosphere of "macro-economics," we encounter not the magnificent opulence one might expect of a trillion-dollar economy but a society deficient in education, transportation, housing and health care, a society in which many vital programs to aid human and community development remain unfunded. During the same decade in which our GNP has more than doubled, our cities have precipitously deteriorated while federal programs created to aid urban areas have been starved for funds. An analysis prepared by the National League of Cities and the United States Conference of Mayors showed that *new* authorizations requested by the Nixon Administration for the fiscal 1973 budget for all agencies and programs having any degree of urban impact amounted to a total of only $7.5 billion.[7] In my own state of Arkansas, to take another example, and in other states as well, it has become all but impossible to travel by train, while many of the nations whose GNP is dwarfed by ours are providing their citizens excellent rail and public trans-

portation service. The list of unfunded projects is a long
one: in Arkansas, for example, in 1972 we had 145 unfunded applications for $35 million in Farmers Home
Administration grants and loans for water and sewer
systems in small communities; preoccupied with the
war and military costs, the Nixon Administration
refused to expend funds appropriated by Congress for
such mundane purposes as water supply and waste disposal. It is ironic indeed that in the land of the trillion-
dollar economy millions of our citizens cannot pay for
and do not receive adequate health care; millions of our
children are denied adequate education; millions of
Americans are compelled to live in rural shacks and
urban slums.

During the decade of the 1960's, while these most
pressing domestic needs went unmet, it was thought
desirable to spend $30 billion so that Americans could
walk on the moon ahead of the Russians. Had we
weighed our priorities more soberly, with greater regard, that is, for the needs and welfare of our own
people, we might well not have seen men land on the
moon in the year 1969. The event might have been
deferred until 1979 or 1989. Would that have been one
of the great tragedies of human history? Suppose that
cautious counsels had prevailed in fifteenth-century
Spain, and Columbus had not made his voyage in 1492.
In all probability Ferdinand Magellan or Sir Francis
Drake—but surely somebody—would have discovered
America a few years or several decades later. America
would still have been there, waiting to be discovered,
its native Indians undistressed and undecimated in
their momentary isolation. With the possible exception
of our own, the planets will still be intact, available for
exploration, in the year 2000.

We have been told many times that, in terms of our
gross national product, we can well afford to do the

things that need to be done at home without reducing our activities abroad. But even if the economic resources were there, the psychological resources are not. The war in Vietnam has drained off not only money but political energy and leadership, and public receptiveness to reform. Until the war is ended, there can be no prospect that the nation's more sober and generous instincts will reassert themselves, no prospect of a renewal of the nation's strength at its vital domestic source.

In the present atmosphere only the military can flourish, and it does. Despite the limited agreement on strategic weapons reached in Moscow in May 1972, defense costs remain staggeringly disproportionate to the rest of our economy. As noted in Chapter 1, the Nixon Administration followed up the 1972 Moscow SALT agreement not with the reduction of military expenditures we might have expected but with a demand for funds for expensive new or accelerated weapons programs such as the missile-launching submarine, *Trident*, the B-1 bomber, and a new submarine-based cruise missile. In addition, one estimate of the cost of the two ABM sites agreed upon in Moscow was actually in excess of the amount estimated for the previously authorized four-site program. Despite the 1972 SALT agreement, the evidence pointed to a dismaying increase in strategic arms spending; the prospective trend as of mid-1972 was difficult indeed to reconcile with claims that SALT would help slow down the arms race. The arms race, far from being curbed as we had hoped, remains a contest in prodigal waste. Only a few years ago Department of Defense officials were suggesting that, as part of a "grand design" for strategic policy, we might be forced to "win" an arms race with the Russians by relying on our superior resources to spend them into bankruptcy. Such a strategy puts one in mind of the practice among the Indians of the Pacific Northwest known as the "potlatch." Starting as a rivalry in gift-giving for the sake of prestige, the practice degenerated as the tribes became wealthier into competitive orgies of waste and deliberate destruction of wealth in which the competing tribes tried to establish their superiority by spending the others—and themselves—into ruin.

Violence has become the nation's leading industry, giving millions of workers as well as industrial magnates a personal economic stake in the "potlatch" of weapons production. For the industrialist a new weapons system means higher profits; for the worker, new jobs and the prospect of higher wages; for the politician, a new installation or defense order with which to ingratiate himself with his constituents. These benefits, once obtained, are not easily parted with. Every new weapons system or military installation soon acquires a constituency—a process which is aided and abetted by the perspicacity with which Pentagon officials award lucrative contracts and establish new plants and installations in the districts of influential members of Congress. Spawned by our global military involvements, the military-industrial complex has become a powerful force for the perpetuation of those involvements. Defense industries, especially the aerospace industry, have become the beneficiaries of what amounts to a socialist welfare system consisting of large subsidies, "restructured" contracts for firms which fail to meet their contractual obligations, and huge federal bail-out arrangements such as the $250 million loan guarantee made to the Lockheed Corporation in 1971. With a vested interest in the expensive weapons systems which provide their livelihood, millions of Americans have acquired an indirect stake in the foreign policy that has kept the United States in a spiraling arms race with the Soviet

Union; made us the world's major salesman of armaments; and committed us to the defense of "freedom" in almost fifty countries, including Vietnam, Spain and Greece, with their "freedom-loving" regimes.

Although we have been unwilling to redistribute income through fundamental tax reform, or to eliminate extreme poverty through extensive revision of our chaotic, wasteful and demeaning welfare programs, we have nonetheless moved far toward a socialized national economy. Through massive subsidies we have already "socialized" much of our agriculture—most of it in large corporate units; we have socialized highway construction and the aerospace industry; especially and above all we have socialized our national defense industry, which, with $80 billion a year, more or less, to dispose of, has organized the armed forces, the armaments industries, powerful labor unions and even some of the great universities into the greatest socialized enterprise on the face of the earth. The question, patently, is not whether we are willing to socialize but what. "The socialization of death," says Michael Harrington, "is, thus far at least, much more generally popular than the socialization of life."[8]

The military have become ardent and dangerous competitors for power in American society. In the absence of effective Congressional "rules for the government and regulation of the land and naval forces"—to quote the language of the Constitution—the armed services have become vigorous and effective partisans for their own favored policies, for new weapons systems and, of course, for funds to finance them. Playing fast and loose in politics, the armed services exert great influence on the executive, actively lobby in Congress, expend enormous sums on contract research in foreign policy, and, in the name of "public affairs," assiduously cultivate public opinion. Constantly improving their

techniques for rapid deployment, or "surgical" bombing, they not only yearn to try them out but actively
seek opportunities by pressing their proposals on political authorities, who all too often are tempted by the
seemingly quick, decisive courses of action proposed by
the military in preference to the endless, wearisome
methods of diplomacy.

For a variety of reasons—to test new plans and equipment, to try out the techniques of counterinsurgency,
and, in the case of the Marines, according to the former
commandant, General Shoup, just to avoid the disgrace
of being left out[9]—all of the military services were en-
thusiastic about the initial involvement in Vietnam. By
now they should have had their fill, but they still seem
game to go on, trying out new weapons and strategies,
although up to now the only military principle which
has been vindicated in Vietnam is Alexis de Tocqueville's maxim, "There are two things that will always be
very difficult for a democratic nation: to start a war and
to end it."[10] For more than a decade out of the last
three we have been engaged in large-scale warfare, and
for the rest of that period we have been engaged in the
cold war and in ever more costly preparations for war.
War, and the chronic threat of war, have consumed our
resources, distorted our priorities, and undermined national security by eroding its domestic base, all the
while carrying us—as Tocqueville warned—"gently"
by our "habits" toward depotism.

II. The Anxious Society

The governing political sentiment in America in recent
years has been fear—fear of communism, fear of crime
and drugs, fear of blacks by whites and of whites by
blacks. Fear has shaped our politics at home and

abroad, distorting perceptions, stifling generosity and idealism, nourishing demagoguery and jingoism.

What is this fear that blights the lives of so many Americans? We are, as we never tire of reminding ourselves, the richest, strongest nation in history. Our factories and farms are among the most productive in the world, our technology the most advanced. Except for the people of a few small countries, our people—most of our people—are fed and clothed and housed and schooled better than any others in the world. Even our poor, for the most part, are poor by a special American standard, a standard which would pass for affluence in most of the world. We are the most favored of societies and quite possibly the most troubled, the richest and strongest and quite possibly the most insecure. Why?

The major immediate source of our anxiety has been the war in Vietnam and its consequences here at home. The war has totally altered the atmosphere of the early sixties when, during the Kennedy Administration, our hopes and confidence were raised high. Domestic changes were obviously needed, but the American people at that time seemed willing to embark upon an era of social reform. And under President Johnson's leadership an excellent start was made with the landmark social legislation of 1964 and 1965, especially in the field of education. Then Vietnam cut that short, diverting the economic resources and political energies that we had only just begun to apply to our domestic needs. Distracted by the war, the Johnson Presidency was ultimately consumed by it. Vietnam provoked dissent and disorder, which in turn gave rise to a middle-class reaction based on the fear of violence and anarchy. The result has been an atmosphere uncongenial to reform, urgently needed though it is.

While the war grew more costly and frustrating and our leaders were distracted, rising racial tensions at home were transforming the civil rights movement into one of angry black militancy, marked by scattered violence. Whether racial violence was directly aggravated by the violent example of Vietnam cannot be judged with certainty, but that seems probable, and there is little doubt that racial antagonisms were exacerbated by the neglect of domestic affairs induced by the war. In any case, the racial violence of the sixties deepened the divisions of the country and heightened popular alarm, especially—for some reason—on the part of middle-class people living in areas far removed from the urban riots.

Taken together, the war, the race crisis and the busing issue which has come to symbolize it, disorderly dissent, crime, drugs and—perhaps most important of all—the vacuum of Presidential moral leadership have had a devastating effect on the American middle-class majority. Peaceful, law-abiding and hard-working, the average American has seen the country threatened, as it seemed, by a tide of violence and anarchy. Under the impact of this national mood of anxiety, the reformist drive of the early 1960's collapsed—notwithstanding the fact that the "Great Society" program had hardly begun, notwithstanding the continuing—indeed the mounting—need of social innovation in America. Social reform movements do not advance simply because they are needed; they prosper, it appears, only when the comfortable majority have been frightened—or enlightened—into awareness of the need for social responsibility.

My premise—more hunch then conviction—is that the mood of national anxiety will abate when it has had its day, but that it will not abate until it has had its day, until the fears of the middle-class majority—of crime and drugs and busing—are recognized as legitimate human problems, no less worthy of compassionate response from government than the problems of extreme poverty and racial injustice. Then and only then—in an atmosphere of restored self-confidence and mutual generosity—is it likely that our society will be prepared to do those things for its poor and racial minorities which it should have done a long time ago, which, but for the war, it might well be doing right now.

Still, one wonders, is the war in Vietnam the cause of all that agitates us or is it more nearly a catalyst, activating underlying ills? What is so frightening and incomplete in American life for the great majority who are not directly affected by war or deprivation? What is it like to be a reasonably well-off and well-educated American in the 1970's? What are the satisfactions enjoyed by the supposedly satisfied classes in our society? Are they really satisfying in the sense of bringing personal fulfillment, or is our affluence narcotic, amusing us with wasteful trivia while numbing us to the spiritual poverty of our lives?

If any tendency can be identified as dominant in contemporary American life, it is the loss of individuality. Jean-Paul Sartre said that there is no greater immorality than the conversion of the concrete into the abstract, of the individual into the dehumanized mass. We are systematically, though heedlessly, converting the American "way of life" into a barren, computerized abstraction. Our names no longer identify us; numbers are now required—to cash a check in the local bank, to register for a course in a university, to fill a prescription in the neighborhood drugstore. Rural and small-town America still retains much that is personal and warm and idiosyncratic, but the daily life of any American city is a ritual of sterile anonymity. Craftsmanship—and the pride of it—are an oddity, quaint and rare; the artifacts of everyday life are chemical synthetics—durable, serviceable, washable, and utterly lacking in in-

dividuality or authenticity. There is no more visible
mark of the way a people live than their architecture;
ours is shoddy, shiny, sterile, anonymous and grimly,
aggressively standardized.

Most ominous of all, perhaps, is the depersonalization
of education. At its best the classroom is a deeply inti-
mate environment, a place in which student and
teacher explore and generate ideas, passing them back
and forth, turning them over like a many-sided prism,
asserting and responding, questioning and criticizing,
above all communicating—with words and without
words. In our great universities today, including the
most famous of them, the classroom is a cavernous lecture hall in which the professor, a remote eminence,
addresses himself to a sea of indistinguishable faces
from a lofty platform and then is gone—no questions,
no answers, no communication. The professor in all
likelihood has bigger things on his mind than the ado-
lescent enthusiasms of undergraduates—the endur-
ance of which in any case makes a suitable novitiate for
promising graduate students. Enticed by a dazzling ar-
ray of foundation grants, by government contracts and
the opportunity to "influence policy," the professor has
become a man on the move, a "scholar" in the new
sense in which that term is used, referring not to a
creator of ideas but to a producer of salable data. As the
trend accelerates, what the teacher teaches becomes as
anonymous as the way he teaches it: philosophy gives
way to behavioral science, imagination to measure-
ment, insight to prediction, appreciation to control. No
longer an end in itself, the human mind becomes cus-
todian to the computer—that mindless, inanimate
mind which "thinks" without knowing that it thinks.

We are moving, so say a number of distinguished
observers of human affairs, into a radically new kind of
civilization. Never in human history have such vast

physical changes been wrought in so short a time as are now being wrought in America, and all that we know for certain about their ultimate effects upon human personality is that they will be both extreme and destructive. Lewis Mumford describes the new age into which we are moving as the age of the "megamachine," an age which "is passing from the primeval state of man, marked by his invention of tools and weapons for the purpose of achieving mastery over the forces of nature, to a radically different condition, in which he will have not only conquered nature, but detached himself as far as possible from the organic habitat."[11] In the psychiatric perspective of Erich Fromm, life in America is being systematically subordinated to the requirements of efficient production. Technology, treated as an end in itself, is gaining predominance over human personality, with the result, as Fromm has put it, that "man is transformed into a soulless consumer who ceases to have genuine feelings, depth of experience, or a sense of identity or integrity. The living human being becomes a thing, manufacturing things, and finding his fulfillment in the use of things. To have and to use become the aim, rather than to be."[12]

That, I suppose, may be what is happening to the affluent urban American majority: we are rich and powerful, but life, somehow, is eluding us. Without intending it, without even knowing it, we have elevated the most advanced technology in the history of man into a kind of deity—a "megamachine," as Mumford calls it— and we are enthralled to it. The human end has been inverted with the technological means and, instead of liberating us from drudgery and insecurity as we had hoped it might, the "megamachine" is inexorably taking possession of our lives, blighting and degrading them in disguised, unrecognized ways. The disguise is in the technological ethic, which equates innovation with progress and work with freedom. From the scientist to the assembly-line worker, the professor to the file clerk, we are caught up in the notion that activity is the same thing as creativity, that, quite aside from questions of usefulness, destructiveness and cost, every new invention is a forward step in the march of civilization, well worth its unmeasured human price.

In our large American cities the supremacy of the machine over man is approaching completeness. Living in an environment of steel and asphalt, an environment almost totally of man's own creation, the daily life of the individual is a losing struggle against man-made impediments. There is a tangible nastiness in the air of any big city—a prevailing mood of unfriendliness and irritability, a sense of isolation in the crowd, of loneliness without the luxury of being alone. Most of all there is the sense on the part of the individual of his loss of control of things, of his thralldom to the things around him, the sense of his needs being denied and his nature violated. I am speaking, bear in mind, of the daily life of those who are well-off, not of the poor, whose teeming slums are the true mark of the primacy of rockets and missiles over schools and homes, the true monument to the victory of the machine over man.

In contrast with life in the big cities there remains something of serenity and grace in rural and small-town America. A small town in Arkansas—or Nebraska or Vermont—is a world away from New York or Chicago. Knowing his neighbors and known to them, free of the crush of crowds and noise, the small-town American is a different kind of human being from the city dweller—friendlier, quieter, less driven, less agitated. His life is not necessarily a bucolic idyll: he may be bored, understimulated, parochial. But he retains— or at least has a good chance of retaining—both identity as an individual and harmony with his natural surroundings.

These are basic human needs, necessities of life, lacking which a man is capable neither of personal fulfillment nor of generosity to others. I suspect that there is an important connection between the loss of identity and harmony in urban, middle-class life and the attitudes of the materially comfortable majority toward the materially deprived minority. There is little room for generosity in the hearts of the spiritually deprived; depression and compassion do not easily coexist. It seems probable that we shall have to focus our political energy, inventiveness and resources not just on the alleviation of acute poverty but on the regeneration of the total urban environment, in order to elicit the deep and enduring sense of social responsibility on the part of the middle classes without which there can be no social justice for our poor and black minorities. It may be, to put it another way, that our prospects for eliminating the material poverty of the few will turn finally upon our ability to alleviate the spiritual poverty of the many.

Whether that can be done or not I do not know. Some observers, such as Professor Brzezynski of Columbia, seem to believe that the trend is irreversible, that we are embarked upon a "technetronic" age in which human conduct will be "programmed" by computer technology, that humanist dissent to the depersonalization of life is a futile rear-guard action against the wave of the future, that all we can do is to try to adapt to the new condition of life, and that the "key" to successful adaptation is the training of a highly educated elite—highly educated, that is, in the technical sense—who will operate the complex new social machinery while the rest of us—unemployed due to automation—thrash around trying to amuse ourselves.[13]

The alienation of so many of our young people is, I believe, in large part a reaction against this repulsive vision of the future. Far from being the revolutionaries that their fearful elders—and they themselves—regard them as being, our alienated youth may well be the last remaining group of deeply committed traditionalists in American society. Asserting freedom of the mind and the autonomy of the individual as their ultimate values, they are far more in the tradition of Jefferson than of Marx. And, I dare say, they have something more than tradition on their side: they have human nature as well —not as expressed in our actual behavior, and not in the sense of an inner force that is destined to prevail, but human nature in the sense of our deeply rooted, largely unrecognized, easily violated, but unalterable human longings.

If American society shows itself incapable of satisfying these longings, of overcoming the material poverty of the poor and the spiritual poverty of the affluent, then our society as presently constituted probably will not survive; nor, in that event, would it be worth saving. Whether it would be replaced by the saner and juster society envisioned by many of our young people, by some zealot's corruption of that vision, by the crude crypto-fascism of the radical right, or the élitist totalitarianism of the new breed of computerized intellectuals, I would not venture to guess. I know only that, except for the first, none of these prospects is enticing, that our society as it has developed since colonial times does have a core of humane and democratic values, that these traditional values are still alive in America, alive to the point of vibrancy in the hearts and minds of many of both the younger and older generations, and that these values are not only worth saving but well worth the struggle to save them in which we are now engaged. So too then is American society worth saving

—not only for what it is but, as Camus would say, for what it is capable of becoming.

What we must hope and strive for is that, with foreign and domestic peace, the decent instincts of the American majority will be enlisted in support of a national program of social reconstruction—a program of economic liberation for the poor but also one of spiritual liberation for all Americans. These two kinds of social action are profoundly interrelated, because fulfillment is the prerequisite of generosity. It seems probable therefore, I stress again, that beyond peace and domestic order, the average, physically comfortable American will find it possible to feel generous toward his poor and black fellow citizens only when he feels certain that the society which is asking his generosity also values *him*, personally and individually, not for what he can do or give or produce but simply for what he is.

We must seek in a time of social injustice, of automation and anonymity, what Erich Fromm has called a "humanist alternative." Whatever that might consist of —new forms of community action and organization, or new—or perhaps revived—life styles emphasizing individual satisfactions and creativity, there must be one guiding principle at its core: the primacy of man over the machine, of human satisfaction over technical innovation, of personal feeling over corporate ideology. Ruling out, as I would, both the coldblooded prognoses of the social scientists and the insubstantial visions of the social revolutionaries for putting right the things which have gone so badly wrong in our society, we are left with the traditional processes of American democracy in which to place our hopes.

Perhaps those hopes will be misplaced; perhaps, despite our best or worst efforts, we will come to grief— to social breakdown or dictatorship, to the living death of the megamachine, or to actual death from the poisoning or exhaustion of the earth's resources, or from starvation due to the population explosion, or from the hydrogen bomb. If any of these calamities does come to pass, however, it will not be brought by fate but by human fallibility. We retain some choice in these matters; we are foredoomed to nothing and that fact alone warrants an act of faith—of faith in American democracy, faith in the decency and good sense of the American people, faith in human nature—which, for all its fallibilities, has shown itself to have certain hopeful possibilities as well. What, when you come right down to it, do we have to lose?

9

Conclusion:
The Price of Empire

The success of a foreign policy, as we have been discovering, depends not only on the availability of military and economic resources but, at least as much, upon the support given it by our people. As we have also been discovering, that support cannot be gained solely by eloquent entreaty, much less by the devices of public relations. In the long run it can only be secured by devising policies which are broadly consistent with the national character and traditional values of the society, and these—products of the total national experience—remain, at least thus far, beyond the reach of even the most effective modern techniques of political manipulation.

History did not prepare the American people for the kind of role we are now playing in the world. From the time of the framing of the Constitution to the two world wars our experience and values—if not our uniform practice—conditioned us not for the unilateral exercise of power but for the placing of limits upon it. Perhaps it was a vanity, but we supposed that we could be an example for the world—an example of rationality and restraint. We supposed, too, as Woodrow Wilson put it, that a rational world order could be created embodying "not a balance of power but a community of power; not organized rivalries, but an organized common peace."[1]

Our practice has not lived up to that ideal but, from the earliest days of the Republic, the ideal has retained its hold upon us, and every time we have acted inconsistently with it—not just in Vietnam but every time— a hue and cry of opposition has arisen. When the United States invaded Mexico, two former Presidents and one future President denounced the war as violating American principles.[2] The senior of them, John Quincy Adams, is said even to have expressed the hope that General Taylor's officers would resign and his men desert.[3] When the United States fought a war with Spain and then suppressed the patriotic resistance to American rule of the Philippines, the ranks of opposition were swelled with two former Presidents, Harrison and Cleveland, with Senators and Congressmen including the Speaker of the House of Representatives, and with such distinguished individuals as Andrew Carnegie and Samuel Gompers.

The dilemma of contemporary American foreign policy is that, while becoming the most powerful nation ever to have existed on the earth, the American people have also carried forward their historical mistrust of power and their commitment to the imposition of restraints upon it. That dilemma came to literal and symbolic fulfillment in the year 1945 when two powerful new forces came into the world. One was the bomb at Hiroshima, representing a quantum leap to a new dimension of undisciplined power. The other was the United Nations Charter, representing the most significant effort ever made toward the restraint and control of national power. Both were American inventions, one the product of our laboratories, the other the product of our national experience. Incongruous though they are, these are America's legacies to the modern world; the one manifested in Vietnam, the cold war, and the nuclear arms race, the other in the hope that the rules of the traditional game of power politics can be changed to make the world safer, more civilized and more humane.

There must be something more substantial for a nation to seek, something more durable and rewarding, than the primacy of its power. The alternative that seems so obvious, so desirable and yet so elusive is the pursuit of public happiness. For reasons that I must confess an almost total inability to understand, large nations seem to be driven by a sense of imperial destiny, as if it would be craven to forego adventure and to concentrate on the intelligent government of a society. We just "have to" play this super-power role, Mr. Nixon said. But what is the greater legacy that any generation of leaders can bequeath: a temporary primacy consisting of the ability to push other people around or a well-run society consisting of cities without violence or slums, of productive farms, and of education and opportunity for all of the country's citizens?

The incongruity between our old values and our new unilateral power has greatly troubled the American people. It has much to do, I suspect, with the rebellion and alienation of our youth, and with the divisions, agitation and unhappiness of so many of our people. Like a human body reacting against a transplanted organ, our body politic is reacting against the alien values which, for the sake of the primacy of our power, have been grafted upon it. We cannot—and dare not—divest ourselves of power, but we have a choice as to how we will use it. We can use it, as Mr. Nixon would have us do, to compel "respect"—or fear—throughout the world for the office of the President of the United States. Or we can try to adapt our power to our traditional values, never allowing it to become more than a means toward domestic, societal ends, while seeking every opportunity to discipline it within an international community.

I. The Competitive Impulse

Like it or not—and I am not at all sure I do—there is no greater spur to human exertion than competition. From the chariot races of ancient Rome to professional football in modern America contests of courage and skill have provided people with thrills and entertainment. Competition is also one of the powerful engines of economic growth and technological innovation. The rivalry of merchants and manufacturers was a powerful force in setting off the Industrial Revolution and is still a major—if somewhat dogmatized—factor in our modern economy. The competitive instinct broke the four-minute mile and sent astronauts to the moon; it also sent tens of millions of people to premature deaths in the two world wars.

Competition between nations differs from the rivalry of individuals in that it is conducted on a far greater scale, brings to bear vastly greater resources, affects the lives of many more people, and is more likely than other rivalries to be conducted without rules or restraints to assure the survival of the participants. In other respects there appear to be no important differences between the rivalries of individuals, teams, corporations, armies and nations. All are engaged in a contest for self-maximization, not just to excel but to exceed, not just to do something well but to do it better than somebody else.

Competition is not the only spur to human exertion. At least in Western cultures the challenge of overcoming natural obstacles has fired the adventurous spirit in man: the mountain challenges the climber, the wave the surf rider, the sea the mariner, the jungle the explorer, the universe the astronaut. By paradoxical contrast, unnatural, which is to say, man-made, obstacles have no such motivating magic. For most of us such unnatural obstacles as decaying cities and polluted water and air are a tolerated nuisance rather than a motivating challenge—the accepted price of something called progress. Western man, it seems, has come close to reversing the ancient stoicism of the East: restless and insatiable in challenging nature's creations, he is becoming passive and fatalistic about his own. He will leap to the stars and yet squat miserably in his own fouled nest. Were it not so paradoxical, eccentric and debilitating, one might even take this for a new form of self-denying stoicism.

Be all that as it may, the competitive instinct is probably the most reliable tool of human creativity. We would not wish to eliminate it but we do need to alleviate its risks, of which the greatest is the constant danger that a zealous competitor will compete too well and so put an end to the competition, robbing mankind of the creative benefits of the competitive process.

The genius of the American Constitution is that, at least up to now, in domestic if not in foreign affairs, it has kept the game going and the competitors in competition. The division of governmental powers among three branches and fifty states puts the various contenders for power in the position of having little chance of victory but an excellent chance of survival in the continuing struggle for power. The system works tolerably well largely because it does not depend too heavily on human conscience and voluntary restraint, which, admirable though these are, must be counted among the less reliable of human attributes. Instead, with unsentimental realism, the framers of our Constitution faced up to the universality of the human drive to self-aggrandizement, recognized it for the creative but dangerous force that it is, and harnessed it into a system of regulated rivalries, free enough to generate political energy, restrained enough to protect the people from despotism.

Difficult as it is to control, the competitive impulse seems even more difficult to acknowledge. Only in sports are competitions conducted in their own name; the game is for its own sake, for the fun of playing and the hope of winning. But in politics we feel a compulsion to dress up our contentious impulses in the vocabulary of ideals and ideology. The landings of American astronauts on the moon, for example, have evoked a great deal of poeticizing about the human spirit bursting its earthly bonds, about the nobility of man's endless search for knowledge, and about the boundless but unspecified benefits for mankind certain to derive from the setting of human feet upon the surface of the moon. In all this one perceives not humbug pure and simple but rather more sententiousness than plain hard truth. Americans went to the moon for a number of reasons, of which the most important by far was our desire to beat the Russians. The kick was not just in getting there but in getting there first; a football team does not celebrate the number of points it got if the other team got more points.

No matter what the issue in politics and who is involved in it, we suppose, almost invariably, that some great principle is at stake, some noble and unselfish purpose, such as realizing our own great ideals or, more commonly, saving people—sometimes against their will—from the wicked designs of our rivals. To hear the Soviet and American leaders talk about the cold war, nothing could be farther from their pristine thoughts than any notion of self-aggrandizement or getting one up on the other. By their own accounting of it the Russian leaders sit up nights in the Kremlin thinking up ways to lift the yoke of oppression from the downtrodden of the earth. President Nixon, for his part, recalled in a speech early in his term of office that the United States had suffered over a million casualties in four wars in this century, and then claimed that it had all been done out of saintly altruism. "Whatever faults we may have as a nation," he declared, "we have asked nothing for ourselves in return for those sacrifices. We have been generous toward those whom we have fought. We've helped our former foes as well as our friends in the task of reconstruction. We are proud of this record and we bring the same attitude in our search for a settlement in Vietnam."[4]

Mr. Nixon was probably sincere in his belief that we had suffered a million casualties in four wars as an act of pure altruism, but that does not make it true. Most of us have a deep and touching faith in our own virtue, and most politicians have an equally tender regard for their own rhetoric. Few people are more moved by a moving speech than the speaker himself—but that does not make what he says true. This is not to suggest that there are no ideals or generous impulses in politics. I suggest only that they are far less controlling than we like to believe; that more often than not what we take for principle is not principle at all but rationalization; that the thing we are usually rationalizing is our instinct for competition; and that if anything approaches being a controlling influence on our political behavior, it is this appetite for contest. I further suggest that there would be much to gain from a candid acknowledgment of our own political nature. Indeed, it is only by recognizing the fragility of our ideals, the limited role they play in guiding our behavior, and their susceptibility to corruption by rationalization that we can have any hope of translating them into reality. The Founding Fathers had no illusions about the behavior of their fellow men and, because of their realism, they were able to discipline the struggle for power so as to protect the people from despotism.

Establishing the primacy of our power in the world —whether through moon flights, the arms race, journeys to the summit, triumphant confrontations, or our "trillion-dollar economy"—will not change the human condition. Men have been achieving technological marvels for the last two centuries, and kings and presidents and popes and preachers have been heralding new eras of brotherly love for the last two millennia. Neither has had an appreciable effect on the moral condition of the human race. The only hope we have of changing that—if it can be changed—is to face up to certain facts of experience, of which the most important is that man, the technological genius, is a moral primitive. If there is ever to be such a thing as a human community, it will have to begin with the candid recognition that man's capacity for brotherly love is limited, and so is his capacity for voluntary restraint of his competitive and destructive impulses. As a species, we do not really like each other all that well, and our problem is to seek out practical ways of restraining the struggle for power on the international level, just as we have restrained it on the domestic level, so as to have some hope of survival. If that is not the most promising of foundations on which to build, it has at least the solidity of truth.

Twice in this century, as was noted in Chapter 5,

honest, hopeful but thus far unsuccessful efforts have been made to bring unrestrained national rivalries under the civilized rules of an international community. These two efforts, the League of Nations and the United Nations, were born of the breakdown of traditional techniques of international relations in the two world wars. It is sometimes said that the League failed and that the United Nations has been ineffective because they were excessively visionary and idealistic—as if they had been undertaken in a recklessly unhistoric spirit, in wholesale disregard for the tried and true methods of the past. In fact they were undertaken only when the traditional techniques collapsed in cataclysms that destroyed tens of millions of human lives. In relation to the failure of the old techniques of power politics and in relation to the needs of the human race, the League and the United Nations were far from excessively idealistic; both represented very modest efforts indeed to lay the foundations of an international community in a world of anarchy and violence.

It is not our needs but our capacities that have been exceeded by the modest experiments in international organization which have been undertaken in this century. The central question about the United Nations—more exactly about the international security community envisioned in the United Nations Charter—is not whether we need it but whether we are capable of making it work. We are caught in this respect in a dilemma: can we devise means of disciplining the competitive impulse in international relations which are both bold enough to eliminate or reduce the danger of nuclear war and modest enough to be within the limits of feasibility imposed by prevailing fears and prejudices?

There is no ready answer to this dilemma but there is hope, and that hope consists primarily in the promise of education for narrowing the gap between our needs and our capacities. There is nothing we can do to reduce our needs: we cannot put the atomic genie back into its bottle. Through their policies of détente with the Soviet Union and China, President Nixon and Mr. Kissinger removed much of the ideological animosity from the relations of the great powers and they may even have laid the groundwork for a new balance of power which could remain stable for some years or even decades to come. In the long run, however, as all past experience has shown, such an equilibrium of power will provide the world with no more than a respite, temporary and precarious. The fundamental defect of the balance-of-power system is that it is hardly more durable than the men who control it. As long as it is manipulated by intelligent or agile statesmen, like Metternich or Bismarck in the nineteenth century, the system is likely to hold up. But clever men pass from the scene, leaving their juggling acts to clumsy or pedestrian successors, who soon enough start dropping the balls, as did Bismarck's successors in the late nineteenth century, the years preceding World War I. In international as in domestic affairs we are in need of a system of laws rather than of men, a system that does not depend upon the cleverness or benevolence of the men who run it. If our lives are to be made secure, there is no alternative to an international community which is capable of making and enforcing civilized rules of international conduct, enforceable upon great nations as well as small ones. What we can and must do is to use whatever respite a new balance of power provides to try to expand the boundaries of human wisdom, sympathy and perception. Education is a slow-moving but powerful force. It may not be fast enough or strong enough to save us from catastrophe, but it is the strongest force available for that purpose, and its proper place, therefore, is not at the periphery but at the center of international relations.

II. The "Empty System of Power"

When he visited America a hundred years ago, Thomas Huxley wrote: "I cannot say that I am in the slightest degree impressed by your bigness, or your material resources, as such. Size is not grandeur and territory does not make a nation. The great issue, about which hangs the terror of overhanging fate, is what are you going to do with all these things?"[5]

The question is still with us. Before the Second World War our world role was a potential role; we were important in the world for what we *could* do with our power, for the leadership we *might* provide, for the example we *might* set. Now the choices are almost gone: we are *almost* the world's self-appointed policeman; we are *almost* the world defender of the status quo; we are well on our way to becoming a traditional great power. And, as with the great empires of the past, as the power grows, it is becoming an end in itself, separated except by ritual incantation from its initial motives, governed, it would seem, by its own mystique, power without philosophy or purpose.

But we have not become a traditional empire yet. The old values remain—the populism and the optimism, the individualism and the rough-hewn equality, the friendliness and the good humor, the inventiveness and the zest for life, the caring about people and the sympathy for the underdog, and the idea, which goes back to the American Revolution, that maybe—just maybe—we can set an example of democracy and human dignity for the world. That is something which none of the great empires of the past has ever done, or

tried to do, or wanted to do, but we were bold enough
—or presumptuous enough—to think that we might be
able to do it. And there are a great many Americans
who still think we can do it—at least they want to try.

That, I believe, is what all the hue and cry has been
about—the dissent in the Senate, the protest marches,
the rejection of and disgust with an endless, futile war
in which few Americans now die but thousands of
Asians continue to die under a rain of American bombs.
Our people have shown that they have no stomach for
this brutalizing crusade, that they think their country
was cut out for better things, for something more enno-
bling than an imperial destiny. Our people are showing
that they still believe in the American dream, and their
protests attest to its continuing vitality.

Nor, so far as I can tell, do the American people
accept the romantic notion that a nation is powerless to
choose the role it will play in the world, that some
mystic force of history or destiny requires a powerful
nation to be an imperial nation, dedicated to what Paul
Goodman has called the "empty system of power,"[6] to
the pursuit of power without purpose, philosophy or
compassion. They do not accept the Hegelian concept
of history as something out of control, as something that
happens to us rather than something that we make.
They do not accept the view that because other great
nations have pursued power for its own sake—a pursuit
which usually has ended in decline or disaster—America must do the same. They think they have some
choice about their own future and that the best basis for
exercising that choice is the values on which this
Republic was founded.

Even the most ardent advocates of an imperial role
for the United States would probably agree that the
proper objective of our foreign policy is the fostering of
a world environment in which we can, with reasonable

security, devote our main energies to the realization of the values of our own society. This does not require the adoption or imposition of these values on anybody, but it does require us so to conduct ourselves that our society does not seem hateful and repugnant to others. At present much of the world is repelled by America and what America seems to stand for. Both in our foreign affairs and in our domestic life we convey an image of violence; I do not care very much about images as distinguished from the things they reflect, but this image is rooted in reality. Abroad we are engaged in a savage and unsuccessful war against poor people in a small and backward nation. At home—largely because of the neglect resulting from decades of preoccupation with foreign involvements—our cities are plagued with crime, our politics with the threat of assassination. America, which only a few years ago seemed to the world to be a model of democracy and social justice, has become a symbol of violence and undisciplined power.

". . . it is excellent," wrote Shakespeare, "to have a giant's strength; but it is tyrannous to use it like a giant."[7] By using our power like a giant we are fostering a world environment which is, to put it mildly, uncongenial to our society. By our unrestrained use of physical power we have divested ourselves of a greater power: the power of example. How, for example, can we commend peaceful compromise to the Arabs and the Israelis when we are unwilling to suspend our relentless terror bombing in Vietnam? How can we commend democratic social reform to Latin America when the crime and poverty of our cities give evidence of our own inadequate efforts at democratic social reform? How can we commend the free-enterprise system to Asians and Africans when in our own country it has produced vast, chaotic, noisy, dangerous and dirty urban complexes while poisoning the very air and land

and water. Far from building a safe world environment for American values, our war in Vietnam and the domestic deterioration which it has largely induced and greatly aggravated are creating a most uncongenial world atmosphere for American ideas and values. The world has no need, in this age of nationalism and nuclear weapons, for a new imperial power, but there is a great need of the leadership of decent example. That role could be ours, but we have, for the time being at least, vacated the field, and all that has kept the Russians from filling it is their own lack of imagination.

At the same time, as we have noted, and of even greater fundamental importance, our purposeless and undisciplined use of power has caused a profound controversy in our own society. This in a way is something to be proud of. We have sickened but not succumbed and, just as a healthy body fights disease, we are fighting the alien concept which has been thrust upon us, not by history but by our policy makers of recent years. We are proving the strength of the American dream by resisting the dream of an imperial destiny. We are demonstrating the validity of our traditional values by the difficulty we are having in betraying them.

Some years ago Archibald MacLeish characterized the American people as follows:

> Races didn't bother the Americans. They were something a lot better than any race. They were a People. They were the first self-constituted, self-declared, self-created People in the history of the world. And their manners were their own business. And so were their politics. And so, but ten times so, were their souls.[8]

Now the possession of their souls has been challenged by the false and dangerous dream of an imperial destiny. It may be that the challenge will succeed, that America will succumb to becoming a traditional empire and will reign for a time over what must surely be a moral if not a physical wasteland, and then, like the great empires of the past, will decline or fall. Or it may be that the effort to create such an anachronism will go up in flames of nuclear holocaust.

But I do not think so. I think rather that the decency and good sense of the American people are astir and making themselves felt. We are, as of this writing in the summer of 1972, still engaged in the terror bombing of North and South Vietnam; we are still neglecting the health and welfare of our own people and the education of our children. But we have moved toward détente, if not yet reconciliation, with China, and we have begun to limit the nuclear arms race with the Soviet Union. With leaders more attuned to the traditional values of the American people we could go on, without great difficulty, to end the debilitating and indecent war, to meet the neglected needs of our own society, and begin to fulfill the promise of the United Nations. The dissenters of recent years have been sending their leaders a message, and there are signs that it is getting through. All things considered, I would place my bet on the regenerative powers of the idealism of our younger generation—this generation who reject the inhumanity of war in a poor and distant land, who reject the poverty and sham in their own country, this generation who are telling their elders what their elders ought to have known, that the price of empire is America's soul and that price is too high.

Notes

INTRODUCTION

[1] *The Arrogance of Power* (New York: Random House, 1966), p. 225.

[2] President Wilson's address to the Senate of January 22, 1917.

[3] Richard M. Freeland, *The Truman Doctrine and the Origins of McCarthyism* (New York: Alfred A. Knopf, 1972), pp. 96–97; Joseph M. Jones, *The Fifteen Weeks* (New York: The Viking Press, 1955), pp. 138–143; Dean G. Acheson, *Present at the Creation* (New York: W. W. Norton & Co., 1969), p. 219.

[4] Arthur H. Vandenberg, Jr., ed., *The Private Papers of Senator Vandenberg* (Boston: Houghton Mifflin Company, 1952), p. 340.

[5] Speech of November 3, 1969.

[6] C. L. Sulzberger, "Nixon, in Interview, Says This Is Probably Last War," *The New York Times,* March 10, 1971, pp. 1, 14.

[7]Herbert Marcuse, "The Problem of Social Change in the Technological Society," in *Le Développement Social,* UNESCO Symposium (Paris: Mouton and Co., 1965), p. 158.

[8]Richard Nixon, *Six Crises* (New York: Doubleday & Co., 1968), p. 317.

CHAPTER 1

[1]X, "The Sources of Soviet Conduct," *Foreign Affairs,* July 1947, pp. 575–6, 582.

[2]Quoted by Alden Whitman in his obituary of Acheson, *The New York Times,* October 13, 1971, p. 50.

[3]Joseph Jones, *The Fifteen Weeks* (New York: The Viking Press, 1955), p. 146.

[4]Chalmers M. Roberts, "The Rages, Charms of Khrushchev," *The Washington Post,* September 12, 1971.

[5]Unofficial notes kept by the staff of the Senate Foreign Relations Committee, inserted in *Congressional Record,* September 15, 1971, p. S 14345.

[6]*The Pentagon Papers* as published by *The New York Times* (New York: Bantam Books, Inc., 1971), p. 432.

[7]Victor Zorza, "Did Kennedy's Misreading Help Topple Khrushchev?" *The Washington Post,* September 16, 1971.

[8]Harrison E. Salisbury, "Khrushchev: Shift in Soviet Path," *The New York Times,* September 12, 1971, p. 77.

[9]Speech of November 3, 1969.

[10]Memorandum issued by the Director, United States Information Agency, March 17, 1972.

[11]"Western Europe and the New Economic Policy," *Report of Senator Mike Mansfield to the Committee on Foreign Relations, U.S. Senate* (Washington: U.S. Government Printing Office, 1971), pp. 7–13.

[12]David Calleo, *The Atlantic Fantasy: The United States,*

NATO and Europe (Baltimore: The Johns Hopkins Press, 1971), pp. 32–3, 124–5.

[13]Haynes Johnson and George C. Wilson, "Army in Anguish," a series in *The Washington Post*, September 12–20, 1971.

[14]Radio address of March 18, 1949. Quoted by Calleo in *The Atlantic Fantasy*, p. 24.

[15]Charles de Gaulle, *Unity* (New York: Simon & Schuster, 1967), p. 88.

[16]Quoted by Chalmers M. Roberts in *The Nuclear Years* (New York: Praeger, 1970), p. 8.

CHAPTER 2

[1]Letter of Transmittal of Department of State publication No. 3573, *United States Relations with China*, signed by Dean Acheson, July 30, 1949.

[2]Dean Rusk in a speech to the China Institute in New York, May 19, 1951.

[3]Warren I. Cohen, *America's Response to China* (New York: John Wiley & Sons, 1971), p. 215.

[4]Lin Piao, "Long Live the Victory of People's War!" *Peking Review*, September 3, 1965, p. 22.

[5]David D. Barrett, *Dixie Mission: The United States Army Observer Group in Yenan, 1944* (Berkeley: University of California, Center for Chinese Studies, 1970); John S. Service, *The Amerasia Papers: Some Problems in the History of US-China Relations* (Berkeley: University of California, Center for Chinese Studies, 1971).

[6]*Dixie Mission*, p. 37.

[7]*Ibid.*, p. 34.

[8]*Ibid.*, p. 43.

[9]*Ibid.*, p. 44.

[10]*Ibid.*, pp. 82–9.

[11]Barrett, *Dixie Mission*, pp. 61–2; Service, *The Amerasia Papers*, pp. 81–2.

[12] *Foreign Relations of the United States, 1944* (Washington: U.S. Dept. of State, Historical Office, Bureau of Public Affairs, 1967), p. 693.

[13] Telegram from Hurley to Truman, May 20, 1945, *Foreign Relations of the U.S., 1945* (Washington: U.S. Dept. of State, Historical Office, Bureau of Public Affairs, 1967), pp. 107–14.

[14] Quoted in Barbara Tuchman, *Stilwell and the American Experience in China* (New York: Macmillan, 1971), p. 486 n.

[15] Quoted by Service in *The Amerasia Papers*, p. 126.

[16] Service, p. 144.

[17] *Ibid.*, p. 162.

[18] *Ibid.*

[19] *Ibid.*, p. 173.

[20] *Ibid.*, pp. 167–73.

[21] *Hearings Before the Senate Foreign Relations Committee*, "Origins of Vietnam War," May 11, 1972.

[22] Quoted by Tom Wicker in *JFK + LBJ* (New York: Penguin Books, 1968), p. 208.

[23] Acheson to U.S. Representative in Hanoi, May 1949, in *U.S.-Vietnam Relations, 1945–1967*, Book 1 of 12, edition published for House Committee on Armed Services (Washington: U.S. Government Printing Office, 1971), Vol. I, "Vietnam and the U.S., 1940–1950," p. C-45.

[24] *U.S.-Vietnam Relations*, Vol. I, p. A-14.

[25] *Ibid.*, p. A-3.

[26] *Ibid.*, pp. C-4, C-60-C-62, C-96-C-97, C-103-C-104.

[27] *Ibid.*, p. C-45.

[28] *Ibid.*, p. C-47.

[29] *Ibid.*, p. C-3.

[30] *Ibid.*, p. C-3.

[31] *Ibid.*, p. C-45.

[32] Woodrow Wilson, in his Fourteen Points speech, January 8, 1918.

CHAPTER 3

[1] Speech at Hampton, New Hampshire, quoted in "Nixon Says He'd End War, Contends LBJ Has Not Used Power Wisely," *The Washington Post*, March 6, 1968, p. 1.

[2] Figures provided by Indochina Resource Center, Washington, D.C.

[3] "The Bombing," *The Washington Post*, April 9, 1972, p. B6.

[4] Quoted by Bernard Gwertzman in "Rogers Defends Bombing; Warns of Further Moves," *The New York Times*, April 18, 1972, p. 1.

[5] Press Conference of February 17, 1971.

[6] Quoted by David Halberstam in "Laos and the Old Illusions," *The New York Times*, February 25, 1971, p. 37.

[7] Quoted by Tom Fox in "The Earth Shakes . . . We Wait to See Who Dies," *The New York Times*, March 21, 1971, p. 2E.

[8] Quoted by Sydney H. Schanberg in "Up Front, Saigon Officer Blames U.S.," *The New York Times*, June 2, 1972, p. 3.

[9] Anthony Lake and Roger Morris, "The Dehumanization of Foreign Policy," *The Washington Post*, September 26, 1971, p.E1.

[10] Henry Kissinger, "Central Issues of American Foreign Policy," in *Agenda for the Nation* (Kermit Gordon, ed., Washington: The Brookings Institution, 1968), p. 591.

[11] James G. Lowenstein and Richard M. Moose, "Vietnam: December 1969," *Report prepared for Committee on Foreign Relations* (Washington, U.S. Government Printing Office, 1970), p. 18.

[12] Speech of November 3, 1969.

[13] Stanley Karnow, "A Marxist Lunch with the Laotians," *The Washington Post*, March 24, 1970.

[14] *A Conversation with U Thant, Secretary General of the United Nations*, by members of the Committee on For-

eign Relations, U.S. Senate, March 22, 1967 (Washington: U.S. Government Printing Office, 1972), p. 2.

15Speech of November 3, 1969.

16Speech of November 3, 1969.

17Henry Kissinger, "The Vietnam Negotiations," *Foreign Affairs,* January 1969, p. 228.

18General Charles de Gaulle, *Memoirs of Hope, Renewal and Endeavor* (New York: Simon & Schuster, translated by Terrenz Kilmartin, 1971—translated from French in 1958).

19Maynard Parker, "Preparing for the Worst," *Newsweek,* November 24, 1969, p. 40.

CHAPTER 4

1I.F. Stone, "Holy War," in *The Israel-Arab Reader* (Walter Laqueur, ed., New York: Bantam Books, 1969), p. 324.

2Quoted in Seth P. Tillman, *Anglo-American Relations at the Paris Peace Conference of 1919* (Princeton University Press, 1961), p. 132.

3Speech to the Central Committee of the Arab Socialist Union, July 24, 1972, quoted in Henry Tanner, "Egyptian Asserts Moscow Caution Caused Ousters," *The New York Times,* July 25, 1972, p. 1.

4Interview on *The Advocates,* a public television network presentation of KCET, Los Angeles, and WGBH, Boston, June 21, 1970, "The Middle East: Where Do We Go From Here? Part II: The Case for U.S. Support for Israel."

5"Sorry Wrong Number," editorial in *The New York Times,* April 10, 1970, p. 38.

6Nahum Goldmann, "Israel and the Arabs—an 'Unrepresentative' View," *Le Monde,* Weekly Selection, May 27, 1970, p. 4.

7Alexis de Tocqueville, *Democracy in America* (New York: Harper and Row, Publishers, 1966), Vol. II, ch. 22, p. 625.

[8]"Nasser Accepts U.S. Plan, but Asks Aid to Israel End," *The New York Times*, July 24, 1970, p. 1.

[9]"Mrs. Meir Asserts Hussein's Plans Skirt Peace Issue," *The New York Times*, March 17, 1972, p.1.

[10]"The Argument Between Arabs and Jews," in *The Israel-Arab Reader*, p. 262.

[11]Quoted in *Search for Peace in the Middle East* (Philadelphia: American Friends Service Committee, 1970), p. 43.

[12]Quoted by Peter Grose in "Israel and U.S. in a Game of 'Diplomatic Chicken,'" *The New York Times*, March 21, 1971, p. 4E.

[13]Interview with John McCook Roots, quoted in "Ben-Gurion Quoted in Article as Favoring Major Pullback," *The Evening Star*, Washington, D.C., March 25, 1971, p. A-3.

[14]Speech to the National Press Club, Washington, D.C., April 10, 1969.

[15]*The Advocates*, June 14, 1970.

[16]Interview with a correspondent of *The London Times*, quoted in "Mrs. Meir Cites Border Changes Sought by Israel," *The New York Times*, March 13, 1971, pp. 1, 6.

[17]*Search for Peace in the Middle East*, p. 36.

[18]Hess, John L., "Sadat Said to Warn Soviet He'll Resist Reds in Middle East," *The New York Times*, August 6, 1971, p. 2.

[19]Speech to the Central Committee of the Arab Socialist Union, July 24, 1972, quoted in Henry Tanner, "Egyptian Asserts Moscow Caution Caused Ousters," *The New York Times*, July 25, 1972, p. 1.

[20]Bernard Gwertzman, "Soviet Role in Mideast," *The New York Times*, August 3, 1970, p. 2.

[21]Televised interview of July 1, 1970.

[22]Background Briefing, San Clemente, California, June 26, 1970, unpublished, p. 20.

[23]Background Briefing, San Clemente, California, June 30, 1970, p. 9; June 26, 1970, p. 23.

[24]Interview with a correspondent of *The London Times*, in "Mrs. Meir Cites Border Changes Sought by Israel," *The New York Times*, March 13, 1971, pp. 1, 6.

[25]Briefing by Secretary of State William P. Rogers, *Hearings Held Before the Committee on Foreign Relations, U.S. Senate*, March 27, 1969 (Washington: U.S. Government Printing Office, 1969), p. 3.

[26]Speech to the National Press Club, Washington, D.C., April 10, 1969.

[27] *Search for Peace in the Middle East*, p. 56.

[28]"Israel and the Arabs—An 'Unrepresentative' View," *Le Monde*, Weekly Selection, May 27, 1970, p. 4.

CHAPTER 5

[1] *Congressional Record*, October 3, 1967, p. S14063.

[2]John Quincy Adams, July 4, 1821, Washington, D.C., reported in *National Intelligencer*, July 11, 1821.

[3]"Nixon Deplores Jubilation of Delegates," *The New York Times*, October 28, 1971, p. 1.

[4]Quoted by Carrol Kilpatrick in "Hill Debate on Support Intensifies," *The Washington Post*, October 28, 1971, p. A-1.

[5]Quoted by Anthony Austin, in "Crushing Defeat for the United States, or a Blessing in Disguise?" *The New York Times*, October 31, 1971, Section 4, p. 1.

[6]Quoted by Henry Tanner in "United States 'Steamroller Tactics' are Blamed for Defeat," *The New York Times*, October 27, 1971, pp. 1, 15.

[7]Kenneth Boulding, "World Economic Contacts and National Policies," in *The World Community* (Quincy Wright, ed., Chicago: University of Chicago Press, 1948), pp. 101–2.

[8]Lin Piao, "Long Live the Victory of People's War!" *Peking Review*, No. 36, September 3, 1965, p. 22.

CHAPTER 6

[1] Maxwell Wiesenthal, "Maine GOP Hears Agnew Rip Muskie," *The Washington Post*, April 29, 1972, p. A16.

[2] Bernard Gwertzman, "Rogers Attacks Democrats on Mining," *The New York Times*, May 16, 1972, p. 14.

[3] Peter Milius, "Connally Assails Democrats," *The Washington Post*, May 11, 1972, p. A18.

[4] "U.S. Commitments to Foreign Powers," *Hearings Before the Committee on Foreign Relations*, U.S. Senate, 90th Cong., First Session, on S. Res. 151 (Washington: U.S. Government Printing Office, 1967), pp. 20, 21.

[5] Executive Comments on the proposed repeal of the Gulf of Tonkin Resolution and other resolutions, March 12, 1970.

[6] "A Bill to Amend the Foreign Assistance Act of 1961," *Hearings Before the Committee on Foreign Relations*, April 18, 1972, p. 241.

[7] "The Southeast Asia Collective Defense Treaty," *Hearings Before the Committee on Foreign Relations*, U.S. Senate, 83rd Cong., 2d Sess., on Exec. K (Washington: U.S. Government Printing Office, 1954), pp. 16–17.

[8] *Ibid.*, p. 25.

[9] *Ibid.*, p. 28.

[10] "Southeast Asia Resolution," *Joint Hearings Before the Committee on Foreign Relations and the Committee on Armed Services*, U.S. Senate, 88th Cong., 2d sess., on a Joint Resolution to Promote the Maintenance of International Peace and Security in Southeast Asia (Washington: U.S. Government Printing Office, 1966), p. 23.

[11] *Congressional Record*, 88th Cong., 2d Sess., Vol. 110, Pt. 14, Senate, August 6, 1964, pp. 18403–4.

[12] *Ibid.*, pp. 18406–7.

[13] *Ibid.*, p. 18420.

[14] *Ibid.*, pp. 18410–11.

[15] *Ibid.*, pp. 18415–16.

[16] *Ibid.*, p. 18456.

[17] *Ibid.*, p. 18459. See also *ibid.*, p. 18462.

[18] Bella S. Abzug, "The House of Semi-Representatives," *The New York Times*, March 29, 1972, p. 43.

[19] "Thailand, Laos, and Cambodia: January 1972," *Staff Report prepared for the Senate Foreign Relations Subcommittee on U.S. Security Agreements and Commitments Abroad* (Washington: U.S. Government Printing Office, 1972), p. 27.

CHAPTER 7

[1] "United States Commitments to Foreign Powers," *Hearings Before the Committee on Foreign Relations*, U.S. Senate 90th Cong., 1st sess., on S. Res. 151 (Washington: U.S. Government Printing Office, 1967), p. 73.

[2] *Ibid.*, p. 72.

[3] "Assignment of Ground Forces of the United States to Duty in the European Area," *Hearing by Committee on Foreign Relations and Armed Services*, U.S. Senate, 82nd Cong., 1st sess., on S. Con. Res. 8, February 1–28, 1951 (Washington: U.S. Government Printing Office, 1951), pp. 92–3.

[4] *The Papers of Thomas Jefferson*, 17 volumes (Julian P. Boyd, ed., Princeton: Princeton University Press, 1955), Vol. 15, p. 397.

[5] *The Federalist*, Jacob E. Cooke, ed. (Middletown, Conn.: Wesleyan University Press, 1961), p. 464.

[6] *A Compilation of the Messages and Papers of the Presidents*, 10 volumes (James Richardson, ed., Washington: U.S. Government Printing Office, 1917), Vol. 2, pp. 489–90.

[7] John Quincy Adams to Don José Maria Salazar, August 6, 1824, quoted in *The Record of American Diplomacy*, Ruhl J. Bartlett, ed., third edition (New York: Alfred A. Knopf, 1954), p. 185.

[8] A letter from Daniel Webster to Mr. Severance, July 4, 1851,

in *The Writings and Speeches of Daniel Webster* (Boston: Little, Brown & Co., 1903), Vol. 14, p. 440.

[9]67 USC 635 (1862).

[10]Justice Robert H. Jackson concurring in *Youngstown Sheet and Tube Co. v. Sawyer,* 343 U.S. 579 (1952), p. 13.

[11]Testimony of Professor Ruhl J. Bartlett, "U.S. Commitments to Foreign Powers," *Hearings Before the Committee on Foreign Relations,* U.S. Senate, 90th Cong., 1st sess., on S. Res. 151 (Washington: U.S. Government Printing Office, 1967), pp. 20–21.

[12]George E. Reedy, *The Twilight of the Presidency* (New York and Cleveland: World Publishing Company, 1970), p. 27.

[13]"Kingdom of Laos," *Hearings Before the Subcommittee on U.S. Security Agreements and Commitments Abroad of the Committee on Foreign Relations* (Washington: U.S. Government Printing Office, 1971), Vol. 1, part 2, p. 547.

[14]Merlo J. Pusey, *The Way We Go To War* (Boston: Houghton Mifflin Company, 1969), p. 138.

[15]"War Powers," *Report by the Committee on Foreign Relations,* 92nd Cong., 2d Sess., No. 92–606, p. 21.

[16]"National Commitments," *Report by Senate Committee on Foreign Relations,* 1969, 91st Cong., 1st Sess., No. 91–129, p. 29.

[17]Leonard C. Meeker, *The Legality of U.S. Participation in the Defense of Viet-Nam* (Washington: U.S. Department of State, March 4, 1966), p. 12.

[18]Merlo J. Pusey, *The Way We Go To War,* p. 138.

[19]*Geofroy v. Riggs,* 133 U.S. 258, 267 (1890).

[20]"War Powers," *op. cit.*

[21]"National Commitments," p. 28.

[22]*The Federalist,* pp. 505–6.

[23]*Congressional Record,* 81st Cong., 2d sess., Vol. 96, pt. 7, Senate, June 27, 1950, p. 9229.

[24]James MacGregor Burns, *Presidential Government, the Crucible of Leadership* (Boston: Houghton Mifflin Com-

pany and Cambridge: The Riverside Press, 1966), p. 330.

[25]George E. Reedy, *The Twilight of the Presidency*, p. 14.

[26]*Ibid.*, p. 80.

[27]Alexander J. Groth, "Britain and America: Some Requisites of Executive Leadership Compared," *Political Science Quarterly*, June 1970, p. 218.

[28]President Nixon's "Memorandum for the Heads of Executive Departments and Agencies," April 17, 1969.

[29]University of Chicago, February 19, 1946.

[30]*Myers v. United States*, 1926, 272 U.S. 293, Mr. Justice Brandeis dissenting.

[31]Quoted in A. T. Mason, *Free Government in the Making* (New York: Oxford University Press, 1965), p. 371.

CHAPTER 8

[1]Charles L. Schultze, Edward R. Fried, Alice M. Rivlin, and Nancy H. Teeters, *Setting National Priorities—The 1973 Budget* (Washington: Brookings Institution, 1972), pp. 77–81.

[2]*1972 Joint Economic Report*, Joint Economic Committee, Congress of the United States (Washington: U.S. Government Printing Office, 1972), p. 55.

[3]"Rostow Blasts Times for 'Misleading' Public," *The Daily Texan*, Austin, Texas, July 6, 1971, p. 3.

[4]*Impact of the Vietnam War*, prepared for the use of the Committee on Foreign Relations, U.S. Senate, by the Foreign Affairs Div., Cong. Research Serv., Library of Congress (Washington: U.S. Government Printing Office, 1971).

[5]The National Urban Coalition, Robert S. Benson and Harold Wolman, eds., *Counterbudget: A Blueprint for Changing National Priorities* (New York: Praeger Publishers, 1971), p. 169.

[6]"The Federal Budget and The Cities," *Congressional Record,* March 24, 1972, Vol. 118, No. 46, p. E3026.

[7]Michael Harrington, *Toward a Democratic Left* (New York: The Macmillan Co., 1968), p. 219.

[8]David M. Shoup, "The New American Militarism," *The Atlantic,* April 1969, p. 55.

[9]Alexis de Tocqueville, *Democracy in America* (New York: Harper & Row, Publishers, 1966), Vol. II, ch. 22, pp. 622–23.

[10]Lewis Mumford, *The Myth of the Machine, Technics and Human Development* (New York: Harcourt, Brace & World, Inc., 1967), p. 3.

[11]The quotation is taken from a personal memorandum given to me by Dr. Fromm in March 1968.

[12]Zbigniew Brzezinski, "America in the Technetronic Age," *Encounter,* January 1968, pp. 16–26.

CHAPTER 9

[1]Address to the Senate, January 22, 1917.

[2]John Quincy Adams, Martin Van Buren and Abraham Lincoln.

[3]Charles A. Barker, "Another American Dilemma," *Virginia Quarterly Review,* Spring 1969, pp. 239–40.

[4]Speech of May 14, 1969.

[5]Thomas Huxley, *American Address with a Lecture on the Study of Biology* (New York: Appleton & Co., 1877), p. 125.

[6]*Like a Conquered Province, The Moral Ambiguity of America* (New York: Random House, 1967), p. 73.

[7]*Measure for Measure,* Act II, Scene 2, Line 107.

[8]Archibald MacLeish, *A Time To Act* (Boston: Houghton Mifflin Co., 1943), p. 115.

J. WILLIAM FULBRIGHT, Senator from Arkansas, is Chairman of the Senate Foreign Relations Committee. He has served longer (since 1959) in that position than any man history. He was first elected to Congress in 1942 and became a member of the House Foreign Affairs Committee, where he introduced the "Fulbright Resolution," calling for the participation by the United States in an international organization to maintain peace and generally considered the forerunner to the establishment of the United Nations.

Senator Fulbright, a member of the Democratic Party, is now serving his fifth term in the Senate. In 1945, he sponsored the international educational exchange program that bears his name. In 1954 Senator Fulbright alone voted against additional funds for the Special Investigating Subcommittee headed by the late Senator Joseph McCarthy, and was a co-sponsor of the censure resolution passed by the Senate against Senator McCarthy. Since 1965, Senator Fulbright has been a leading and persistent critic of the war in Vietnam.

In recent years, in addition to its normal legislative functions, the Senate Foreign Relations Committee has conducted extensive inquiries into American policy in Southeast Asia, relations with China, and United States commitments abroad.

Senator Fulbright, who formerly chaired the Senate Banking and Currency Committee, also serves on the Senate Finance and Joint Economic Committees. He has been particularly concerned with reasserting the constitutional role of Congress and with reordering national priorities so as to bring about a more rational allocation of the country's resources.

Senator Fulbright's home is in Fayetteville, Arkansas. He is married to the former Elizabeth Kremer Williams.